TILOPA'S WISDOM

Tilopa's Wisdom

His Life and Teachings on the
Ganges Mahamudra

Khenchen Thrangu

BASED ON TRANSLATIONS FROM
ORAL TEACHINGS BY
Lama Yeshe Gyamtso, Jules Levinson,
and Jerry Morrell

SNOW LION
BOULDER
2019

Snow Lion
An imprint of Shambhala Publications, Inc.
4720 Walnut Street
Boulder, Colorado 80301
www.shambhala.com

9 8 7 6 5 4 3 2 1

First Edition
Printed in the United States of America

⊗ This edition is printed on acid-free paper that meets
the American National Standards Institute z39.48 Standard.
♲ Shambhala Publications makes every effort to print on recycled paper.
For more information please visit www.shambhala.com.

Snow Lion is distributed worldwide by Penguin Random House, Inc.,
and its subsidiaries.

LIBRARY OF CONGRESS CATALOGING-IN-PUBLICATION DATA
Names: Thrangu, Rinpoche, 1933– author. | O'Hearn, Peter, 1959– translator. | Levinson,
Jules B., translator. | Morrell, Jerry, translator.
Title: Tilopa's wisdom: his life and teachings on the Ganges Mahamudra / Khenchen
Thrangu; based on translations from oral teachings by Lama Yeshe Gyamtso, Jules
Levinson, and Jerry Morrell.
Description: First edition. | Boulder: Snow Lion, 2019. | Includes bibliographical
references and index.
Identifiers: LCCN 2019007662 | ISBN 9781559394871 (pbk.: alk. paper)
Subjects: LCSH: Tillopāda, 988–1069. | Buddhist priests—India—Biography. |
Meditation—Tantric Buddhism. | Mahāmudrā (Tantric rite)
Classification: LCC BQ990.I57 T47 2019 | DDC 294.3/92092 [B]—dc23
LC record available at https://lccn.loc.gov/2019007662

In this world there have been many beings, chiefly human beings, but other beings as well, who have produced great benefit by offering their intelligence, their mind, their talents. Tilopa was like that. He was able to benefit an immense number of beings through his realization and greatness. For example, if medicine that can cure a serious illness is kept secret and not given to those who need it, then it will not benefit anyone. But if that medicine is spread throughout the world and made available to everyone, then it will be of great benefit and will save many lives.

So therefore, in order to understand Tilopa's contribution, it is very important to understand what realization means, the wisdom that Tilopa represents. To understand this, we have to look into the story of Tilopa, how he went through difficulties, how much effort he made, how he attained understanding, wisdom, and qualities of loving-kindness and compassion.

—THE KARMAPA, OGYEN TRINLEY DORJE

CONTENTS

Editor's Preface   ix

Part One: The Life of Tilopa

1. Introduction   3

2. Childhood   7

3. Renouncing Samsara and Meeting His Teachers   11

4. Teaching Mahamudra at Pancapana   19

5. Receiving Secret Instructions   29

6. Gaining Disciples   35

Part Two: Teachings on the Ganges Mahamudra

7. Tilopa's *Ganges Mahamudra*: Root Text   47

8. Introduction   55

9. The View of Mahamudra in Six Metaphors   67

10. The Conduct of Mahamudra   89

11. The Commitments of Mahamudra   101

12. The Benefits of Practicing Mahamudra   107

13. The Defects of Not Practicing Mahamudra   111

14. How to Practice the Preliminaries   115

15. How to Practice the Main Body of Mahamudra   135

Afterword   155

Appendix A: Tilopa's Six Points for Mahamudra   157

Appendix B: The Five Buddha Families   161

Appendix C: The Eight Consciousnesses   163

Glossary   165

Glossary of Tibetan Terms   179

Notes   183

Annotated Bibliography   191

Index   197

Biographical Note about Khenchen Thrangu   207

Editor's Preface

When the Buddha passed away 2,500 years ago, he left a vast collection of teachings from his forty years of guiding laypeople and monastics. There were several main teachings of the Buddha that were quite radical given the religious beliefs and practices dominant in India during his lifetime. First, the Buddha denied the existence of any creator(s) of the world, a god, or gods, who must be worshipped. He taught that everything in this world came about because of cause and effect—much like way that modern scientists describe the evolution of living creatures on earth. This contrasted greatly with the prevalent Hindu culture that posited that the world and everything that happened to the people and animals in it were due to the actions of the gods. Second, he taught that all men and women regardless of their nationality, race, or caste could practice what he taught and eventually reach complete enlightenment or awakening. This also differed greatly from Hinduism in which only the men of the highest Brahmin caste could learn Sanskrit and then perform religious ceremonies and achieve awakening. That only some people could learn Sanskrit was significant because people believed that while conducting a religious ceremony one had to pronounce each Sanskrit syllable absolutely correctly or the whole ceremony, or puja, would be defiled and become ineffective. Third, he taught that people should live in harmony with their environment, which means that animals should not be needlessly killed. This was in conflict with the prevalence of animal sacrifices at the time. Finally, the Buddha did not designate a person to head the Buddhist "church," and he did not give any instructions on how they should set up a hierarchical religion after his passing away. Rather, the Buddha laid down a set of rules for the ordained Buddhist sangha and suggested a fairly democratic way of making decisions and handling disputes based on respect, love, and compassion.

As the number of Buddhists grew and the Buddhist teachings spread to many different countries, Buddhism began slowly to develop two different methods for achieving awakening. On the one hand, monastic universities developed where a large number of monks from different traditions including Hindu specialists in the Vedas, rhetoric, medicine, and so on congregated and studied together, sharing the culture of India. Many pilgrims from Tibet and China visited these universities and brought back descriptions of these universities and what was taught in them, and actually brought back many of the texts that were taught there. As a result, we know who many of the great teachers were and what they taught. This immense learning, however, was totally unavailable to the ordinary person in India who spoke only their local language and therefore did not know Sanskrit, which was the language that most of the Buddhist Dharma was taught in. These monastic universities were mostly sponsored by rich patrons or the ruling kings, and they were mainly organized as feudal organizations.

On the other hand, there were also the yogi mendicants who were said to live "in the forest" (but more likely lived outside towns and larger cities) and who followed the *siddha* tradition of India; they taught ordinary people in their own local language. The siddha tradition in India goes back to before the time of the Buddha. Siddhas were wandering religious men who mainly engaged in various ascetic practices. Even today we can see these siddhas all across India doing ascetic practices such as not wearing any clothing, standing on only one leg for great lengths of time, rubbing themselves with ashes, and so on. Since the Buddha had actually engaged in these practices himself for six years and found that they did not lead to awakening, Buddhist siddhas do not particularly practice asceticism. Instead they attempt to reach awakening by breaking all their conventional conditioning and conceptual thinking and by acting in unconventional ways such as eating meat, intermarrying with members of the lowest castes, insulting officials and important people, and the like. The Buddhist siddhas that are best known are called *mahasiddhas*, and they were made famous by a compilation of short biographies about them called the *Eighty-Four Mahasiddhas* (composed by Abhayadatta, who lived in the early twelfth century). Tilopa and his main disciple Naropa are both considered to be part of this group of eighty-four mahasiddhas.

Tilopa (988–1069) was born in Bengal, India. Peter Alan Roberts gives a rare physical description of Tilopa as "a solitary dark-skinned wanderer with bulging eyes and long, matted hair."[1] Tilopa received his name from *til*, which means "sesame seed" in Sanskrit. Because the great scholars, or *panditas*, worked and practiced in monastic universities with great libraries, their lives and works were much better documented than those of the mahasiddhas who often lived away from civilization; no one followed them into the jungles and small towns where they taught and wrote down any details about their lives. Also this was a time when dates were not considered important. In fact, the official calendar of Tibet began in 1067, just two years before the death of Tilopa. Because we don't have a documented history of Tilopa's life, we have many conflicting stories about him. For example, the most important event of his life—when he attained enlightenment after pounding sesame seeds for many years—is told differently in several of his biographies: Several accounts state that Tilopa went to a town and asked to be chained there. He then remained there for twelve years before reaching realization. The biographies of Marpa and Wangchuk Gyaltsen tell the story that Tilopa was told by his guru Matangi to go to a town and pound sesame seeds during the day and to be a procurer for the prostitute Dharima at night without telling anyone that he was a mahasiddha. In a version told by the Seventeenth Karmapa, based on Taranatha's account, Tilopa was living in a monastery as a celibate monk and left the monastery and began living with the prostitute Dharima. There he pounded sesame seeds during the day and at night practiced Mahamudra with Dharima and thus reached enlightenment.[2]

In India, the tenth century was a time when many people told elaborate stories about the powers of siddhas, and therefore many Western scholars have dismissed these stories outright. However, some of the stories about the powers of siddhas are true and others are intended to be merely symbolic. For example, in modern times, there are a number of great practitioners who have "traveled" to another dimension and received teachings from a famous but long-dead siddha (or accomplished one). Upon returning, they furiously write down these teachings and then give them to their students. Or realized teachers will sometimes know exactly what is going on somewhere out of their sight, even as far away as in a distant country. For example, when Lama Norlha, who lives in New York State, was visiting the young Seventeenth Karmapa in Tibet and describing his center, the Karmapa suddenly said, "What is that hole in your backyard?" The lama was taken aback and said that the hole was to be a swimming pool that he was building. Other lamas such as Adzom Rinpoche and the Seventeenth Karmapa have placed their hands on rocks and melted the surface enough to form a fingerprint or a handprint. Finally, many Buddhist practitioners have witnessed the practice of *thukdam*, in which a lama tells his students that he is going to die and then adopts a perfect meditation posture and remains there for days after his heart and breathing have stopped. In normal persons, the body slumps to the floor at death and the body becomes cold, but for the practitioner of thukdam, the heart area (where it is believed the mind resides) remains warm for days and the body doesn't lose its upright meditation posture. These siddhis or "powers," which are based on meditation practice, may not be as great as Tilopa's being able to conjure up a huge army (as one story about him has it), but they are powers not presently explainable by modern science.

Sometimes the story about a siddha's powers is intended to be merely symbolic; for example, a story about a siddha being burned alive and yet being unscathed by the fire. This is a symbolic way of saying that they had mastered the element of fire. Or a story that a siddha was drowned and yet survived may be a way of saying that they had mastered the element of water. It's even possible that a story of a siddha creating the illusion of a great army symbolically indicates that they had mastered the practice of the illusory body (Tib. *gyü lü*).

When Thrangu Rinpoche was asked about these miracles, he said that in a sacred biography (Tib. *namtar*), it really doesn't matter where the persons were born, where they traveled, and so on, because the stories are presented to explain how that siddha achieved enlightenment and that is what is really important. If we study these biographies, we can learn in a very interesting and nonacademic way what the path to enlightenment can be like and how extraordinary practitioners attained realization. This is why I have included Thrangu Rinpoche's teachings on Tilopa's life in the first part of this book.

The first biography of Tilopa was written by Marpa (1012–1097), who received the information from Tilopa's only major pupil, Naropa. This text has been translated by Fabrizio Torricelli and Sangye Naga and published as *The Life of Mahasiddha Tilopa*. A second major biography of Tilopa was written by Wangchuk Gyaltsen (1317–1405), who was a student of Tsangpa Heruka. Wangchuk Gyaltsen collected ten different Tibetan biographies of Tilopa and assembled them into a single coherent story. This biography has been translated into English by Ives Waldo. A third significant biography of Tilopa was composed by Pema Karpo (1527–1592) in his *Pekar Chöjung* (History of the Dharma), which is the text that Thrangu Rinpoche used in his oral teachings on Tilopa's life, which form the basis for some of the chapters in this book. This book has been translated by both Helmut

Hoffman and the Nālandā Translation Committee. Finally, Khenpo Kön-chog Gyaltsen translated Dorje Dze Öd's *The Great Kagyu Masters*, which recounts the lives of the masters of the Drikung Kagyu lineage (Thrangu Rinpoche is of the Karma Kagyu lineage) and that has a fairly long retelling of Tilopa's life and also of his main pupil, Naropa.

The second part of this book includes the twenty-nine stanzas of Tilopa's *Ganges Mahamudra*, followed by Thrangu Rinpoche's commentary on it in eight chapters. The *Ganges Mahamudra* is a *doha* (song), a form of poetry written in rhyming couplets. Since the mahasiddhas taught in the language spoken by the people they lived among, and Tilopa was from Bengal, India, where people spoke the Apabhramsha language, this doha was originally written in Apabhramsha. Dohas were not ordinary songs or poetry, how-ever. They were sung spontaneously by siddhas as an expression of their spir-itual realization. So a more accurate translation of *doha* would be "spiritual song" or "a song of realization." They were not like a poem that you might write down, then come back to later in order to edit and improve it. The initial composition was final. However, since these dohas were passed on orally from teacher to student, several different versions of a doha may exist.

The term *doha* comes from Sanskrit where *do* comes from the word meaning "two," which refers to the two lines forming the rhyming couplets. When these couplets were translated into Tibetan, however, they were often transformed into four-line verses that did not rhyme. The Tibetan transla-tions usually have the same number of syllables per line so they can be sung to many different melodies.

Saraha, who most likely lived in Bengal, which is in the eastern part of India, at least a century before Tilopa, is credited with giving the first recorded teachings on Mahamudra in his *Three Cycles of Doha*. Saraha was the king's main Brahmin and led an exemplary life. However, one day he met a lower-caste woman who was making arrows in the marketplace, and she ended up teaching Mahamudra to Saraha. He began living with her and started to act more like a mahasiddha than the king's head religious leader. Some citizens of the kingdom then came to Saraha and asked him to return to the palace; Saraha's reply was *The Citizen's Doha*, which described Mahamudra meditation. Then the queen came to ask him to return, and he replied with *The Queen's Doha*. Finally, the king himself came and made the same request, and Saraha replied with *The King's Doha*, again describing Mahamudra.

The next important Mahamudra texts that we know of were taught by

Tilopa, who was also born in Bengal, where there were several monastic universities such as Somapuri. Some of the biographies say that Tilopa visited, and may have studied at, one of these monasteries. He most likely also spent a great deal of time teaching in small towns and forests and cremation grounds. As already mentioned, the several accounts of Tilopa's life do not always agree with each other.

According to James Robinson, Tilopa has eight different teachings in the Tengyur. This volume includes translations of two of his most famous dohas on Mahamudra along with Thrangu Rinpoche commentaries on them. The first is a four-verse teaching that Tilopa gave at the Pancapana marketplace where he attained enlightenment. The second is the *Ganges Mahamudra* that Tilopa taught to his most prominent student, Naropa, on the banks of the Ganges. The *Ganges Mahamudra* is by far his most famous teaching, and it has been translated at least a dozen times. Tilopa's third most important work was the teachings that he gave Naropa called *Instructions of the Six Yogas* (Skt. *Saddharmo-padesha*, Tib. *Chos drug gi man ngag*). These teachings were systematized and expanded by his student Naropa and are now popularly known as *The Six Dharmas of Naropa* (Tib. *Na ro'i chos drug*), or *The Six Yogas of Naropa*. While Thrangu Rinpoche has not publicly given teachings on *The Six Dharmas of Naropa*, he does teach them in his three-year retreat programs.

What is so remarkable about the *Ganges Mahamudra* is that a thousand years ago it laid out the practice of Mahamudra in just twenty-nine verses. Moreover, Tilopa's description of how to engage in Mahamudra is almost identical to the descriptions of Mahamudra practice that have been given by contemporary Tibetan masters, including Thrangu Rinpoche. The Mahamudra tradition's ability to keep its practice free from adulteration for ten centuries is quite remarkable especially if we compare, for example, how the Christian church changed its doctrine and practice radically in its first one thousand years.

The reason why Mahamudra has remained unchanged is that it was transmitted in a special way. The persons who mastered it found it to be real and profound because it was not based on conceptual thought or cultural conditioning but on carefully examining the mind. Since all humans have a mind that is readily accessible and this mind is much deeper than its superficial thoughts and cultural concepts, it is available to anyone interested in examining it. The transmission began by encouraging people to practice Mahamudra. If a practitioner fully realized Mahamudra, then the teacher would allow that person to become a teacher. Moreover, the many students who practiced Mahamudra but did not reach full awakening did not lose anything thereby because the blessings of doing the practice helped them along the path of full enlightenment.

THE ORIGINS OF THIS BOOK

In 1988 the Nālandā Translation Committee asked Thrangu Rinpoche to teach on Tilopa because they were translating an independent biography on him.[3] Thrangu Rinpoche gave these teachings in Boulder, Colorado, that year, with Jerry Morrell doing the oral translating. Namo Buddha Publications was fortunate to receive an audio copy of these teachings, and the audio copy was transcribed and edited by Gaby Hollmann in 1990.

Thrangu Rinpoche also gave teachings on Tilopa in Nepal in 1991 while doing a pilgrimage to Lumbini, the birthplace of the Buddha, with Jules Levinson translating.

In 1994 Thrangu Rinpoche also gave teachings at Thrangu Tashi Chöling in Nepal on *The Song of Tilopa*, which was the teaching on Mahamudra that Tilopa gave at the Pancapana marketplace. These teachings were translated by Lama Yeshe Gyamtso.

Then in 1998 Thrangu Rinpoche gave a series of teachings in Vancouver, with Lama Yeshe Gyamtso translating, on the *Ganges Mahamudra*. For this volume, I have used Lama Yeshe Gyamtso's translation of the root verses, as well as his oral translations of Thrangu Rinpoche's commentary.

Finally, I have included Tilopa's famous six-line teaching on Mahamudra meditation in appendix A, which includes Thrangu Rinpoche's commentary on it that was orally translated by Jules Levinson and the full spiritual song from which the six-line teaching was taken.

Since Thrangu Rinpoche emphasized certain points in one teaching and other points in others, I decided to compose a single volume of these teachings on Tilopa that would make them more useful to the practitioner who desires to learn more about Mahamudra meditation and where it comes from.

ACKNOWLEDGMENTS

I would like to thank Jerry Morrell for translating the teachings given in Boulder, Jules Levinson for translating the teachings given in Nepal and for translating the six-line Mahamudra teaching in appendix A, and Lama Yeshe Gyamtso for translating the *Ganges Mahamudra* teachings. I would like to thank Gaby Hollmann for transcribing and editing the Boulder teachings and Tilopa's *Song of Realization* and Clarke Fountain for editing, and Margaret Neuman for transcribing, the Nepal teachings. I would also like to thank Lama Tashi of *Shenpen Ösel* magazine for providing us with additional materials on the *Ganges Mahamudra*. Also, I would like to thank Michael Wakoff at Shambhala Publications for his editing. Finally, this book would not have been possible if it weren't for the oral translations provided by Jerry Morrell, Jules Levinson, and Lama Yeshe Gyamtso.

Clark Johnson, PhD

PART ONE

THE LIFE OF TILOPA

Tilopa and Vajradhara. Tilopa received his teachings from Vajradhara through
a wisdom dakini. He wears a meditation belt and sits on a deerskin. Behind
him is a treasure vase, and in the sky a dakini is raising a victory banner.
Drawing by Jamyong Singhe, courtesy of Namo Buddha Publications.

1

Introduction

A spiritual biography of a great mahasiddha or any great lama is called a *namtar*[4] in Tibetan, which means "a hagiography" or "a story of realization." This type of spiritual biography is not a biography that discusses when and where a person was born and other biographical details but rather a story of the events that led to the individual's realization. A spiritual biography discusses how that individual began to practice meditation, how he or she applied themselves to the Dharma, what methods that person used to attain realization, and how this realization led to the helping of others. Since they are stories of complete liberation from all suffering, they are called *namtar*, with the syllable *nam* meaning "liberation" and the syllable *tar* meaning "complete."

Spiritual biographies usually have few references to the more mundane things of a mahasiddha's life, such as what kind of clothes were worn, what kind of food was eaten, or where he or she went. The reason for this is that the main purpose of a spiritual biography is to show the student of Buddhism how to practice the Dharma and to illustrate the results of practicing the Dharma by using the example of an individual who has actually attained buddhahood.

Many people say that Tibetan stories and spiritual biographies present only the good deeds and qualities of an individual, leaving out all their bad deeds. One Tibetan author, Gendun Choephel, who wrote *The White Annals*, makes the point that Tibetan stories and biographies don't present the complete truth and often gloss over the faults of lamas. There is some truth in this, but the purpose of a spiritual biography is for the student to discover what the practice of Dharma is actually like, what meditation is like, and how love and compassion are expressed by the great practitioners. So the purpose of a namtar is to inspire the student, and this is why they present all the marvelous qualities of the lamas and leave out the negative ones.

Western scholars complain, "How can these biographies be taken seriously? They don't provide a birth date or mention the actual places the mahasiddha lived and taught and other details." This is true, but why do we need to know when these people lived? Perhaps Tilopa lived in the seventh century, perhaps in the eleventh century. But who actually cares? Tilopa was not an ordinary human being anyway. We should remember Tilopa's and Naropa's great kindness and the great efforts they made to propagate the teachings of Mahamudra and the Six Yogas of Naropa,[5] making them available to everyone in Tibet, and now to students all over the world.

The Buddha gave numerous teachings of the sutras and the tantras that make up the eighty-four thousand classes of Dharma. He taught the entire path of Dharma in an extremely vast way. However, if we were to try to study all these sutras and tantras, it would be very difficult to extract their pith instructions on how to practice and discover how to actually travel on the path.[6] The great mahasiddha Tilopa, however, extracted the very essence of these vast teachings of the sutras and tantras and explained exactly how we should develop our practice. An analogy is that if we go into a forest in the high mountains, we may be aware that the forest is full of medicine. However, this knowledge is useless unless we also know which particular plant is a medicinal plant and which particular illness can be cured by that plant.

Tilopa (988–1069) was an emanation of Chakrasamvara. He practiced the Dharma completely and attained enlightenment. Tilopa was not able to see the supreme nirmanakaya emanation of the Buddha Shakyamuni, who had passed away many centuries before.[7] However, the dharmakaya is replete with the unbelievable power of compassion that manifests continuously to all sentient beings. This dharmakaya aspect, as well as the compassion aspect of the sambhogakaya, goes on for the benefit of all sentient beings. Tilopa had direct experience of this dharmakaya aspect and received all the pith instructions from the buddha Vajradhara on how to practice directly. Tilopa was different from the other Kagyu lineage holders such as Marpa and Milarepa because Tilopa was an actual emanation of Chakrasamvara and therefore had a direct experience of Vajradhara. Marpa, in contrast, was an ordinary person who gained enlightenment through his practice. However, Tilopa still had physical limitations due to his karmically conditioned body. The traditional example of this is the *garuda*, a bird that is born with wings and has the power to fly but is still contained in a fine envelope of an eggshell. In the same way, until that last piece of eggshell of his karmically conditioned physical form was broken, Tilopa could not develop full realization. Without a doubt, Tilopa was an emanation of Chakrasamvara. However, because of the obscurations and disturbing emotions possessed by most sentient beings, they were not able to perceive the form of Chakrasamvara directly.

The deities Chakrasamvara, Vajrayogini, and Chenrezik are not individual entities like living beings. The best way to understand them is to see them as the dharmata (the true nature of reality), the completely vast state of emptiness that is replete with the guru's wisdom and has extreme power and luminous clarity.[8] The very nature of this luminous clarity is compassion. There is a great amount of power in the completely empty space of dharmata. That power is such that without any particular intention or direction by any kind of thought, it will manifest to benefit sentient beings in a myriad of different ways. This emanation could be as Chakrasamvara, as Vajrayogini, or as a king, an animal, a queen, or even a beggar. The power of this luminous clarity and compassion is such that without making some sort of decision, for example, "I will manifest in this way to benefit so and so," it just happens spontaneously. This is how we should understand the nature of these deities. They have arisen from the power of luminous clarity and compassion of the buddha nature, which is the emptiness of dharmata itself.[9]

So Chakrasamvara emanated as an impure being, an ordinary manifestation, being born among humans as Tilopa. This emanation was visible to human beings who needed to be taught how to gain liberation. If Chakrasamvara were to emanate gloriously in the human realm without relying on a particular teacher or doing any particular practice or following any particular tradition, human beings would think, "Well, this is some kind of magical being from outside this world, and it isn't possible for me to be like him in any way." In India, the great mahasiddha Tilopa took up the practice of Dharma and achieved enlightenment. He brought the pith instructions of Mahamudra and the Six Dharmas of Naropa into our world. These teachings went directly from him to Naropa, and were then carried to Tibet by Marpa, where they flourished widely. Even today, a thousand years later, these very same teachings are spreading throughout the world and even to Western countries. This is a sign of the great wisdom, compassion, and power of the mahasiddha Tilopa.

The great translator Marpa received the transmission of Mahamudra meditation and the Six Dharmas of Naropa mainly from Tilopa's student Naropa. He received these in the form of practicing the Hevajra tantra and, more specifically, the Chakrasamvara tantra. In the mandala of Chakrasamvara, Marpa received the essence of skillful means (Skt. *upaya*) as Chakrasamvara and the essence of wisdom (Skt. *prajna*) as Vajrayogini. The mandala of the union of skillful means and wisdom is the basis of the Chakrasamvara tantra. When we visualize ourselves as Hevajra or Chakrasamvara in the practice of these tantras, we are engaging in the creation stage of meditation. The meditation on the Six Dharmas of Naropa is the completion stage of the Chakrasamvara tantra.[10]

2

CHILDHOOD

Tilopa was born in eastern India in 988. When Tilopa was a young boy, he had the special qualities of being extremely compassionate, kind, and loving. He was a cowherd and played in the forest without a care. At that time, the great Nagarjuna was out walking in the vicinity.[11] He had the special insight that in this region there was someone who was an ideal vessel to receive the Vajrayana teachings. Pondering this, he proceeded to the place between the town and the river where Tilopa was taking care of water buffaloes. Nagarjuna wanted to cross the river and pretended not to know where to ford it. He went to a point in the river with rapids and high waves and pretended that he was going to walk into the raging river. Tilopa came running up to him and said, "I will help you by carrying you across. There is no need for you to be afraid or to trouble yourself." Nagarjuna instantly saw that this child had great potential for developing intense devotion and compassion and that he had the capacity for extreme courage and diligence. He allowed the boy to carry him into the river. Although Tilopa was young and Nagarjuna was an adult, by his miraculous power Nagarjuna made his body so light that the boy could carry him quite easily.

Tilopa carried him into the river and when they got to the middle of the river, Nagarjuna used his miraculous powers again to make the river rise very high. The raging torrent almost carried the boy away so that he was about to disappear beneath the waves. The young Tilopa didn't think, "Oh, I've made a mistake. We shouldn't have tried this," but rather developed a firm determination to get to the other side and wasn't afraid at all.

Nagarjuna tested him even further and exclaimed, "All is lost. We are done for. There is nothing to grab on to. We will never get to the other side of the river." But Tilopa developed even greater determination and said to

Nagarjuna, "Just hold on tight to my neck, and I'll get you to the other side. Don't worry. We are going to do this." So Nagarjuna saw that Tilopa had great courage and potential and was indeed a fit vessel for all the Dharma teachings.

On another occasion, Nagarjuna was again traveling in the neighborhood and came upon young Tilopa playing that he was a king. He was sitting at the bottom of a tree with a couple of girls pretending to be his queens, four little children pretending to be his inner court, other children pretending to be the outer court, and twenty-five children acting as his subjects. Seeing this, Nagarjuna came up to them smiling. The young Tilopa jumped up and prostrated to Nagarjuna and said, "How are you? Did you have a hard time on your journey?" Nagarjuna said, "I have the means by which you can become a real king." The young Tilopa responded, "Oh please, you must tell me how!" Nagarjuna then spent seven days consecrating a special treasure vase. He wrote down on a piece of paper the name of the king, the names of the queens, what kinds of ministers he would require, and what kind of wealth and riches would be needed by the kingdom, and put the paper into the treasure vase. He then gave it to Tilopa and said, "Say 'I will be king' three times into this vase." Tilopa took the vase, put it to his mouth, and shouted inside it, "I will be king" three times.

It so happened that the king of that region suddenly became totally exasperated with his kingdom and decided he must give it up and go somewhere else. This was due to the great blessings and power of Nagarjuna and the magic treasure vase. Furthermore, this thought of leaving came to the king without anyone else knowing about it. He dressed himself as an ordinary person and just left.

This kingdom also had a most extraordinary elephant who had clairvoyant powers and would predict events in the kingdom. For instance, if there were any threats from enemies, the elephant would plow up the earth and toss it around. When a plague of some kind would threaten the kingdom, the elephant would cry and shed many tears. When good things happened in the kingdom, the elephant would rush into the local park and pull up the flowers and throw them all around. This elephant was also responsible for determining the future king. The elephant would pick up a crowning vase with its trunk and place it on the head of the person who was next to be king.

Not many people had noticed that their king had gone. One day the elephant went to the vase he used to crown the next king, picked it up, and began marching out of the palace toward the forest where young Tilopa was still playing his game of royal court. All the ministers and people ran behind the elephant, muttering to each other, "What's going on? Either the king is dying or our kingdom is finished." They followed the elephant to the group of children, and the elephant placed the vase on top of Tilopa's head. Because the people of the kingdom believed completely in the elephant's choice, they took the young boy back to the palace and placed him upon the jeweled throne and made him their king.

At first the ministers and later all the subjects treated this boy-king with suspicion. They didn't obey his commands because they thought that he was an ordinary person and his selection was actually some sort of mistake. So Tilopa prayed to Nagarjuna for guidance, and Nagarjuna instructed Tilopa to mount his elephant, take a sword in one hand, go out into the park, slap the trees in the park, and then tell them to go to war. Tilopa did this, and when he slapped the trees, the trees turned into warriors, ready to go to war. When the subjects and ministers saw this, they thought, "Oh, this is a great king with incredible merit" and brought him back to the palace and accepted him as their true king.[12]

Another time, a city in Tilopa's kingdom was approached by what looked like a horde of Persian merchants. They arrived on horseback dressed as ordinary merchants with big packs on the backs of their animals. The people and ministers of the kingdom saw them and didn't give them another thought. However, they were actually Persian warriors disguised as merchants. When they stopped in front of the city, they got off their animals, undid their packs, put on all their armor, and prepared to advance into the city.

At this point everyone in the kingdom was terrified that there would be a great war and they would be destroyed. But Tilopa told them, "Don't be afraid. I'll take care of it." He went out in front of this horde of Persian warriors with his mantle, holding a stick with a globe on it in one hand and his sword in the other. He stood before the approaching army and an incredible light radiated from his mantle, dazzling all the Persian warriors so they couldn't look in his direction. Then Tilopa held up his sword and brandished it until many soldiers came flying out of it, scaring the Persian enemy completely away. After that, the subjects and ministers were extremely happy with their king and celebrated and rejoiced.

This concludes the second chapter on the childhood of Tilopa, which tells how the poor cowherd became a king. This chapter shows us that one does not have to become poor and be an ascetic to practice the Dharma.

3

RENOUNCING SAMSARA AND
MEETING HIS TEACHERS

The outer action of any mahasiddha has three stages. The first stage is called the "completely virtuous stage," the second is called the "stage of vanquishing negative behavior," and the third stage is called the "victorious in all actions." A mahasiddha goes through these stages one by one. The first is called the "completely virtuous stage" because the beginner must take up the practice of being extremely peaceful and calm and carefully watch his or her actions by having extremely controlled and noble behavior. The beginner who engages in this behavior is able to advance along the path and then at a certain point he or she must enter what is called "vanquishing behavior" or *tül shuk* in Tibetan. The syllable *tül* means "to vanquish" or "to subdue" and refers to subduing one's disturbing emotions (Skt. *kleshas*), especially one's arrogance, which is to be completely subdued by the practice. The syllable *shuk* means "entering."

So in this second stage, the practitioners actually submit themselves to conditions such as rage or desire that would normally evoke disturbing consequences. In the first stage of completely virtuous behavior, beginners avoid these situations, but in the vanquishing stage, meditators actually seek them out. The meditators have to destroy their arrogance, pride, and hatred by throwing themselves into situations that evoke a response that allows them to work with these emotions. The third stage of "victorious in all actions" is the final expression of total fearlessness; a total lack of any inhibition about anything that is done. An example of this third kind of behavior would be to fearlessly ride on the back of an incensed tigress. This stage is the final expression of realization.

The story proceeds with Tilopa abandoning his life as a king and becoming a monk and entering the Foundation path. This took place when, as a king, he developed great revulsion for samsara. Setting up his own son as the royal heir, Tilopa left the kingdom and went to a cemetery called Somapuri where there was a temple erected over a spontaneously arisen form of the *heruka*.[13] At the time of Tilopa, this temple was considered to be holy by both Buddhists and non-Buddhists alike. There Tilopa received full ordination as a monk (Skt. *bhikshu*) and resided in Somapuri for a long time practicing diligently. At this point, Tilopa began practicing the first stage of completely virtuous behavior by maintaining his vows as a monk and studying very diligently.

TILOPA BEGINS VAJRAYANA MEDITATION

However, one day Tilopa's meditation was interrupted by a very ugly hag who had a bluish-gray complexion and yellow-colored hair who suddenly appeared in front of him. She distracted him by asking him what he was reading. It was the Prajnaparamita, and she asked, "Would you like to understand and directly experience the meaning of the Prajnaparamita?" At that moment, Tilopa recognized that she was a real dakini and said to her, "Yes, I would like to really understand the meaning of this teaching. I want to understand it directly." The dakini then said to him, "Although what you have been studying is the pure and perfect teaching of the Buddha, it requires a great deal of hardship to actually attain fruition. To attain buddhahood, you must practice virtuous behavior for many lifetimes. This is a path with many obstacles, and it is a difficult path to travel, taking a great deal of time. The teachings I have to teach you are of the fruition tantra. With this practice, you can attain fruition within one, three, or at most seven lifetimes. This practice is very easy to do, and there are few obstacles on this path. I am going to let you enter into the secret Mantrayana.[14]

The dakini transformed herself into the mandala of Chakrasamvara in the sky in front of Tilopa and gave him the pith instructions of the creation and completion stages of practice. In the creation stage, we visualize ourselves as the deity and the purpose of this practice is to destroy our current neurotic fixation on gross and mundane phenomena. Since we can develop a fixation upon the deity itself, the dakini then taught Tilopa the pith instructions of the completion stage, which is basically the instruction on how to dissolve the immeasurable palace of the mandala into the deity, the deity into a seed syllable, and the seed syllable into emptiness. With these two pith instructions, Tilopa attained a degree of realization and the dakini said, "Now throw out your *bhikshu* ordination (monk's vows) and go about acting like a madman, practicing in secret so that nobody knows what you are doing." Then the dakini vanished into the sky.

The dakini who bestowed these instructions and empowerments on Tilopa was called Karpo Sangmo. The reason for doing this second stage of vanquishing behavior of acting like a madman is that one has to test one's samadhi by enduring the bad conditions that this practice places one in, such as being thrown in jail, being beaten up and robbed, and so on. One combines the experience of these unfavorable conditions with the samadhi to experience the power of one's samadhi. This vanquishing behavior is a very powerful method to eliminate one's neurotic conceptions.

This part of Tilopa's biography corrects the notion that people can attain enlightenment by themselves and they don't need a teacher. Tilopa took a dakini as a teacher. That is why Marpa in his commentary on this part of Tilopa's life wrote, "He received the blessing from the great dakini Karpo Sangmo and she gave him the four empowerments."

THE FOUR EMPOWERMENTS OF KARPO SANGMO

The first empowerment is called the "vase empowerment," which points out that the nature of our five aggregates (Skt. *skandhas*) is actually the five buddha families.[15] There are five aspects of the vase empowerment: the vase empowerment of Akshobhya, the crown empowerment of Ratnasambhava, the vajra empowerment of Amitabha, the bell empowerment of Amoghasiddhi, and the name empowerment of Vairochana. Through these five stages of the vase empowerment, we recognize the five aggregates as being the five buddha families.

The second empowerment is called the "secret empowerment," and this takes place through the actual experience of tasting and swallowing the healing nectar (Skt. *amrita*) that is passed out in the empowerment. If we are completely receptive and swallow this amrita,[16] then all the knots and blockages within the subtle channels (Skt. *nadis*) in the body and the life force (Skt. *prana*) are untied or liberated. With this empowerment, if we are receptive to it, we will experience an extremely even flow of the energy within the body. This is the empowerment of the energy flow, the channels, and the energy drops within the body, and especially the flow of the mantra itself.[17]

The third empowerment is called the "knowledge and wisdom empowerment," in which we actually experience great bliss. By experiencing great bliss, we recognize that it is inseparable from the nature of mind, that it is emptiness. So we attain an experience called "bliss-emptiness."

The fourth empowerment is called the "empowerment of the word," which explains the real nature of wisdom itself. These four empowerments are called "ripening empowerments" because when we receive these empowerments, this does not mean that we have attained all the stages and never need to practice anymore. Rather, ripening empowerments should be taken as symbolic moments that eventually lead to the fruition of our practice. Having received these empowerments, we should feel that we have had the great fortune of receiving the empowerments and these empowerments are connected with the full realization of these empowerments with further practice.

TILOPA MEETS MATANGI

After practicing the pith instructions for a long time, Tilopa found that he had reached a point where he could progress no further. He wanted to go to southern India to find Nagarjuna once more. To do this, he began walking through the jungle. In the jungle, he saw a beautiful straw hut and wondered who lived there. Inside he found a yogi who had no food, utensils, or clothes. Tilopa said to him, "What are you doing?" The yogi replied, "I am teaching Dharma to the *gandharvas* (celestial musicians and spirits who live off smell). I was told to teach the gandharvas by the great Nagarjuna himself. I have nothing here." Tilopa asked him, "Who feeds you?" He answered, "All the nature spirits and the deities of the forest bring me food." Tilopa then inquired, "What is your name?" and the yogi replied, "My name is Matangi" and he told Tilopa that Nagarjuna was deceased and had entered parinirvana.

Tilopa asked Matangi to accept him as his student, and Matangi accepted him. Matangi then created the mandala of Guhyasamaja and gave him all the pith instructions of the creation and completion stages of this tantra. The Chakrasamvara tantra that Tilopa had received from the dakini Karpo Sangmo was from the mother tantra. The instructions of Sangvadhupa from Matangi were from the father tantra. The basic difference between the mother tantra and father tantra is that the mother tantra emphasizes the completion stage, which relies more on the emptiness aspect of the nature of mind, whereas the father tantra emphasizes the creation stage, which relies more on the luminous clarity aspect of the nature of mind.[18] Based on Matangi's instructions, Tilopa fully achieved the creation stage to the point where it was almost like he was seeing the meditational deity (Tib. *yidam*) face to face. Tilopa had attained the wisdom arising from the creation stage and was now on the verge of completely achieving the completion stage.

But Tilopa decided that he needed further instructions and left southern India to go to northeastern India where he sought out the teacher Nagpopa. Tilopa received the instructions and empowerments of the Chakrasamvara practice from Nagpopa, although he had already received these from Karpo Sangmo. However, there are three lineages of Chakrasamvara, with one coming from Luipa, the second from Nagpopa, and the third from Dribupa. This lineage of Chakrasamvara came from Nagpopa, who became Tilopa's third teacher.

Tilopa received all the pith instructions of Nagpopa and became a fully accomplished practitioner in the completion stage. Even though he had completely accomplished the creation and completion stages of practice, he still hadn't attained the ultimate view. So he left that part of India and went to the west of India where he encountered the great mahasiddha Lavapa. From Lavapa he received the pith instructions of Mahamudra instructions, especially the "three heart spheres."[19] In summary, Tilopa had traveled to the four directions of India and had become the disciple of four great mahasiddhas: Matangi, Lavapa, Karpo Sangmo, and Nagpopa, from whom he received the mother tantra, the father tantra, and the Mahamudra instructions. He had not only received these instructions but he also practiced them until he had fully mastered them.

Tilopa received one further instruction from Matangi, who told him, "Now you must meditate continuously on the very essence of suchness, the nature of phenomena and mind. To do this, you must find some kind of activity to engage in. Previously, you were a king, so you still have some vestiges of class arrogance and this must be destroyed." Matangi ordered Tilopa to take the job of extracting oil from sesame seeds by beating them, which was an occupation performed only by the lowest caste. Furthermore, Matangi told Tilopa that in the state of Bengal in eastern India there was a kingdom ruled by a very divine king, who was no ordinary king but an incarnate king called Raja Udmakemara. He had blessed the land so that whoever practiced meditation there would travel very rapidly on the path to enlightenment and attain exceedingly good results. Matangi also explained that in this kingdom there was a town called Harikila that had a market-place and a brothel. Tilopa must become a pimp and a servant to a prosti-tute in this brothel. Matangi explained to Tilopa that at this point in his life he should begin engaging in the second type of mahasiddha behavior of "vanquishing behavior." This outer activity, supported by the power of samadhi, is not a meditation practice but rather it is a practice in which one puts oneself in lowly jobs to destroy any vestiges of arrogance. Matangi also predicted that if he practiced in this way, Tilopa would attain perfect powers (Skt. *siddhis*) and benefit many beings.[20]

So Tilopa went to Bengal in eastern India and did exactly as his guru Matangi told him. During the day he pounded sesame seeds to extract oil to be sold, and at night he was a servant to the prostitute Dharima. All the time that he was engaged in this outward behavior, his mind was completely absorbed in the samadhi of suchness (that is, phenomena as it really is).

By doing this practice for twelve years, Tilopa reached enlightenment. He was then seen by the people around him in different marvelous ways. Some saw him flying through the sky like a blazing ball of fire surrounded by fourteen butter lamps. Others saw him in the midst of brilliant light, sitting as a yogi surrounded by women and dakinis who were circumam-bulating and making prostrations to him. Still others saw him sitting as an ordained monk absorbed in samadhi in the midst of brilliant light. When people began to see these things, they began to tell Dharima that something had happened to Tilopa. Dharima was really shocked at hearing this, and when she went out to see for herself, she saw Tilopa in the sky before her, radiant and brilliant. In his left hand he held a mortar, and with his right hand, Tilopa was crushing sesame seeds with a pestle. Dharima was upset and confessed to Tilopa that she had no idea he was such a holy person and felt very sorry that she had ordered him around as a prostitute's servant for all these years. She then offered him her deep confession.

Tilopa replied, "You are not at fault. You didn't know I was a mahasid-dha. Actually, I have attained all the siddhis because of you. I needed to work as your servant to become enlightened. There has been no harm done." Dharima developed great faith in Tilopa, who then touched her on the head with a flower. He blessed her saying, "May all the experience and wisdom I possess arise in you at this very instant." Because of her strong connec-tion with him, she immediately had a profound experience of realization and became a yogini. Everyone around them was completely amazed and rejoiced. Word quickly spread to the king who came in regal splendor riding on an elephant to see what was going on. As he approached, he noticed that Tilopa and Dharima were floating in the sky at the height of seven plantain trees.

Tilopa then sang a song of realization (doha) to the king and everyone assembled there. This doha condensed all the pith instructions Tilopa had received of the mother tantra, the father tantra, and the Mahamudra teachings. In this spiritual song he used several metaphors. We will discuss this doha sung at the marketplace in the next chapter.

4

TEACHING MAHAMUDRA AT PANCAPANA

To review: after Tilopa had practiced for twelve years and was seen float-ing in the sky, the news traveled to the king who heard that the prostitute Dharima had been liberated by an incarnate yogin. The king, riding on his elephant, with a large retinue went to see Tilopa. Both the yogin and Dharima were sitting at the crossroads of the marketplace in the town of Pancapana and had risen into the sky to the height of seven plantain trees. Tilopa then sang this famous spiritual song of realization in the resonant and harmonious voice of Mahabrahma:[21]

1. Sesame oil is the essence.
Although the ignorant know that it is in the sesame seed,
They do not understand the way of cause, effect, and becoming,
And therefore are unable to extract the essence, the sesame oil.

2. Although innate coemergent wisdom
Abides in the heart of all beings,
If it is not shown by the guru, it cannot be realized,
Just as sesame oil that remains in the seed does not appear.

3. If one removes the husk by pounding the sesame seed,
The sesame oil, the essence, appears.
In the same way, the guru shows the truth of reality (Skt. *tathata*),
And all phenomena become indivisible in one essence.

Kye ho!

4. The far-reaching, unfathomable meaning
Is apparent at this very moment.
O how wondrous![22]

Thus in ultimate reality there is no path to be practiced, no difference between what is to be abandoned and what is to be used as an antidote. However, on the conventional level of reality, all phenomena depend on causes and effects. This difference between conventional and ultimate reality is illustrated by the example of sesame seed and sesame oil. If one has a mortar, pestle, and sesame seeds, but there is no one to grind the seeds, one cannot obtain the oil. This is because everything produced is not created by just one cause or one condition, but rather things are produced through the collective force of causal conditions. In the same way, although the dharmakaya pervades all sentient beings, if the guru does not point out this fact or if the path of realization is not practiced, the end result of practice will not be actualized. The relative level of phenomena depends on a series of cause and effects; the realization of this wisdom of suchness is illustrated in terms of the pounding of sesame seeds to extract the oil.

As Tilopa sang this spiritual song to all the people assembled there, just by hearing the sound of this song, they were liberated from the bondage of the disturbing emotions. They saw the wisdom of things as they actually are and attained the siddhi of the celestial realm. So, the country of Sahor was emptied of people who were confused and unvirtuous and thus Sahor became famous for this.

I shall now explain the meaning of this spiritual song in terms of Mahamudra in three parts: the view of Mahamudra, the practice of the path of Mahamudra, and the benefit of the result of having practiced Mahamudra.

THE VIEW OF MAHAMUDRA

1. Sesame oil is the essence.
Although the ignorant know the oil is in the sesame seed,
They do not understand the way of cause, effect, and becoming,
And therefore are unable to extract the essence, the sesame oil.

The first verse of Tilopa's spiritual song presents the principal metaphor concerning buddha nature. This buddha nature or buddha essence is presented in the same way that "the ground" (as in ground, path, and fruition) is presented in the Mahayana sutras and the Vajrayana teachings.

In the second turning of the wheel of Dharma, there is a presentation of emptiness in terms of the Middle Way (Skt. *Madhyamaka*) school, particularly in the Consequence (Skt. *Prasangika*) school, that demonstrates that the ground or foundation of phenomena is emptiness. Emptiness (Skt. *shunyata*) is important in understanding the Perfection of Wisdom or Prajnaparamita teachings.

However, in the third turning of the wheel of Dharma, buddha nature is taught as being present within each and every sentient being. The belief that buddha nature is present in all beings is also the same understanding of buddha nature that is found in Mahamudra meditation. The main difference between the presentation of buddha nature in the Middle Way school and in Mahamudra teachings is that, in the Middle Way school, the understanding of emptiness is arrived at through inferential reasoning, whereas in the tantric or Vajrayana path, emptiness is arrived at by directly experiencing it when examining the mind. The Middle Way school teaches that all things or phenomena are empty. For example, the Middle Way school begins by saying that to understand the reason that phenomena are empty, we must first demonstrate that the subtlest indivisible particles (atoms) have no inherent existence. Then it reasons that coarse substances that are made up of these atoms must also have no inherent existence. Furthermore, this means that composites such as trees and people, which are composed of these coarse substances, can then logically be shown not to have any inherent existence either and so forth. In other words, they prove, using logic, that phenomena are empty. However, as already mentioned, in the third turning of the wheel of Dharma and in Mahamudra practice when we look nakedly at mind, we find nothing substantial and this leads to the understanding that phenomena are empty.[23]

Whether we are using the Rangtong Middle Way presentation or the Shentong Middle Way presentation of emptiness,[24] they both agree that the presence of buddha nature is in the continuum of the mind of every being and that both of these presentations are effective in leading to a realization of ultimate truth (Tib. *döndam*). However, because the Mahayana Middle Way approach relies on inference rather than direct experience, it is very difficult to develop a conclusive experience and realization of this emptiness using logical reasoning. The reason this is such a difficult and long process is that inference uses conceptual understanding, which relies on a belief in something, and this type of understanding takes a great deal of time to develop. For that reason, in the sutras and their commentaries it says that the Middle Way path of inference takes three eons, during which one has to gather vast accumulations of merit and wisdom before such realization can occur.

According to the tradition of the Vajrayana, and especially Mahamudra, it is unnecessary to engage in this process of gathering the two accumulations for three innumerable eons. In Mahamudra practice, buddhahood can be attained in one body and in one lifetime. The reason for this is that Mahamudra uses the mind of the practitioner as an object of direct experience. The recognition that ensues from this is the foundation for the accomplishment of supreme attainment. There have been many siddhas in the Kagyu tradition who have attained full awakening in one lifetime through this use of direct experience. For example, in the *Biography of Milarepa* we find that his student Rechungpa and other students assembled in Milarepa's presence and said to him: "Whether one looks at your fortitude in undergoing the austerities presented to you by your guru Marpa, or your fortitude in practice, or the manner in which you have attained buddhahood, whatever aspects of your life one looks at, it is evident that you are not an ordinary person, that you must be the emanation of either a buddha or a bodhisattva. Would you therefore please tell us which buddha or bodhisattva you are an emanation of?"

In response to this Milarepa said, "Well, I know you all think that I am an emanation of some buddha or bodhisattva, and that is evidence of your pure view, your sacred outlook on me as your guru. However, it is also evidence of your severe misunderstanding of Dharma." Milarepa then went on to explain, "Thinking that the reason your guru is great and must therefore be an emanation of a buddha or bodhisattva comes from your having no confidence in the actual effectiveness of the Dharma as a means of awakening. This is a misunderstanding of the Dharma. I am not an emanation of a buddha or bodhisattva; in fact, in my life I was a black magician who killed many people by causing hailstorms. Yet later I met my guru Marpa, received extraordinary instructions from him, and by practicing these without any laziness I was able to become enlightened. The fact that I was an evildoer in my youth and now I am an awakened person comes from the power and effectiveness of Dharma. It is very important for you to understand this." For that reason, in Mahamudra, direct experience is taken as the path for practice.

Although this doha by Tilopa is primarily an instruction in Mahamudra, it can also be explained at the sutra level, as in the first few lines of this first verse. The example of sesame oil being within the sesame seed is an analogy for the sutra view that the nature within sentient beings is the fact that phenomena are empty or without true existence. This means that even the suffering of samsara is empty; even the disturbing emotions of hatred, attachment, ignorance, jealousy, and pride are empty; and even virtuous and unvirtuous actions are empty. Yet if this is not properly understood, there is no benefit in believing this experience of phenomena to be empty. The essential emptiness of phenomena does not prevent beings from suffering if this emptiness is not recognized. That interpretation of the metaphor is in accordance with the second turning of the wheel of Dharma that emphasizes the Prajnaparamita teachings on the recognition of emptiness.

If we go back and explain the same lines from the point of view of the third turning of the wheel of Dharma that emphasizes the aspect of luminous clarity and all-present wisdom, there is a further implication to this metaphor. In the third turning of the wheel of Dharma, the Buddha explained that the ground or basic nature of mind is not just empty; within this basic nature are all the qualities of enlightenment, and these qualities exist within the continuum of all living beings. In the Vajrayana context, the sesame oil refers to the fact that while all beings have buddha nature, as long as this buddha nature is not recognized, the person will not know how to make these qualities manifest and benefit others.

Tilopa began this spiritual song with the statement that everyone knows that there is sesame oil within the sesame seed, but they don't know how to extract it. If they do not know that it can be extracted by being beaten, pressed, or cooked, then they cannot obtain the pure sesame oil. This is very similar to spiritual realization, with the sesame oil representing the inborn, innate wisdom of mind. This explanation of the nature of mind is somewhat beyond the view explained in the Rangtong Middle Way and the Mind-Only (Skt. *Chittamatra*) schools. The Rangtong view basically points out that the nature of mind is actually only emptiness. The Shentong Madhyamaka school holds the belief that in Mahamudra there is an actual essence or nature of mind that is innate, primordial wisdom and that is recognized and actualized in practice. In the Foundation schools, the realization is the same as in the Middle Way schools, but it is achieved through gradually developing meditation through progressive stages and deepening the view. In the Mahamudra view, by hearing the explanation and receiving the introduction to the mind's nature as being unborn,[25] innate spontaneous wisdom or realization is attained. With this realization, all our neurotic pre-conceptions then collapse into awareness itself and we attain Mahamudra directly. This is the meaning of the oil in the sesame seed.

Continuing with this metaphor, there is buddha nature or buddha essence (Skt. *tathagatagarbha*) in the sutra tradition and the "essence of pri-mordial wisdom" in the Mahamudra tradition. Buddha essence is found in the minds of all sentient beings. Just as we cannot extract sesame oil unless we know the process, we can't realize the unborn natural wisdom of Maha-mudra without instructions from a qualified guru. This can take place in a myriad of ways. Some gurus may point out the mind's true nature merely by explaining what it is and saying, "Your mind is Mahamudra." Others may explain it through symbols or hand gestures. Still others may explain it in a completely special way such as when Tilopa hit Naropa in the face with his sandal or when Naropa introduced the nature of mind to Marpa by creating a mandala of a yidam in the sky. Even though there are numerous ways of introducing the nature of mind, it is impossible to actualize this wisdom without the proper conditions in the student's mind.

The Practice of the Path

> 2. Although innate coemergent wisdom
> Abides in the heart of all beings,
> If it is not shown by the guru, it cannot be realized,
> Just as sesame oil that remains in the seed does not appear.

The second verse uses a sesame seed and its oil as a metaphor to show that it is necessary to have a spiritual friend to realize this nature. From the sutra view, the second verse explains that the nature of phenomena is empty of inherent existence and this is difficult to realize because the understanding of this emptiness goes against our conventional daily experience that every-thing is solid and real. Also the sutra presentation of buddha nature makes it seem that emptiness is very difficult to experience directly because it is so veiled or hidden by disturbing emotions and other obscurations. These apparent difficulties are the problem with using inference as the path.

In Mahamudra, however, emptiness and buddha nature are not difficult to experience or far away; rather they are referred to as "innate coemergent wisdom." The term *coemergent* (Tib. *lhenchik kyepa*) literally means "born together," and it shows that this wisdom, which is the ground to be realized, is not something that has to be acquired because it has always been present within us. The term *innate* (Tib. *nyük ma*) means "natural," which means that this state has to be acquired by removing the quality of our ordinary experience. In fact, this ground is far more natural, far more central, to our being than the obscurations that veil it. This also means that the desire that we must acquire or create this wisdom is a mistake. In fact, the realization of this ground does not depend upon any attempt to end our ordinary experience and replace it with something else. That is why siddhas of this tradition have referred to the presence of this ground as being "coemergent," "natural," or "innate."

The wisdom of Mahamudra, this coemergent wisdom, abides innately within each and every being, and since it has not been recognized, it has not yet manifested. The reason it has not manifested is that its recognition depends upon relying upon an authentic guru who can show us the presence of this coemergent wisdom within us. In other words, the recognition of coemergent wisdom does not automatically happen at a certain time in a person's life and it does not happen for no particular reason.

> 3. If one removes the husk by pounding the sesame seed,
> The sesame oil, the essence, appears.
> In the same way, the guru shows the truth of reality (Skt. *tathata*),
> And all phenomena become indivisible in one essence.

In this third verse, pounding the sesame seeds to produce the oil is a metaphor for going through the process with a teacher of beginning to recognize this nature that has always been present within us. We have always possessed coemergent wisdom since beginningless time, but since we have not met a teacher and received instruction, we have not recognized it. Again, what we have not recognized is referred to in the sutras as "buddha nature" and in the Vajrayana as "coemergent wisdom."

The last two lines describe how this nature has always been present and can therefore be recognized. Pounding the sesame seeds to reveal the oil that has been hidden within the seeds is similar to the guru revealing the nature of the mind, and when we recognize it, we can derive benefit from this recognition. So the benefit of the sesame oil is compared to the effect of our direct experience of mind.

The Sanskrit word *tathata* (Tib. *de shin nyi*) means "suchness" and refers to things as they really are. The use of this term here points out that the nature of mind is already there; it is not newly created, and it is not something that is being added to. Finally, in the last line, the term *phenomena* refers to two aspects of experience—the experience of external objects and the experience in which they became internal subjective cognition. The last line, "All phenomena become indivisible in one essence," means that when we gain the direct experience of the indivisibility of external objects and internal cognition we have achieved our goal.

In the sutras, the discussion of the nature of phenomena is usually explained with the statement that all things that appear are actually without true existence. In Mahamudra, however, we are not concerned with the nature of external objects but with the direct experience of the mind that is experiencing these external objects. So the foundation for our attention is the mind—our consciousness and our thoughts. Thoughts manifest in many forms. We have good thoughts (of faith, compassion, and so forth) and bad thoughts (of attachment, hatred, and so forth). But if we look directly at these thoughts, we will see that we can perceive or "see" them directly because thoughts are not distant or hard to find. For example, we can try to determine where our thoughts are actually located. Are they inside our body? If so, where in the body? Can we find where they are from by examining their origin from the top of our head down to our toes? Or are thoughts outside of our body? If so, where outside the body are they located? Through this kind of examination we begin to discover that thoughts are nowhere. And this experience is a direct experience of emptiness that does not depend upon logical analysis or inferential reasoning. If we directly experience the fundamental nature of the emptiness of thought, then we realize that this experience of the emptiness of mind has the same nature as all external phenomena.[26] So this true experience of the emptiness of our own thoughts can result in understanding that emptiness is the nature of all things. In the sutra approach, this is what is referred to in the *Heart Sutra*, where it is said, "No eyes, no ears, no tongue, and so forth." But in this Mahamudra approach, we are not dealing with it on the level of reasoning but on the level of direct experience.

So, it is possible to look directly at the nature of our own mind, and when we do so, we experience that the nature of this mind is not anything—it has no substantiality, it has no true existence, and therefore we call it "empty." And yet it is not nothingness in the sense of voidness, like in empty space, nor is it a "dead" emptiness, like the absence of thinking of a corpse. Rather this empty mind has the ability to think and to experience at the same time. This emptiness of mind is referred to as "the unity of luminous clarity and emptiness" or "the unity of space and wisdom." Even if we have never recognized the nature of mind, it has always been with us, and recognition of this emptiness does not affect the actual nature of mind in any way.

THE BENEFIT OF THE RESULT

While this nature of mind is totally unaffected by the presence or absence of the recognition of the mind's nature, nevertheless the recognition of this nature is of very great benefit to ourselves. As discussed earlier, if we have the direct experience of the emptiness of phenomena, then ordinary circumstances that would normally cause us to suffer greatly will now no longer cause us harm. Also the presence of conditions for suffering—even the passing of disturbing emotions through our mind—all become self-liberated because the mind has no substantiality; therefore there is nothing to be harmed by these negative circumstances. This means that the supreme peace of this realization of the nature of mind is the freedom from the danger of being harmed by apparent causes of suffering; this peace is called "great joy" or "great bliss." This joy produces tremendous confidence and delight, which is expressed in this spiritual song by Tilopa with the words *Kye ho!* a traditional expression of delight.

We could say this doha (or "song of instruction") is of greater value than conventional Dharma instructions. Conventional instructions cause sadness and renunciation by reminding us of the suffering of samsara in order to make us practice Dharma. This spiritual song is even more powerful, causing us to become diligent because it produces a delight and a confidence in the central meaning of Dharma. In fact, even if we do not fully recognize the true nature that is presented in this spiritual song, just partially understanding it will give us a method to free ourselves and this is a cause for great delight. To explain this, the song gives the fourth verse:

> 4. The far-reaching, unfathomable meaning
> Is apparent at this very moment.
> O how wondrous!

In this verse, "far-reaching" means that what is being presented in the doha can carry us all the way along the path. It is this realization that is the nature of the path, and therefore it traverses the path that, in the sutras, is said to take three periods of innumerable eons to amass the accumulation of merit. The "unfathomable meaning" presented here—the ultimate nature of all phenomena—is unfathomable by using inference. And yet here in this short spiritual song it is presented in an effective, brief, concise, and clear manner. Having understood this, we need not place our hope for enlightenment in our future lives, but we can accomplish full awakening, full buddhahood, in this very lifetime. Because such a profound point has been so clearly and easily demonstrated, it is "wondrous." What could be more wonderful than to have these means at our disposal?

QUESTIONS

Question: I have a lot of difficulty with understanding how to look at the nature of mind. Is the instruction to look at external appearances without altering them the same technique that one uses when one looks at one's mind, and if not, what are the actual mechanics of how to look at the nature of your mind?

Rinpoche: These two techniques are slightly different. There is a difference between looking directly at appearances and looking directly at the nature of the mind. Because we have from beginningless time developed a habit of samsara, we experience external appearances as substantial and we will continue to experience them as though they had substantial existence until we develop some extraordinary level of realization. It is very difficult to work with external appearances in meditation in the beginning because these appearances seem so solid, and therefore it is recommended to just leave appearances alone, since they are not the problem. They do not pose any particular harm or help to us. Our mind, on the other hand, is manifestly insubstantial, and we can experience this by looking for solidity within it. If we find it difficult to look directly at the mind and perceive its insubstantiality, then we can select various substantial characteristics and look for them in turn. For example, we can look for a color, look for a location, look for a shape, look for a size, and so on. And if we take it step by step in this manner, sooner or later we will definitely begin to directly experience the mind's insubstantial nature.

5

RECEIVING SECRET INSTRUCTIONS

We begin Vajrayana practice with the beginning level of "totally virtuous behavior" and gradually work toward the final level of the practice of "victory in all directions." As beginners, we must begin practicing completely virtuous behavior until true wisdom and realization arise and this becomes a stable experience for us. We cannot begin our practice at the level of vanquishing behavior by doing such things as wearing bone ornaments and behaving like a madman. These things are meditative practices for later on when we have gone through the various other spiritual stages.

The biography of Tilopa has two aspects: a "shared" biography, in which it is assumed that Tilopa was a normal person who relied on four human teachers for training, and an "unshared" biography, in which it is assumed that Tilopa was a direct emanation of Vajradhara. The first part of his spiritual biography has already been discussed—Tilopa's meeting with these four great lamas. The second part of his biography concerns his direct experience of Vajradhara; that is, meeting the wisdom dakinis and receiving instructions and teachings directly from them through visions. These two sides of the biography in no way conflict with each other. Actually, the whole story of Tilopa is quite inconceivable. It would be foolish to attempt to put all of these events in some kind of order and say, "At this specific time, Tilopa received this particular instruction from such and such a lama and had the vision of this particular wisdom dakini." These things happened simultaneously and in no chronological order. It is quite possible that Tilopa was receiving direct visionary experience from the wisdom dakinis while he was searching for a teacher on the worldly level.

This chapter begins with telling how Tilopa obtained instructions from the secret treasure house of the wisdom dakinis in the western realm of

Urgyen. The "western land of Urgyen" refers to the land of total enjoyment of the dakas and dakinis who have reached the profound levels of realization and mastery of the nature of phenomena. "Urgyen" here refers to a level of realization. However, it also seems that there were many mahasiddhas who came from a particular area in the western part of India (usually said to be the Swat Valley in Pakistan), and this place was called Urgyen. For example, in the seven-line prayer to Padmasambhava, it says, "You who have gone to the northwest border of Urgyen." There is also a very symbolic meaning to these cardinal directions, so it is hard to locate this place literally. At the same time, these symbolic meanings are involved with actual directions as we think of them.

While Tilopa was still a youth, one day he was sitting in a wooded area under a tree taking care of a herd of cattle and studying the alphabet by himself in accordance with the Indian tradition of those times. A wisdom dakini appeared to him in the form of a very ugly old woman who was disgusting to look at. She then asked him, "Who is your father? What is your country? What book are you reading? What are these cattle?" and so on. Tilopa answered, "My country is the land of Sahor. My father is the Brahmin Salwa, my mother is the Brahmini Saldanma, and my sister is Zaldren." He also answered the other questions, saying that the cattle that he was taking care of were the source of his family's wealth and that he was reading a book to learn the Dharma.

This hag became extremely angry with him and said, "You know nothing. This isn't true! Your land and country is the western realm of Urgyen. Your father is Chakrasamvara, your mother is Vajrayogini, and I am your sister and my name is Sukhada." Then she said, "The place where you are sitting is amid bodhi trees, and the herds you need to take care of are the degrees of your samadhi. The Dharma you are studying is the inexpressible Dharma of the whispered lineage.[27] The Dharma you are reading is in the hands of the wisdom dakinis."

He asked the wisdom dakini, "Will I be able to obtain teachings of this whispered lineage?" She answered, "You have the three prophesied qualities of having perfect samaya and being an emanation yourself."[28] She continued, "With these three qualities, you are entitled to go to the western land of Urgyen and demand the teachings directly from the wisdom dakinis there. In order to get there, you need three things: a crystal ladder, a bridge adorned with precious jewels, and a magical key made of grass."

The items mentioned in this story are, of course, symbolic. For instance, in the life story of Padmasambhava (Tib. Guru Rinpoche), it was predicted that many obstacles to his receiving the Dharma would arise. Padmasambhava wanted to go to the hidden realm called Beyu that required a special way to enter it. It was said that there was a raging river that no one could cross with any ferry, and there was a tree on this side of the river that was the gate to this secret kingdom, but it couldn't be cut down with any kind of ax or sword. However, at the base of the tree was a crystal knife, and the tree could be cut down with this crystal knife. When the tree fell across the river, it would serve as a bridge to the hidden kingdom in which there were many kinds of precious metals in this pure land of nirmanakaya-sambhogakaya-dharmakaya. The adept capable of going through the process of cutting the tree could attain many kinds of samadhi and great teachings in this realm. Khenpo Gangshar has written a treatise about this particular realm. He said some people think that they can just go find the river that nobody can cross, find the tree, chop it down, and cross the river. He explains that this is impossible for someone who has accumulated negative karma. He also writes that, in the literal sense, a river impossible to cross does not exist and a tree that can't be cut down with an iron ax and yet can be cut down with a glass knife also doesn't exist. He then shows that these parts of the story are symbolic. The incredible torrent that can't be crossed is the turbulence of samsara. The tree that can't be cut down by ordinary means is the tree of ego-clinging. The crystal knife nestled in the tree of ego-clinging is the knife of wisdom. This metaphor shows that the practice of Dharma involves traversing samsara by means of walking over one's ego-clinging. At the beginning of the path, ego fixation is an integral part of the practice. Traversing over this tree of ego-clinging is the path itself, and entering into the wondrous hidden kingdom of the nirmanakaya-sambhogakaya-dharmakaya is the richness of the fruition that one will attain after completing the path. As we can see, these symbolic stories are very profound teachings.

I believe that this story about Tilopa is also symbolic. The crystal ladder is a metaphor for the pure view of realizing emptiness, which is like a crystal. The jeweled bridge is a metaphor for meditation because meditation on resting on the nature of the mind is so uncommon that it is like a bridge covered with jewels that are considered very pure. The grass key is a metaphor for taking action without attachment. The key that can do this is made of grass because one doesn't become attached to something made of grass. The key actually represents mastering the subtle channels and the energy flowing within the vajra body.

In accordance with the prophecy of the wisdom dakini, Tilopa asked his parents for permission to go to Urgyen. Tilopa told them that he had received a prophecy that he was to go to the western realm of Urgyen and receive instructions from the wisdom dakinis there, and his mother and father assented. So, he went to the western realm of Urgyen and confronted many dakinis guarding this land who tried to scare him away with projections of many different wrathful and frightful manifestations. He was very proud of the fact that he was able to overcome any fear they projected at him and wasn't afraid of their manifestations in the slightest. He went past the nirmanakaya and the sambhogakaya dakinis right into the very heart of the mandala, which was the dharmakaya court in the center of the realm of Urgyen.

As Tilopa entered the center of the mandala, which was the temple of fragrance (Skt. *gandhalaya*), he sat down comfortably without any inhibition before Bhagavati, the great mother of all the dakinis. All the other dakas and dakinis were very upset that he just strode into the center of the mandala without offering any respect to the mother of all buddhas. They voiced this opinion to Bhagavati, and she replied, "He is, in fact, the father of all buddhas—the emanation of Chakrasamvara himself. Even if you were to produce a huge hailstorm of vajras, he would not be harmed in any way. He has every right to sit with me without offering obeisance." So the dakas and dakinis settled back in their places to witness the next stage.

The mother of all buddhas asked Tilopa, "What do you want? Why did you come to this western realm of Urgyen?" He answered, "My sister Sukhada, the wisdom dakini, told me I should come here to receive the special unwritten pith instructions that come from the lineage of direct hearing. I have come here for these instructions, so please give them to me." Then Bhagavati made three symbolic gestures. The first symbol she made was a physical symbol. Then she said a seed syllable for the speech symbol, and following that she made a hand gesture (Skt. *mudra*) for the mind symbol.

Tilopa knew what these symbols meant and knew that he had to explain their meaning to go further. He said, "I recognize that this physical symbol (*tsakali*) is the treasury of the body, of physical experience. I need to receive all the instructions of the lineage from the dharmakaya manifestation of Vajradhara himself for this." When he heard the seed syllable, he recognized that this represented the treasury of speech. From the great treasury of speech, he requested all the teachings, all the empowerments, and all the different degrees of practice of the path of ripening. Seeing the hand gesture, he recognized that it was the symbol of the treasury of mind. He therefore asked Bhagavati for all the teachings on Mahamudra, the path of liberation. He requested all these teachings of the "path of ripening" and the "path of liberation"[29] by directly understanding the meaning of the symbols.

Bhagavati replied, "It is true. In my treasure house is the body where the wish-fulfilling jewel of the lineage lies. But the door to this treasure house is locked with the lock of samaya. Those who don't have the key of samaya cannot enter. It is also true that in my treasure house of speech are the teachings of the path of ripening. All the yidam deities in this treasure house are closed to those who don't have a prophecy. Finally, it is true that in my treasure house of the mind there is the dharmakaya, which contains all the correct instructions of Mahamudra, the path of instantaneous liberation. But this is closed to those who have not attained full accomplishment."

The "treasure house" should not be thought of as an actual place that can be entered using a key. What this passage means is that if one has perfect samaya by keeping all one's vows, and one has received a command that predicts one's enlightenment, and one has also attained a deep level of realization, then these treasures and the richness of the pith instructions will be available to one and this is like opening a door so one can go in and take whatever instructions one wants. Without perfect samaya, one cannot receive the legacy of this lineage. Without the prophecy, one cannot receive all the teachings of the path of ripening. Without the direct experience of the nature of dharmata, one cannot understand Mahamudra.

Tilopa replied to Bhagavati, "My sister the dakini gave me a key to get into these treasure houses." At this, Bhagavati and the dakas and dakinis roared with laughter. Bhagavati responded laughingly, "A blind man can't see an image. A deaf man can't hear a sound. A mute can't talk. And a cripple can't stand up and run. So whatever prophecy you have comes from some demon and is a fake." Tilopa was unperturbed by all this joking and replied, "I have the first key, the key of perfect samaya, because I have recognized the self-arisen clear nature of mind. I have the second key of the prophecy because I have recognized my mind as Mahamudra, the dharmata itself. I have the third key of actual accomplishment, having merged my mind totally with the Dharmakaya and have direct, continuous experience of it. So, I am fully authorized to enter the treasury."

When Tilopa said, "I have the key of prophecy because I have realized Mahamudra," he was referring to instantaneous prophecy. The word *prophecy* in Tibetan is *lung ten*, which means "prediction," and there are two kinds of prophecies. The first kind of prophecy is when a realized individual says, "In the future time so-and-so will attain such-and-such state of realization." The second kind of prophecy is when an individual, through direct experience, knows something and has attained something. That is the instantaneous prophecy of having attained Mahamudra that Tilopa was referring to.

The Bhagavati was extremely impressed with Tilopa and said, "You are the father of all buddhas; you are the actual emanation of Chakrasamvara. You have perfect samaya, the prophecy, and are fully accomplished. Therefore, I bestow upon you these jewels from each of my three treasuries." So she revealed to him these three jewels. Tilopa understood them instantly, saying, "Through these three jewels from the three treasure houses I will attain enlightenment. I am fearless and fly in the sky like a bird, and there is nothing that can obstruct me. I am Sherab Sangpo ("good and deep wisdom"). From this time on, Tilopa was known as Tilopa Sherab Sangpo.

Bhagavati and all the dakas and dakinis told Tilopa, "You must reside with us here in the land of Urgyen." Tilopa answered, "No, I cannot. I have my disciples—Naropa, Rerepa, and Kasuriva—and I must take these three jewels from the treasury to bestow them upon my many disciples."[30] Having said this, he left the land of Urgyen and was constantly followed by nine formless dakinis who made the prophecy that he would achieve all attainments and be able to guide and help all sentient beings.

In this way, these teachings or pith instructions that Tilopa brought from the land of Urgyen became extremely widespread in the land of Tibet.

6

GAINING DISCIPLES

The main disciple of Tilopa was the great Naropa. However, the whole story of Tilopa accepting Naropa as his student and the story of all the difficulties Naropa had being trained by Tilopa are not given in any detail in Tilopa's spiritual biography because they are vividly described in Naropa's spiritual biography.

Naropa was a prince and an extremely learned scholar. Consequently, he was arrogant and had a great deal of pride. For Naropa to progress along the path, Tilopa had to destroy his arrogance. Naropa had already mastered a great deal of knowledge, so in training Naropa, Tilopa did not give Naropa empowerments or specific teachings. Rather, Tilopa provided an environment for Naropa to destroy his pride and arrogance by giving him all kinds of hardships to undergo. The transmission of Mahamudra teachings to Naropa took place through symbols,[31] and the empowerment that did take employed Tilopa's skill at using symbols to subdue Naropa's pride. Finally, Naropa gained realization when Tilopa slapped him across his face with a shoe. Naropa's wisdom and realization somehow naturally manifested by means of Tilopa's way of dealing with him.

The depiction of Tilopa holding a fish is based upon the story of Naropa's first meeting with him. When Naropa went to look for Tilopa, he had no idea exactly where Tilopa was. Naropa was just going on a prediction that he had received that the one who would be his guru was somewhere in eastern India and that his name was Tilop or Tilopa. He had no idea what Tilopa looked like or exactly where he was, and this caused him great hardship in finding Tilopa. Having gone through a lot of difficulty already and still not having found him, one day he tracked Tilopa down to a certain locality, and when he arrived there, he asked the local people if the mahasiddha

Tilopa lived there. The person he spoke to said they had never heard of any mahasiddha Tilopa, but that there was a beggar named Tilopa who was right over there, indicating a place nearby. Naropa was inspired by this because he thought Tilopa was a mahasiddha, and therefore he could be living as a beggar. When he went over to meet him for the first time, he saw Tilopa sitting there with a pile of fish that he had caught, snapping his fingers and thereby causing the consciousness of each fish to be liberated into the dharmadhatu, after which he would eat the fish. Since this was the first of Tilopa's more famous recorded miraculous displays and was the first time that Naropa actually came into his physical presence, it is commemorated by the traditional depiction in drawings and paintings of Tilopa holding a fish.

Tilopa. Drawing by Jamyong Singhe,
courtesy of Namo Buddha Publications.

The Tilopa Cave. Tilopa meditated and gave teachings to Naropa in this cave at Pashupatinath, one of the most sacred places in Nepal, about ten miles outside of Kathmandu. The cave has since been faced with a door and portico and has a statue of Tilopa inside. Photo courtesy of Clark Johnson.

Unlike Naropa, the eight disciples mentioned in this particular spiritual biography did not have a natural inclination toward practicing Dharma and had to be subdued through miracles and magical displays. The first of these eight main disciples of Tilopa became a disciple because a certain king was always concerned about his mother's happiness. He asked his mother, "How can I make you happy?" His mother replied, "You must gather all the panditas and mahasiddhas and yogins together and sponsor a great feast-offering ceremony." So the king made the arrangements, but in a feast-offering ceremony someone has to act as the master of ceremonies. They decided that the master of ceremonies should be the yogin Marti, who was a renowned and accomplished yogin. He naturally accepted the position of master of ceremonies. But Tilopa's ugly sister appeared and told the assembly, "You've got the wrong person in charge of this feast offering." They replied, "Who then do you think should be the leader?" She answered, "My brother, Tilopa," and then she vanished.

A few minutes later she returned with Tilopa and this started a contest between Tilopa and Marti to see who was, in fact, the best master of ceremonies. In the beginning of the contest, Tilopa equaled all of the miraculous displays that Marti performed. Finally, at the end of this contest, Tilopa made the sun and moon fall to the ground and turned his body completely inside out, revealing whole universes in each of his pores. At that point, Marti realized that he was no match for this great yogin. He developed great faith in Tilopa and requested transmission from him. Tilopa agreed and gave him all the pith instructions and empowerments that he requested. Thus the mahasiddha Marti became the first of Tilopa's eight renowned disciples. He became known as Nuden Lodro.

During this time, the Buddhists were having a great deal of trouble in southern India because there was an extremely clever and erudite Hindu who was defeating them in debate. According to the tradition of those times, whoever lost a debate had to reject his own teachings and convert to the religion of the winner. Therefore, the Buddhists were suffering terribly. Tilopa received news of this and headed there disguised as a monk. When he arrived where the Hindu was causing all the trouble, he was extremely rude to the Hindu, irritating him. The Hindu said, "I challenge you to debate. If I lose, then I will reject my teachings and convert to yours. If you lose, the same applies to you." He was fairly confident that he would win. However, Tilopa won the debate. The Hindu then displayed his miraculous power, by trying to make the sun set by pushing it down toward the western horizon. Tilopa quite easily changed the direction of the sun and kept it from setting. When the sun returned to its normal position, Tilopa made the sun set, and no matter how much the Hindu tried to make the sun come back up again, he had no effect on it. So he lost and admitted that he had. At this point, Tilopa pulled out a knife and told the Hindu, "Now I am going to give you a haircut because you have to enter the Buddhist way, which requires the cutting of your hair."[32] The Hindu was really upset about this and ran away while Tilopa chased after him. The Hindu then turned around, and blazing fire from his mouth, burned Tilopa. Tilopa returned the fire with more of his own fire, which was much more powerful than the Hindu's fire. Tilopa's fire mixed with the Hindu's fire and turned toward the Hindu, who was severely burned. At this point, he gave up and the Hindu Nagpogowa became the second of Tilopa's great disciples.

The third disciple was found during the time that the kingdoms in Bengal, which were very rich, were under attack from an extremely vicious and deceitful magician. This magician had been progressing through the various kingdoms in the south of India, creating enormous armies with his magic and causing these kingdoms to surrender out of fear of war. After he robbed and pillaged the palaces of one kingdom, he continued on to the next king-dom, each time using his magical power to defeat his enemies. The magician arrived one day with his horde of magically produced armies in a city of one of the kingdoms of Bengal, and all the people in the city were extremely frightened and convened a large meeting to discuss what they should do in the face of this attack.

Then along came Tilopa's ugly old sister and asked those gathered at the meeting, "What are you doing?" They answered, "We are deciding what to do about this invasion." She suggested, "You can't win unless you use the services of my brother." They asked where he was, and she answered, "He is waltzing with corpses in the charnel ground." Of course, the citizens did not believe her and thought she was crazy. But they decided to go take a look anyway, and when they did, they saw Tilopa was doing exactly what the old lady had said. He was dancing with corpses hanging from a tree by a single horse hair. Seeing that spectacle, they decided that he must have magical power and invited him to defend their city. Tilopa did this with the power of his samadhi by completely dissolving the magical illusion created by the magician. He then grabbed hold of him and threw him into jail. This magi-cian then became the third of Tilopa's main disciples.

The fourth disciple was a woman who ran a brewery in central India with the help of a young servant. She had become very famous for the quality of her beer and was extremely proud and attached to her business. One day, when the young male servant was away from the brewery, Tilopa entered it and began pulling all the stoppers out of the kegs of beer, letting the beer flow onto the ground. The woman was furious and became very abusive toward Tilopa, who then disappeared. The lady then sat down, weeping over her fate of having lost all of her wonderful beer. The young servant returned, and having heard what had happened, shouted, "We should kill the person who did this." At this point, Tilopa transformed himself into a cat and began jumping among the beer barrels and pulling out the rest of the stoppers until the entire supply of beer was gone. The woman and the young servant began chasing the cat, trying to beat it, but it always jumped out of the way because it was a manifestation of Tilopa. Both were completely in despair when Tilopa came nonchalantly strolling in, saying, "What's the matter with you? Why are you so upset?" The woman answered, "You ruined my supply of beer! You destroyed my entire business, and I have no more livelihood." Tilopa replied, "No, wait. Look inside the barrels, and you will see that they are refilled with even better beer." She didn't believe this but went to see. She found that all the barrels were full of a wonderful new brew. Then she instantaneously had great faith in Tilopa and became his fourth disciple, named Nyi Öd Dronma.

At another time, Tilopa heard of a butcher who slaughtered animals for a living. He wanted to make him his disciple so he entered the butcher's premises and with a magical trick made the lower side of beef that was cooking in the pot look like the butcher's son and left. The butcher came home and wanted to look at the meat that was boiling all day; he lifted up the lid and there was his only son, well cooked in the pot. He was completely heartbroken and was so depressed that he couldn't do anything more for seven days. Meanwhile, Tilopa caused the actual son to disappear from the scene. At the end of seven days, Tilopa arrived. When he returned, he saw the butcher crying and asked, "What's the matter with you?" The butcher said, "You did it. You killed my son and put him in the cooking pot and now he is dead." Tilopa replied, "Well, look at how much suffering you had to undergo by being a father and seeing your child killed. Don't you think that the fathers and mothers of animals suffer seeing their children being taken away from them and slaughtered?" The butcher was then moved from his depression and said, "This is really true. I've caused so much suffering to those mothers of the animals I've butchered." Tilopa said, "If I could bring back your son, would you completely give up your work as a butcher?" The butcher replied, "Without a doubt I would if you can bring back my son." So Tilopa brought the son out of hiding and said, "This is your son who is alive again." At this point the butcher developed great faith in Tilopa, received all the teachings and instructions from him, and became his fifth major disciple, the mahasiddha De Je Gawa.

The next disciple lived in Srinagar, India. He was a great singer who was very famous. He was proud of his accomplishments and very arrogant about his talent. He traveled from town to town, receiving payment for his performances, and enjoyed the great deal of applause he received. One day he was in Srinagar singing his heart out in the middle of the village when Tilopa, having manifested himself as a singer, came from the other side of the square, singing even more beautiful and sweet melodies and outdoing this most famous of singers. A battle arose between them. No matter how sweetly he sang, the singer couldn't sing better than Tilopa. Then he said,

"Until now I thought I was the greatest singer in the whole world. Now that I've met you, I see you must be a god, a *naga*, or some other kind of spirit. How is it that you can possibly have such a wonderful singing voice?" Tilopa then showed his real form, and the singer was so astounded with this miraculous display that he requested to become his disciple. Tilopa assented and bestowed upon him the teachings and instructions, and the singer became his sixth disciple, called Jangden Kukpa.

The seventh disciple of Tilopa was discovered when Tilopa heard about an ongoing debate between a great Hindu scholar and a Buddhist scholar who were always debating the law of cause and effect (karma). The debate went on for a long time, with each side using excellent logic. At every turn of the argument, the Hindu scholar refuted the law of karma, which is the cornerstone of Buddhist philosophy. Tilopa heard about this and entered the debate. He said, "Listen, you two don't have to continue the debate. Just take hold of my garment, and I'll show you something." As soon as they took hold of his garment, Tilopa took them to the hell realms with all its intense suffering. In particular, there were great cauldrons full of boiling iron with the hell beings being tortured and screaming in the pot of molten metal. They were being stirred by a guardian of the hell realm. Then Tilopa asked, "What is it they have done to experience such great suffering?" The guardian of the hell realm answered, "These are people who did not believe in the law of karma. They have therefore developed many negative tendencies and did many evil deeds. The result of these actions is rebirth in the midst of this boiling metal." The Hindu then became extremely terrified and said, "Oh, I was wrong. It's true about the law of karma." He looked around and there was another cauldron completely empty of beings, but full of boiling metal. He then asked the guardian, "What is this one for? Why is it empty?" The guardian said, "We are preparing this for those people who have refuted the law of karma." The Hindu was then extremely terrified and gave up all doubts about the law of karma and thought that he had actually died and said, "Is this it? Is this the moment I'm to be born in the hell realms?"

Tilopa then went to one of the heavenly realms with the two scholars still holding on to his garment and made them witness an orgy of sensual delights of the god realm. The Hindu looked at this and asked why these beings were experiencing such pleasure and happiness. The reply came, "It's because these people have practiced great virtue and developed their noble qualities. The result of this is the blissful experience of the god realm." Just over to one side there was a celestial palace empty except for a harem of gorgeous women in it. The Hindu asked, "Why is no one there to enjoy this?" They said that they were preparing for the future bliss of those who had a strong belief in the law of karma and were developing the noble qualities of practicing virtuous behavior." The Hindu was then completely convinced of the law of karma and became Tilopa's seventh major disciple and was called Nagatanga.

Tilopa realized that he had to go to one more place to subjugate a great sorcerer who was extremely vicious and sadistic and loved to use his black magic upon the terrified population. He liked to cast spells on people, and the curse would kill them immediately, and in general he loved causing great harm so that everyone was afraid of him. Tilopa traveled to where he was and said something extremely rude to the sorcerer, who was delighted at another opportunity to perform his evil magic. He said to Tilopa, "I'm going to cast a spell on you." Tilopa replied, "Go right ahead. What kind of power do you have that you can cast a spell on me?" So the sorcerer cast a spell as hard as he could while Tilopa just sat there and watched the spell taking place. As it took place, all of the sorcerer's relatives fell sick and died because Tilopa had turned the power of the magic spell upon them. Tilopa then said to the sorcerer, "Well, you did your magic, and I don't even have a toothache. But look at your relatives; they're all dead." Then the sorcerer became overwrought and began crying and weeping. "Look how much you're suffering because your magic has caused the death of all your relatives." Tilopa then added, "If I could revive all your relatives, would you have faith in me and abandon your ways?" The sorcerer insisted that he would never again do any black magic. Tilopa then revived all his relatives and the sorcerer became the eighth disciple of Tilopa and was called Luje Denma.

QUESTIONS

Question: What are the higher realms of existence?

Rinpoche: There are three higher realms of existence—the human realm, the jealous god realm, and the god realms. These realms are superior in that the beings in these realms don't have to experience a great deal of pain and suffering. They do experience degrees of happiness and joy because of their previous virtuous actions. These states are still part of samsara and beings in them still maintain their clinging to ideas of reality; they haven't subdued them by realizing that all phenomena are uncreated. In the god realm, for example, beings are so distracted by their experience of pleasure that they have no inclination to gain liberation. Unlike the human realm where we have moments of satisfaction, in the god realm there is a continual craving and continual gratification of that craving. However, there are many beings in the god realm who do practice the Dharma because they are not totally confused by their experience of pleasure.

PART TWO

TEACHINGS ON THE
GANGES MAHAMUDRA

7

TILOPA'S *GANGES MAHAMUDRA*
Root Text

THE TITLE

Sanskrit: *Mahamudra Upadesha*
Tibetan: *Phyag rgya chen po'i man ngag*

THE HOMAGE

Homage to Vajradakini!

A BRIEF EXPLANATION OF THE TEXT

1. Although Mahamudra cannot be taught,
Intelligent and patient Naropa, tolerant of suffering,
Who is engaged in austerity and is devoted to the guru,
Fortunate one, do this with your mind.

I. THE VIEW OF MAHAMUDRA IN SIX METAPHORS

2. For example, in space, what is resting on what?
In one's mind, Mahamudra, there is nothing to be shown.
Rest relaxed in the natural state without attempting to alter anything.
If this fetter of thought is loosened, there is no doubt that you will be
    liberated.

3. For example, it is like looking in the middle of the sky and not seeing anything.
In the same way, when your mind looks at your mind,
Thoughts stop and you will attain unsurpassable awakening.

4. For example, just as the vapor that arises from the earth becomes clouds and dissolves into the expanse of space,
Not going anywhere else and yet not continuing to abide anywhere,
In the same way, the agitation of the thoughts that arise from the mind and within the mind is calmed the instant you see the mind's nature.

5. For example, just as the nature of space transcends color and shape,
And therefore is unaffected and unobscured by the various colors and shapes that occur within it,
In the same way, the essence of your mind transcends color and shape,
And therefore is never affected by the various colors and shapes of virtue and wrongdoing.

6. For example, it is like the luminous heart of the sun,
Which could never be obscured even by the darkness of a thousand eons.
In the same way, that luminous clarity that is the essence of the mind is never obscured by the samsara of innumerable eons.

7. For example, just as we apply the term *empty* to space,
In fact, there is nothing within space that we are accurately describing by that term.
In the same way, although we call the mind clear light or luminosity,
Simply calling it so does not make it true that there is actually anything within the mind that is a true basis for that designation.

8a. In the same way, the nature of the mind has from the beginning been like space,
And there are no dharmas that are not included within that.

II. The Conduct of Mahamudra

8b. Abandoning all physical actions, the practitioner should rest at ease.
Without any verbal utterance, your speech becomes like an echo, sound
    inseparable from emptiness.
Think of nothing whatsoever with the mind and look at the dharmas of
  · the leap.

III. The Meditation of Mahamudra

9. The body is without meaning, empty like a bamboo stalk.
The mind is like the midst of space. It is inconceivable.
Rest relaxed within that; do not let it go or force it to rest.
If mind has no direction, it is Mahamudra.
With this you will attain unsurpassable awakening.

IV. The Commitments of Mahamudra

10. Those who follow tantra and the vehicle of the paramitas,
The Vinaya, the sutras, and the various teachings of the Buddha with an
    attachment for their individual textual traditions and their individual
    philosophy
Will not come to see luminous Mahamudra,
Because the seeing of that luminosity is obscured by their intention and
    attitude.

11. The conceptualized maintenance of vows actually causes you to impair
    the meaning of samaya.
Without mental activity or direction, be free of all intentionality.
Thoughts are self-arisen and self-pacified like designs on the surface of
    water.
If you do not pass beyond the meaning that is not abiding and not
    conceptualizing or focusing,
Then through not passing beyond that, you do not transgress samaya.
This is the torch that dispels all obscurity or darkness.

V. THE BENEFITS OF PRACTICING MAHAMUDRA

12. If free of all intention you do not abide in extremes,
You will see without exception the meaning of all the Buddha's teachings
from all the sections of the Buddha's Dharma.

13. If you rest in this, you will be liberated from the prison of samsara.
If you rest evenly within this, all of your wrongdoing and obscurations
will be burned.
For these reasons, this is called the torch of the doctrine.

VI. THE DEFECTS OF NOT PRACTICING MAHAMUDRA

14. Foolish people who have no interest in this will only be continually
carried off by the river of samsara.
Those foolish people experiencing intolerable sufferings in lower states of
existence are worthy of compassion.

VII. THE MANNER OF PRACTICING MAHAMUDRA

Kye ho!
15. Wishing to attain liberation from intolerable suffering, rely upon a
wise guru.
When the guru's blessings enter your heart, your mind will be liberated.
These phenomena of samsara are pointless and are the causes of suffering.
And since all of these things we have been doing are pointless, look at that
which is meaningful.

16. If you are beyond all grasping at an object and grasping at a subject,
that is the monarch among all views.
If there is no distraction, that is the monarch among all meditations.
If there is no effort, that is the monarch among all conduct.
When there is no hope and no fear, that is the final result and the fruition
has been attained.

17. It is beyond being an object of conceptual focus, and the mind's nature is lucidity.

There is no path to be traversed and yet, in that way, you enter the path of buddhahood.

There is no object of meditation, but if you become accustomed to this, you will attain unsurpassable awakening.

18. Thoroughly examine mundane things of the world.

If you do, you will see that none of them persist,

None of them are capable of permanence,

And that they are all like dreams and magical illusions.

Dreams and magical illusions are meaningless.

Therefore, generate renunciation and abandon mundane concerns.

19. Cut through the bonds of attachment and aversion toward those around you and your surroundings.

Meditate in isolated retreats, forests, and so forth, living alone.

Remain in that state without meditation.

When you attain that which is without attainment, you have attained Mahamudra.

20. For example, if the single taproot of a tree with many branches, leaves, flowers, and fruit is cut,

Then all will automatically die.

In the same way, if the root of mind is cut through,

Then all the branches and leaves of samsara will dry up.

21. For example, just as the darkness that has accumulated over a thousand eons is dispelled by the illumination of one lamp,

In the same way, one instant of the wisdom of the clear light of one's mind dispels all the ignorance, wrongdoing, and obscurations accumulated throughout numerous eons.

THE MAIN PRACTICE OF MAHAMUDRA

Kye ho!

22. The intellect cannot see that which is beyond conceptual mind.

You will never realize that which is uncreated through created dharmas.

If you wish to realize that which is beyond the intellect and is uncreated,
Then scrutinize your mind, and strip awareness naked.

23. Allow the cloudy water of thought to clarify itself.
Do not attempt to stop or create appearances.
Leave them as they are.
If you are without acceptance and rejection of external appearances,
All that appears and exists will be liberated as Mahamudra.

24. The all-basis is unborn, and within that unborn all-basis, abandon bad
habits, wrongdoing, and obscurations.
Therefore, do not fixate or reckon, but rest in the essence of the unborn
nature.
In that state, appearances are fully apparent,
And within that vivid experience, allow concepts to be exhausted or
dissolve.

25. Complete liberation from all conceptual extremes is the supreme
monarch of views.
Boundless vastness is the supreme monarch of meditations.
Being directionless and utterly impartial is the supreme monarch of
conduct.
Self-liberation beyond expectation is the supreme result.

26. For a beginner, it is like a fast current running through a narrow
ravine.
In the middle, or after that, it becomes like the gentle current of the
Ganges River.
In the end, it is like the flowing of all rivers into the mother ocean,
Or, it is like the meeting of the mother and child of all the rivers.

27. If those of little intelligence find they cannot remain in that state,
They may apply the technique of breathing and emphasize the essence of
awareness.
Through many techniques such as gazing and holding the mind,
Tighten your awareness until it stays put,
Exerting effort until awareness comes to rest in its nature.

28. If you rely upon a karmamudra, the wisdom of bliss and emptiness will arise.

Enter into the union, having consecrated the upaya and the prajna.

Slowly send it down, coil it, turn it back, and lead it to its proper place.

Finally cause it to pervade your whole body.

If there is no attachment or craving, the wisdom of bliss and emptiness will appear.

29. You will possess longevity without white hair, and you will be as healthy as the waxing moon.

Your complexion will be lustrous, and you will be as powerful as a lion.

You will quickly attain the common siddhis, and you will come to attain the supreme siddhi as well.[33]

DEDICATION AND ASPIRATION

These instructions of the essential point of Mahamudra, may they abide in the hearts of fortunate beings.

May these essential instructions in Mahamudra abide in the hearts of worthy beings.

THE COLOPHON

This was bestowed on the banks of the Ganges River by the great and glorious siddha Tilopa, who had realized Mahamudra, upon the Kashmiri pandit Naropa, who was both learned and realized, after he had engaged in twelve hardships or austerities. This was translated and written down at Pullahari in the north by the great Naropa and the great Tibetan translator, the king among translators, Marpa Chokyi Lodro.

8

INTRODUCTION

In this chapter I am going to discuss an important teaching that Tilopa gave to his pupil Naropa on the banks of the Ganges River in India. This teaching is called the *Ganges Mahamudra*, and Tilopa gave this teaching to Naropa; later Naropa taught it to Marpa, who brought it to Tibet and translated it into Tibetan. This short text is an instruction in Mahamudra meditation and is considered to be the source of the tradition of Mahamudra in the Kagyu lineage. So I feel very fortunate to have the opportunity to explain it to you.

MAHAMUDRA

Mahamudra is a practice that can be done by anyone. It is an approach that engulfs any practitioner with tremendous blessings that makes it very effective and easy to implement. This is true in our present time, and especially true for Westerners, because in the West there are very few obstacles to the practice of Mahamudra. When His Holiness the Sixteenth Karmapa, Rigpe Dorje, went to spread the Buddhist teachings to the West, he was asked by a student, "Since the Kagyu teachings are now spreading throughout the world, what Tibetan texts should be translated into English?" His Holiness answered that the first text of great importance should be *Moonbeams of Mahamudra* by Dakpo Tashi Namgyal.[34] It should be translated as soon as possible because it is a very important source for the study and practice of Mahamudra. So in accordance with His Holiness's vision, the *Moonbeams of Mahamudra* was translated and is now readily available in English.

From time to time I have suggested and encouraged Dharma students to read *Moonbeams of Mahamudra* and have said, "It is a very good book.

You should read it." Often students will respond, "Well, it is too long and it doesn't seem to be so important. It is too dry." Or something like that. So to encourage students to actually use this text, I have taught on it extensively.[35] However, in order to suit those who need a more abbreviated explanation of Mahamudra, I will teach this present text, the *Ganges Mahamudra*, which is very concise and also full of blessings.

What makes Mahamudra so special? There exists extremely profound practices such as the Six Limbs of the Completion Stage of the Kalachakra Tantra and the renowned instructions on the Great Perfection (Tib. Dzokchen) that are really extraordinary. But for ordinary practitioners there seem to be some problems in implementing these instructions. For example, sometimes practitioners try to practice Dzogchen in a dark retreat. It is possible by spending a month or two in total darkness that you can have uncommon experiences and realization, but it is also quite possible that an ordinary practitioner might go completely crazy in a dark retreat. Or if the practitioner were to do the Leap Over (Tib. *tögal*) practice, which uses the rays of the sun as an external condition, it is possible to develop extraordinary and ensuing wisdom from gazing at the sun in a careful way, but sometimes when it isn't done properly, there will be permanent damage to the eyes. Mahamudra, in contrast, has no such dangers. It is a practice that does not bring about these problems and can be done in a state of relaxation and ease.

The term *Mahamudra* in Sanskrit was translated into Tibetan as *phyag gya chen po* (pronounced *chak gya chen po*). The first Sanskrit syllable, *maha*, which means "great," was translated into Tibetan as *chen po*. The second Sanskrit syllable, *mudra*, means "a seal," for example, the seal that a king affixes to a proclamation to show it was made by the king and covers his whole kingdom. The Tibetan syllable for *mudra* is *phyag gya* (pronounced *chak gya*), which has the additional meaning of "vast." One of the implications of *phyag gya* is that the true nature of phenomena, the emptiness of all phenomena, is vast and unfathomable. If this same nature is recognized within the mind of the practitioner, then this recognition in its vastness is a seal that pervades all of a person's experience. That is why *mudra* is called "a seal" with the connotation of vastness. The reason Mahamudra is called the "great seal" is that it encompasses something far greater than a monarch's seal on a document. Mahamudra is actually the greatest seal of all.

The siddhas who translated *mudra* from Sanskrit into Tibetan added a third word: *phyag*. On a literal level, the word *phyag* is the honorific word for "hand." However, the uncommon meaning in this context is somewhat more profound because *phyag*, as the honorific word for "hand," is also applied to the hands of the Buddha, the hands of bodhisattvas, the hands of one's guru, and so forth. Moreover, this term is also used in an ordinary sense to refer to cleaning tools, such as a broom, which is called a *phyag-ma*. Also someone who uses a broom might simply be called a *phyag*. So the term *phyag* in Mahamudra has the connotations of being both the sacred word for "hand" and also "that which cleans." Putting these two connotations of the word *phyag* together, we get the symbolic meaning "the work that is done by the hands of buddhas, bodhisattvas, and gurus is to cleanse or purify the minds of their students." For example, this term could also be used by the king's ministers to describe actions that promote goodness or healthiness in the lives of the people they govern, which is also an act of cleansing. Putting this all together, the practice of Mahamudra has a cleansing effect, in the sense that it purifies, or cuts through, one's disturbing emotions, and that is why it is called *phyag gya chenpo*. So, that's the reason why the term *Mahamudra* was translated in this way.

There are even more implications of the Tibetan translation of *Mahamudra*. In commentaries, you will find that the first syllable of the Tibetan word *phyag gya* also means "emptiness"—*phyag* refers to the emptiness that is to be realized. The second syllable, *gya* (which itself could simply mean "a sea" or "vastness"), refers to the wisdom that realizes emptiness. What is being pointed out in *phyag gya* is that these two are not separate from each other—Mahamudra is the inseparability of emptiness and wisdom or the inseparability of space and wisdom, which is indicated by the Tibetan word *chenpo,* which means "great." The point is that the supreme pacification of all suffering and all causes of suffering—the disturbing emotions and so forth—is the wisdom of emptiness. It is emptiness itself that is the stable clarity of Mahamudra. And the word *chenpo*, "great," also implies the nonduality of emptiness and the wisdom that recognizes emptiness, which indicates the all-pervasive quality of this realization.

The Importance of the *Upadeshas*

We have the extreme good fortune to have this opportunity to study Tilopa's *Ganges Mahamudra*, which is also called *Mahamudra Practice Instruction* (*Mahamudra Upadesha*). This practice instruction (Skt. *upadesha*) is an extremely useful and beneficial text to study. When we examine the practice of the great siddhas of Tibet, we find that in their study, and also in their practice, they emphasized not the Buddha's original teachings but rather the commentaries on the Buddha's teachings (Skt. *shastras*) composed by the great siddhas and scholars of the past. One might think that the original teachings of the Buddha would be far more important and practical to use. However, in Tibet, there was a greater emphasis placed on both the study and the practical implementation of the shastras for the simple reason that these commentaries contain the condensed essence of the Buddha's teachings and were therefore more convenient to study and implement.

Of the various types of commentaries, the ones that are of the greatest importance are those called "practice instructions." These are the most important texts because they actually explain how we go about meditation practice—how we are to practice the generation stage, the completion stage, and so forth. By emphasizing these texts and their practical implementation, many individuals have been able to obtain the realization of Vajradhara in one lifetime and in one body. There are also others who, after living a life devoted to practice, have been able to attain the state of Vajradhara in the intermediate state (Tib. *bardo*) immediately upon their death.

Some advantages of these practice instructions are that they are easy to remember, easy to understand, and easy to apply. Therefore, upadeshas, especially those in the style of a spiritual song, are of foremost importance. The importance of these dohas is indicated by the fact that practically every siddha from both India and Tibet has left us with a wealth of such spiritual songs.

THE IMPORTANCE OF TILOPA'S DOHAS

These upadeshas were composed by all of the great siddhas of India, including the eighty-four mahasiddhas, for the benefit of their immediate disciples and also for their students and future generations. There are quite a number of dohas. However, the ones that bear the greatest blessings and are the most beneficial are those composed by Tilopa. This is because, unlike other teachers, Tilopa met Vajradhara face to face and received the transmission of Mahamudra directly from him. Therefore, Tilopa's spiritual songs are extremely important. In particular, the *Ganges Mahamudra* is perhaps the most important of the upadeshas on Mahamudra, especially for those practitioners who have had the good fortune to practice Mahamudra, but also for the world in general.

Some of you may not know who or what Vajradhara is and wonder, "Is Vajradhara a person or not, and if Vajradhara is not a person, what is he or she?" As you know, what we call the Dharma are the teachings of the Buddha Shakyamuni. Therefore, the fundamental source and teacher of all Buddhists is Buddha Shakyamuni. As you also know, Buddha Shakyamuni was born about 500 BCE in India and attained buddhahood at Bodh Gaya. The Buddha first turned the wheel of Dharma at Varanasi, then taught for about forty years, and then passed into parinirvana at Kushinagara around the age of eighty. Saying that the Buddha passed into parinirvana means that although his physical body passed away, his mind and wisdom did not pass away; that is, the qualities of his enlightenment—the wisdom that knows the nature of each and every thing and the variety of phenomena, the compassion that is dedicated to the liberation of all beings, and the actual ability to bring about the liberation of all beings—these three qualities of wisdom, compassion, and ability—will never change. This unchanging wisdom mind of the Buddha is called the "dharmakaya." What passed away at Kushinagara 2,500 years ago is called a "supreme nirmanakaya." The dharmakaya does not stop and does not change. Because of its unchanging quality, the dharmakaya is permanent, and because it is permanent, we call the dharmakaya "Vajradhara." The Sanskrit word *vajra* means "permanent," or "that which does not change," and the syllable *dhara* means "that which holds," so "Vajradhara" means that the mind of the Buddha holds this wisdom beyond fluctuation or change.

The dharmakaya Vajradhara is that awakened mind of loving-kindness, wisdom, and the ability to actually benefit beings. In that sense, it is the root of all actual achievement of benefit for beings. But, on the other hand, it cannot itself act directly because the dharmakaya cannot be experienced directly by ordinary human beings. For the dharmakaya to benefit beings, it must therefore display itself in a different form and this form is called the "nirmanakaya." We say that the Buddha who lived 2,500 years ago as a human being is the "supreme nirmanakaya" because this appearance was experienced by ordinary beings. The Buddha can also present himself to realized beings in the form called the "sambhogakaya," which is a pure environment or pure realm available to persons with purified perception. The Vajradhara who is depicted in paintings as being blue in color, holding a vajra and bell crossed in front of him, dressed in fine clothes, and sitting cross-legged on a lotus is the sambhogakaya Vajradhara. This sambhogakaya form is the display of the dharmakaya Vajradhara in a pure environment, which can be experienced by those with pure perception. Bodhisattvas on any of the ten bodhisattva levels can encounter and receive instruction and transmission from the sambhogakaya.[36] This is exactly what happened in Tilopa's case. He encountered the sambhogakaya Vajradhara in a pure realm and received instruction from him.

This means that Tilopa was quite unlike other mahasiddhas in that he would sometimes go to the pure realms to receive instruction and at other times appear in impure realms to teach what he had received. Normally, bodhisattvas and mahasiddhas may choose to be reborn in either a pure or an impure realm, but if they are born in a pure realm, then they remain in that pure realm, and if they are born in an impure realm, then they remain for the duration of that life in that impure realm. They do not usually have the ability to move freely from one to another within a given life. Tilopa, however, had this ability, which is extraordinary because he was one of the few people who is supposed to have been able to do this, and in doing so he received a vast number of tantras and transmissions in the pure realms from Vajradhara and he then brought them back and taught them to his disciples in our world.

Among all of Tilopa's teachings on Mahamudra, the one that has the greatest significance is this short text, which is referred to as the *Mahamudra Upadesha*. This practical instruction is significant both in its title and its explanations. It is taught in the sutras and in the commentaries on the sutras that for ordinary individuals to attain buddhahood, they must first go through three periods of innumerable eons in which they gather the accumulations of merit and wisdom. The significance of the term *upadesha* in the title is that it refers to practical methods that are so efficacious that they obviate the need for such a long path to enlightenment. This text of instruction by Tilopa, who is regarded as being like the king of all mahasiddhas, is quite concise, consisting of only twenty-nine stanzas. It is really valuable because every line in it has a distinct meaning that is worthy of reflection and investigation. We should read it again and again and think about what it means and use it as a basis for our actual practice of meditation. We might have a number of different reactions to this doha. For example, by working with this instruction and practice, we might develop some realization of our mind's nature. We might have received a great deal of instruction from various teachers and have some realization from these. But if we have some recognition of our mind's nature, we should not be satisfied with just that. We should use this experience as the basis for a continued lifelong application of mindfulness and alertness until we have attained full awakening so that we can truly free ourselves from suffering forever. Or we might think, "What exactly is this Mahamudra, what is this nature of mind? I want to know what it is, and I want to realize it." If we have that inquisitiveness and that kind of enthusiasm, it will bring us to the recognition of the mind's nature. Or we might not be that interested in Mahamudra practice to begin with. That is why Tilopa gives us reasons for why we should be extremely interested in Mahamudra. The reason for being interested in Mahamudra, being interested in working with our own mind directly, is that only by directly realizing our mind can we be of genuine and great benefit to ourselves and to others. In any case, whether we presently have some realization of our mind's nature or not, and whether we are particularly interested in this or not, if we look at our mind, we will get it.

EXPLANATION OF THE TITLE

The actual title of this text is the *Mahamudra Upadesha*, but it is commonly known as the *Ganges Mahamudra* because it was taught on the banks of the Ganges River in India. Tilopa couldn't give this particular Mahamudra teaching to all his students—it was given only to his foremost disciple, the pandita Naropa, in a very simple and direct way. Tilopa gave Naropa these teachings after he put Naropa through twelve great trials. This particular teaching is considered to be the cause of Naropa's realization.

In general, some Buddhist texts are named after the student who requests the instruction, others are named after the topic taught, and still others are named after the place where the instruction was given. This text was obviously named after the place, the banks of the sacred Ganges River.

THE TITLE

Sanskrit: *Mahamudra Upadesha*
Tibetan: *Phyag rgya chen po'i man ngag*

This text begins with the name of the text in Sanskrit, followed by the name of the text in Tibetan. This is almost always the case with texts that have been translated into Tibetan from Sanskrit.[37]

THE HOMAGE

> Homage to Vajradakini!

The text proper begins with a homage. There are different editions of this root text in Tibetan, and the first difference between the two most common editions is found in this first line. In some editions, it says, "Homage to glorious coemergence," and others say, "Homage to Vajradakini." The text we are using begins with the latter. The homage is to "Vajradakini," which means that it is to Mahamudra or the Prajnaparamita, where Vajradakini is the mother of all buddhas or, one could say, the realization that produces all the buddhas.

A BRIEF EXPLANATION OF THE TEXT

Each section of the text begins with a brief topical analysis or overview. The headings used here are from a commentary composed by the Third Gyalwa Karmapa, Rangjung Dorje, which we are using. The first verse by Tilopa is the promise to teach.

> 1. Although Mahamudra cannot be taught,
> Intelligent and patient Naropa, tolerant of suffering,
> Who is engaged in austerity and is devoted to the guru,
> Fortunate one, do this with your mind.

Because Tilopa is presenting the view of direct valid cognition or direct experience, he begins by saying, "Although Mahamudra cannot be taught" because Mahamudra is on the ultimate level of reality and therefore cannot be expressed in words or even in concepts. As was said by Shantideva, "Absolute reality is not an object of the intellect because the intellect itself is an object of conventional reality." The intellect is an aspect of ignorance and therefore the intellect is always ignorant.[38] The intellect is always wrong and never sees phenomena correctly and thus never perceives things just as they are. The intellect, being a symptom of delusion, can perceive only in a deluded way. So, we cannot use the intellect to experience Mahamudra. Therefore, Mahamudra cannot be described in conceptual terms. The only thing that we can do is practice meditation and allow the innate intelligence that is aware of itself to emerge.

The second line refers to his student Naropa, who underwent many austerities while he was searching for Tilopa, and also while he was attending Tilopa. He underwent what are called the "twelve major and twelve minor hardships or austerities."[39] The reason for Naropa's earnest seeking and hardship was that even though he had already met a number of extraordinary teachers and mahasiddhas before meeting Tilopa, his yidam had predicted that Tilopa was to be his karmically destined root guru. His search for Tilopa was based upon strong confidence in the prediction that he had received. In this verse, Tilopa refers to Naropa as "a fortunate one." "Fortunate" or "worthy" here means that Naropa had such great faith and devotion and was able to engage in these austerities and find his teacher. It was appropriate for Tilopa to give these instructions to Naropa because of his faith and devotion; only a person with faith and devotion would be capable of understanding the teaching's meaning and actually implementing these teachings as a basis for practice.

Devotion plays two functions in the practice of Mahamudra. One provides an immediate benefit, and the other is the main function of devotion. The immediate benefit occurs sometimes when you supplicate the root and lineage gurus with intense devotion and your outlook changes completely. In an instant, there is a great change in how you experience the world, and the result is right there; you will make considerable progress. For example, if you have had no experience of your mind's nature, then whatever recognition and experience you have had will increase with devotion. So that is the short-term benefit of devotion, which is simply that devotion brings blessings, and blessings bring about progress in your practice. But the true function of devotion is even more basic than that. It is that the more trust, the more interest and confidence that you have in something, the more effort you will put into it. If you have trust in Mahamudra and you believe it is authentic and trustworthy—that is the extent that you will actually engage in practicing it. If you lack devotion or are suspicious of Mahamudra, thinking, "How could it be so easy, how could this actually work—something so simple as this?" or you do not trust it, obviously you are not going to practice it. And when someone takes on this uninterested attitude, no matter how many times Mahamudra is taught to them and no matter how much instruction they receive, it is obviously not going to do them any good. If you have 100 percent confidence in your teacher and 100 percent confidence in Mahamudra, you will have 100 percent diligence. If you have 50 percent confidence, you will have 50 percent diligence. Clearly, this is actually common to all endeavors, whether they are spiritual or mundane. To summarize, the more confidence you have in something, the more you will put into it, and the more you will get out of it.

It is important to understand the reason why Naropa underwent these austerities. He did not undergo them for any mundane reason, such as wanting food or clothing. He underwent them to find and please the guru. It is necessary for a student to prove to a teacher that he or she has enough confidence and trust in him or her and in the instructions to be able to undergo such austerities because only someone who has that much longing and trust can actually practice this kind of teaching. If a student diligently practices the teaching, there will be a positive result; if a student does not practice it, there will obviously be no point in the whole process. Therefore, the ability to practice depends upon the ability to undergo hardships. And if there is no willingness to undergo hardships, then this is an indication that the student has no trust in either the guru or the instructions given by the guru.

Generally, in Buddhism there is no belief that physical suffering is a prerequisite for practice and for awakening. Yet Naropa and Milarepa both underwent inconceivable physical suffering in the process of their training. They underwent this not for the sake of the suffering itself but to show their complete trust and confidence in their guru. Because Naropa was absolutely certain that if he succeeded in receiving instructions from Tilopa, he would attain full enlightenment, this gave him the courage to undergo all these austerities. So in this first verse, Tilopa thanks "intelligent and patient Naropa." In the last line, when Tilopa says to "do this with your mind," he means that now that he has proven himself, if he does this, he will realize the fruition of this practice.

Questions

Question: In the stories of Naropa and Milarepa, it seems that before they actually realized the nature of mind, each one of them underwent tremendous difficulties. In modern times, do we need to undergo similar hardships? Is this somehow a preparation for us to leap over?

Rinpoche: A distinction needs to be made between the simple recognition of the mind's nature and the full realization of the mind's nature. In order to recognize the nature of your mind, heroic austerities like those of Milarepa are not necessary. But in order to fully realize the nature of your mind, these hardships might be necessary. For example, when Milarepa first received instruction from Marpa, he instantly recognized the nature of his mind because that is what Marpa had explained to him and Milarepa understood it. But he had to go through all the subsequent austerities and practice in order to fully realize what he had already recognized. But you should not think that the success or failure of your practice is based upon your ability or inability to do what Milarepa did. This is because any degree of realization of the mind's nature will make your practice and your life completely worthwhile and meaningful. If you can achieve the complete realization that Milarepa did, of course, that would be magnificent. But even having 50 percent or 25 percent or 5 percent or even 1 percent of this realization would still be extraordinary. You should not think that you are in some way disqualified as a practitioner merely because you cannot equal the experience of Milarepa. Any amount of Mahamudra practice you do will be very beneficial.

9

THE VIEW OF MAHAMUDRA IN SIX METAPHORS

OVERVIEW OF THE TEXT

According to Rangjung Dorje's analysis, there are seven main topics presented in the *Ganges Mahamudra*. Different editions of the *Ganges Mahamudra* have different orders of these topics, but the most common order is the following: (1) the view of Mahamudra, (2) the conduct of Mahamudra, (3) the meditation of Mahamudra, (4) the samaya of Mahamudra, (5) the benefits of practicing Mahamudra, (6) the problems of not practicing Mahamudra, and (7) the practice of Mahamudra itself.

I. THE VIEW OF MAHAMUDRA IN SIX METAPHORS

The first of these seven major topics is the "view," and the function of the view is to reveal what is literally called "the ground" or we could say, "the foundation." The ground here means the ground on which everything occurs and within which everything arises. The ground includes the ground of meditation, the ground of conduct, the ground of samaya, and so on.

The ground is the true nature of phenomena (Tib. *nye luk*), and this view can be pointed out in two ways: the common view and the uncommon view. The common view consists of the view arrived at through logical reasoning or inferential valid cognition. This consists of using logic to determine that emptiness is the nature of phenomena. The uncommon view, which is the view of this practice instruction, uses direct experience or direct valid cognition. The reason this teaching is called the "uncommon view" is that one can then avoid using the intellect because ultimate reality is not an object of the intellect—the intellect itself belongs to relative truth or conventional reality. This means that because the intellect is itself bewildered or confused, it cannot transcend its own realm of bewilderment. So in the uncommon view, we simply look directly at our own mind to determine its nature. This is using direct experience to arrive at the view and that is a special characteristic of the view of Mahamudra.

The view of Mahamudra is presented in terms of six examples or metaphors in Tilopa's spiritual song. Perhaps it would be more correct to say that there are six metaphors rather than six examples because, as you will see, space is used as a metaphor in the first, the second, and fourth points of this topic. This shows one of the main differences between a poetic composition and the spontaneous composition of a spiritual song (doha). Normally, when we compose a poem, we write part of the poem, then look at it, and then improve it a little bit. Later we examine it again and improve it a little more, and so on. Nowadays, we would do this on a computer. In contrast, a spiritual song is spontaneously sung with a melody by the lama and is never changed after it is first sung. So there is less attention paid to the restrictions of poetic traditions, which is the reason why the same metaphor of space is used again and again.

FIRST METAPHOR: SPACE AS AN EXAMPLE OF THE ABSENCE OF SOLIDITY

> 2. For example, in space, what is resting on what?
> In one's mind, Mahamudra, there is nothing to be shown.
> Rest relaxed in the natural state without attempting to alter anything.
> If this fetter of thought is loosened, there is no doubt that you will be liberated.

Tilopa begins the first metaphor by using the image of space to communicate something about the ground of Mahamudra. "Space" by definition is physical emptiness; it is an expanse. As such, it is the fundamental medium that allows other things to be present.[40] But because space is nothing in and of itself, it does not require any kind of support. Space does not have to rest on something or be supported by something. Therefore, space itself cannot support anything else. Nothing can rest on space. Things can only rest within space. In the same way, because Mahamudra is emptiness, the absence of substantiality of the mind, it cannot be seen or identified.

Because it is not anything, it cannot be pointed out as being anything. This is described in the second line that says, "In one's mind, Mahamudra, there is nothing to be shown."

Now, if there is nothing to be shown and nothing to be said about it, what are we to do? The next line tells us to "rest relaxed in the natural state without attempting to alter anything." When we hear that we cannot use logical inference to realize Mahamudra and it cannot be taught at all, it makes understanding Mahamudra sound hopeless. But in fact it is not. We can know the meaning of Mahamudra and we can realize it without logical reasoning. We also do not need to have it pointed out to us by a teacher. The only thing that we need to do is "rest relaxed in the natural state"— meaning that we should rest in the nature of our mind without making any alteration to it.

When the text says, "in one's mind," it should be taken to refer to our mind just as it is. Normally, when we think about our mind, we think of it as being full of worries, desires, regrets of what we have done wrong, and so on. Indeed, our mind from time to time may seem to us to be just like that. But, in fact, that is not the true condition of our mind. Saraha has said, "Homage to the mind that is like a wish-fulfilling jewel." A wish-fulfilling jewel is a legendary object that is supposed to be able to grant a person any wish he or she desires. The reason the mind is compared to a wish-granting jewel is that if we look at our mind, we will come to realize the nature of everything. And in order to do this, we do not need to alter our mind. "Not altering the mind" means that we simply rest in our mind as it is. If our mind is something, then rest in that something; if our mind is nothing, then rest in that nothing. Do not feel that you have to turn it into nothing if it seems to be something. Of course, the mind is not something because it has no substantial characteristics. And yet it also is not nothing because it is continually engaging in lucid cognition. It is simply our mind, and we just rest in it as it is without attempting to make it into anything other than what it is. And if we can do that, we will realize Mahamudra.

Maybe it is easy to rest our mind in a relaxed way in its own nature without altering it.[41] But maybe it is very difficult to do so. We might ask, "How do I do this? I have never done this before. I do not know how to relax my mind in its own nature." This is not an unreasonable question. We normally take what we experience—for example, strong disturbing emotions, confused thoughts, and so forth, to be solid and real. The last two lines of this verse tell us that this is an incorrect belief because believing that these experiences truly exist and are solid and real is exactly what binds us or puts us in bondage. If we can let go of this incorrect belief, then automatically we will experience liberation.

SECOND METAPHOR: SPACE AS AN EXAMPLE OF PRACTICING MAHAMUDRA

The second point concerning the view also uses space as a metaphor.

> 3. For example, it is like looking in the middle of the sky and not
> seeing anything.
> In the same way, when your mind looks at your mind,
> Thoughts stop and you will attain unsurpassable awakening.

In the previous verse, space, or the sky, was used as an image to illustrate that Mahamudra has no solidity. In this verse, the sky is used to communicate what happens when Mahamudra is practiced. When we look into the middle of a cloudless sky, we don't see anything at all; there is no form to be seen. Whereas when we look at the ground, of course, we see all sorts of things. This example is used to indicate what it is like when we look for our own mind in the practice of Mahamudra. From a logical point of view, it makes no sense that our mind is looking at our mind. It is like thinking that a sword can cut itself or we can stand on our own shoulders. Nevertheless, in actual experience, it is not only quite possible for mind to look at or observe mind; it is not that difficult. The reason that we can do this is that our mind is very, very close to us; it is inseparable from us. In that sense, we could say that it is not extremely difficult to find our mind because it is right there with us all the time—it is the same cognition and the same awareness that we have always had.

However, if our mind were a solid object and had some kind of substantiality, then when we looked at it, we would see something. Yet, when we look directly at our mind, we don't see anything. The Third Karmapa, Rangjung Dorje, in his *Aspirational Prayer for Mahamudra*, says, "It is not existent— even the victorious ones have not seen it." This means that, from a certain point of view, we can say that there is nothing there, so there is nothing to see. The reason we don't see anything when we look directly at the mind is not because it is obscured in some way or that we don't know how to look at it or that we have to overcome obstacles to see it directly. That's why

Rangjung Dorje said that even the victorious ones (the buddhas) do not see it.

We usually explain Dharma in terms of view, meditation, and conduct. There are two approaches to the view; the first approach is the sutra approach. In this approach, we can develop understanding and confidence in the view through analysis and inferential reasoning. We can become confident that we have sufficiently analyzed a particular topic and that we have determined its nature. The second approach to understanding the view is the Vajrayana approach when "mind looks at our mind"; this approach relies on our direct experience in our meditation. It is this second approach to the view that is referred to in the last two lines of verse 3. In other words, using direct experience, we can see the mind directly, and yet we will not see anything.

How does it actually happen that looking at the mind somehow causes thoughts to dissolve or stop, as it says in the verse? There was a very important terton called Yonge Mingyur Dorje (1641–1708) who discovered a practice or sadhana called *Sampopang* ("Proper Container"). In that liturgy, he talks about the nature of anger and makes the point that anger is meaningful only if it is outwardly directed. We can't have anger that is not outwardly directed, which means that if we turn anger in on itself, if we look directly at our anger, then it doesn't seem to be anything. We can't find where the anger is. We can't discover what shape it has or what color it is or discern any other substantial quality that it has. If anger has none of these substantial qualities, then what does it have? What could it possibly be? What we think of as being "anger" is merely the appearance of anger and not really anything at all. It is like looking for the wind while looking at the empty sky—we can't see anything. So if we look at our own anger, we won't see it, and that pacifies the anger. In the Foundation Vehicle, this same experience is described as the selflessness, or egolessness, of persons. In the Mahayana Vehicle, this is described in terms of emptiness. But whether this was taught by the Buddha or not, when we look at our own mind, we can directly experience the mind's essential emptiness.

This insubstantiality, or emptiness, is true not only of anger but also of other disturbing emotions such as desire, attachment, jealousy, pride, and so forth. It is not only true of negative thoughts, it is also true of positive thoughts. Whatever form a thought takes, if we look directly at it, we will see that in its nature it is nonexistent, and that recognition pacifies the thought, or causes it to cease.[42]

Normally, we never look at our mind in this way. From the time we wake in the morning until the time we go to sleep, our mind is just a stream of one thought after another, one thought producing a second, which produces a third, and so forth, and that is our whole life. Not only that, but while some of these continuous thoughts are virtuous, most of them are unvirtuous. Under the influence of negative thoughts, we engage in harmful actions that cause us to wander around and around in cyclic existence (samsara), and we are often completely miserable. We can see that thoughts that are expressions of delight and uplifted happenings are, in fact, comparatively rare for us. We spend most of our time thinking about how miserable we are. Well, if we rest in Mahamudra, all of that stops. It is through the process of stopping our continuous internal dialogue that we gradually develop awakening.

The last two lines "When your mind looks at your mind, thoughts stop and you will attain unsurpassable awakening" mean that regardless of what is arising in your mind, if you look directly at it, it will dissolve. When thoughts appear in your mind, they do so by arising and then remaining as an experience and then dissolving. If at any point in this process you look directly at the thought, it will dissolve. For example, when a thought or emotion arises, you look to see whence it arose, how it arose, and what this arising means in the case of a thought. If the thought is still present, you look to see where it is and what it is and how it is. Finally, when this thought or emotion dissolves, you look to see where it is going, how it is going and what it is that is going. If you look at the thought in this nonconceptual manner, it will dissolve; it will not be there any more. And if you cultivate this practice again and again, then gradually it will lead to liberation from the bondage of thought, which is unsurpassable awakening. Therefore, Tilopa says, "You will attain unsurpassable awakening."

We sometimes experience this view of Mahamudra and we sometimes do not. When you do not experience it, do not become discouraged. We should not think, "This is impossible. I cannot practice this. Even if I try to practice this, I will not realize it." This process is quite possible and quite workable. But we really need to emphasize this in our practice. We need to actually take the time to look at our mind because by doing so we can experience and realize it directly.

Often we think thoughts like, "Of course, the mahasiddhas can realize this. That is what makes them mahasiddhas. But I cannot possibly do this." It is okay to think about and be impressed by the qualities of mahasiddhas, but we have to remember that mahasiddhas started out as ordinary practitioners like ourselves, and they became mahasiddhas by doing this practice. So it is not impossible.

THIRD METAPHOR: MIST ILLUSTRATES THE WAY THOUGHTS DISSOLVE

The third metaphor describes Mahamudra using a slightly different image—mist or clouds—illustrating the way thoughts dissipate or dissolve by themselves:

> 4. For example, just as the vapor that arises from the earth becomes clouds and dissolves into the expanse of space,
> Not going anywhere else and yet not continuing to abide anywhere,
> In the same way, the agitation of the thoughts that arise from the mind and within the mind is calmed the instant you see the mind's nature.

While we are still within samsara, we have a lot of mental and physical suffering. Mental suffering consists of disturbing emotions arising in our mind that make us suffer at the time they arise. They make us miserable right away and cause us to become even more miserable, depressed, and worried later on. And there are, of course, all kinds of physical suffering: damage or harm to our body, loss of possessions, and so on. Physical suffering and mental suffering can be prevented through the practice of Mahamudra.

How the practice of Mahamudra relieves and prevents mental suffering is explained in this verse with a new image. Tilopa says, "For example, just as the vapor that arises from the earth becomes clouds and dissolves into the expanse of space." He continues, "In the same way, the agitation of the thoughts that arise from the mind and within the mind is calmed the instant you see the mind's nature."

The mental suffering that we experience consists of all the thoughts that arise in our minds, with most being of the nature of suffering—thoughts of worry, agitation, and so on—as well as all the various disturbing emotions that are not only unpleasant at the time they arise but also are the causes of future suffering as well. At any given time, we are both experiencing suffering and creating the causes of future suffering. If we ask, "Can we just stop this?" we will find that we cannot. Even though we try to stop this process, it will still continue to happen.

In this case, what is called mind's nature, which is also called "original mind" (Tib. *thamel gyi shepa*), is luminous clarity because the agitation of thoughts that come out of the mental sixth consciousness is calmed by this luminous clarity. In this verse, original mind is distinguished from all the different thoughts, conceptualizations, mental formations, and experiences that we undergo that arise from the mind. These include the fifty-one types of mental factors, including the five mental factors that must be present for a volitional action to occur, the various virtuous and unvirtuous factors, and so forth.

In the practice of Tranquillity meditation, we are trying to weaken the power of our thoughts. By making these thoughts less strong and influential in our thinking, we begin to relax into the state of tranquillity. In the practice of Mahamudra, these thoughts are not suppressed or weakened, rather they are purified. This is done by examining the direct experience of our mind, which is that it has no substantial existence but definitely has this innate cognitive clarity. Whether we call this "luminous clarity," "true nature of the mind," "emptiness," "clarity," "the unity of emptiness and clarity," or "the unity of space and wisdom," this is not experienced as something that exists or as something that does not exist. Rather it is a genuine and direct experience that causes the waves of discursive thought to naturally dissolve.

The practice of Mahamudra is an alternative to attempting to forcibly stop this seemingly ceaseless flow of thoughts, kleshas, and suffering. It entails looking at the nature of the thoughts that arise, which enables us to transcend them. When a thought arises in our mind, we can look directly at it to see what exactly it consists of: What is a thought? Does a thought have a certain shape, a certain size, a certain substance? Does it have a certain color? If it has any of these characteristics, exactly what shape, color, size, and so on does it have? If it does not have any of these characteristics, what characteristics, if any, does it have? If a thought had any such characteristics, we would surely be able to see them because they arise in the mind. But, in fact, thoughts do not have any such characteristics; they are by nature pure. Previously, I quoted the mahasiddha Saraha as saying, "Homage to the mind that is like a wish-fulfilling jewel." The significance of the image of the wish-fulfilling jewel is that it is something that is completely flawless and always beneficial.[43] The mind, which we erroneously regard as somehow inherently miserable, is, in fact, in its true nature, flawless and inherently free of misery.

There is a song of instructions that Milarepa gave to Paldarbum that is found in *The Rain of Wisdom*. This song consists of five images of which one is appropriate here. Milarepa said, "Look at the depths of the ocean, and meditate. Look at the mind, and meditate without thought." In response Nima Paldarbum asked Milarepa, "I can look at the ocean, but what do I do with all those waves? I can look at my mind, but what do I do with all those thoughts?" This means that she can look at the mind, nevertheless she is disturbed by the thoughts arising within it. Milarepa's response was, "If you can meditate on the ocean, then you will experience that the waves on the ocean's surface are merely the expression of the ocean itself. If you can meditate on the mind, then the thoughts that arise are nothing other than the expressions of the mind."

In other words, if we see our own mind, then what we see is the mind's essence or emptiness. When we see that, we will also see that the nature of whatever thoughts arise in the mind are also emptiness. When this is experienced directly, these thoughts dissolve in their own place, which means right there. Thoughts are not driven out nor do they go somewhere else. They do not go away; they simply dissolve naturally because they are directly perceived. So, that is how the third image of mist illustrates the dissolving of thoughts.

It is very important to practice these instructions, both in formal meditation and in our daily activities, by using the practice of mindfulness. It is important to remember that each of us presently has the extraordinary opportunity of being a human being with eighteen special characteristics.[44] Modern life is very busy, and it seems that we lead full, active, and productive lives and therefore have no time to meditate or that when we spend our time in the practice of meditation, we are then dissatisfied with the quality of our daily lives. Many students are always saying to me, "Oh, I don't have time to practice," or "My life is no good." From a Mahamudra point of view, however, there is no such contradiction. Mahamudra should be practiced formally as much as possible in sitting meditation, but when you cannot do that, you always have the opportunity to apply these instructions to whatever activities you are doing. There are many illustrations of this in the history of our lineage, such as Tilopa who practiced continually while pounding sesame seeds for a living and through that practice he attained full awakening. This is an important example for us. So practice according to this example, and don't let yourself be overpowered by disturbing emotions.

FOURTH METAPHOR: SPACE AS AN EXAMPLE OF NOT BEING OBSCURED

The next stanza again uses space as the image:

> 5. For example, just as the nature of space transcends color and shape,
> And therefore is unaffected and unobscured by the various colors
>   and shapes that occur within it,
> In the same way, the essence of your mind transcends color and
>   shape,
> And therefore is never affected by the various colors and shapes of
>   virtue and wrongdoing.

Here we have to be clear about which of the various meanings of *space* or *sky* we are referring to. In the *Abhidharmakosha*, Vasubandhu explains the two main uses of the term *space*. One meaning of *space* is something that is not anything; it is not a composite of anything and therefore has no visible characteristics, and that is called "empty space." The other use of the term *space* is to describe the sky that is perceived as being blue. In these images (of Tilopa's doha), we are not talking about the blue sky; so when we say that space in its nature has no color, it should not be seen as a contradictory statement. In fact, in the Abhidharma, there is a specific term used to refer to the blue sky, which is *ornamental space* because it is an object of visual perception. In addition, we can think of space as having a shape, as being a certain aperture that is governed by the shape of what it is within. For example, we can think of a square hole as a square space. But Tilopa is talking about space itself, which has no shape, just as it has no color and therefore, as the second line says, it is never obscured or affected by the various colors and shapes.

The third line goes on: "In the same way, the essence of your mind transcends color and shape." We have discussed the specific type of space that Tilopa is referring to, and in the same way, we have to distinguish between two things that could be meant by *mind*. When we talk about mind in the context of conventional reality (Tib. *kunsop*), we are talking about how we experience our mind as being filled with lots of thoughts of happiness, suffering, and so forth. But in this verse we are talking about the nature or essence of the mind, so the mind is being discussed in the context of ultimate truth or reality (Tib. *döndam*). On the ultimate level, there are no characteristics of color and shape to the mind; in other words, there is nothing that would indicate any kind of solidity or true existence. Although we tend to regard our mind as being truly existent, when we directly experience its awareness, we find mind has no solidity, no color, no shape, and so forth. When using logical reasoning as the path—whether in the Rangtong or the Shentong school—there is a lot of discussion about the conventional and ultimate levels of reality. In these explanations, it is often said that conventional reality is experienced within confusion in the mind and ultimate reality is experienced without that confusion. But in the view of Mahamudra, there is little discussion of conventional and ultimate reality. While it is true that ultimate truth is beyond conceptual mind, nevertheless, emphasizing the fact that conventional truth is the experience of confusion makes ultimate truth sound like it is something that is so far away that it can't be directly experienced. The purpose here is to explain that we reach realization from the direct experience of the nature of our own mind. For that reason, the two truths or realities are not used in the example in this text. This verse explains that when you experience the nature of your own mind, it is something that is extraordinarily peaceful, extraordinarily pleasant, and blissful.

It is often said that virtuous actions produce states of happiness and harmful actions produce states of misery. When we experience the mind's nature, we find it possesses an inherent blissfulness that transcends the temporary experiences of happiness or suffering produced as a result of our actions. Because this total peace is experienced, there is no need to hope for temporary states of pleasure produced by virtuous actions and there is also no need to fear temporary states of suffering produced by negative actions. The last lines of this verse say that the nature of mind is "never affected by the various colors and shapes of virtue and wrongdoing." The implication of this verse is that the practice of Mahamudra will help alleviate our physical suffering because the essential quality of our mind is like space and therefore is inherently unaffected by what occurs within it. When we engage in wrongdoing, we accumulate karmic seeds (Tib. *bakchak*) and these karmic seeds or latencies that are stored in the eighth consciousness will not disappear by themselves, but will ripen, that is, express themselves, later. And when they ripen, we experience them as upheaval, impediments, and various kinds of unpleasant circumstances. However, since the experience of suffering occurs within our mind, and because the nature of our mind is itself free of solidity and the characteristics of a solid object, then when we rest in that nature through the practice of Mahamudra, we will not experience what would otherwise be experienced as suffering at all. Or, if we experience it as suffering, it will be far less intense than it would be in ordinary circumstances.

The fundamental reason for the practice of meditation is that it initially pacifies mental suffering and then it also eventually helps us deal with external and physical suffering as well. But we might ask, "Does it do anything else? Does one actually generate any qualities or virtues through the practice of meditation?" The answer is yes. Although the nature of our mind is emptiness, it is also free of possessing any basis for the presence of inherent defects; at the same time, the mind is not absolutely nothing. As we have said before, in the *Heart Sutra* it says, "No eyes, no ears, no tongue, no nose, no tactile consciousness," and so on. And it goes through a list of all the things that you might think to exist—all the relative truths that appear to you—and points out that all of them have no inherent, substantial existence and therefore are empty. The Buddha taught that this mind is empty, but he also taught in the sutras that buddha nature (Skt. *sugatagarbha*), which is to say, emptiness, which is the nature of our mind, contains within it the inherent potential for all of the qualities of buddhahood to develop.

FIFTH METAPHOR: SUNLIGHT AS MIND'S BEING BOTH EMPTY AND LUMINOUS

The fifth metaphor primarily explains that the nature of the mind is not just empty but also has luminous clarity at the same time. The primary metaphor used in this stanza is the sun.

> 6. For example, it is like the luminous heart of the sun,
> Which could never be obscured even by the darkness of a thousand eons.
> In the same way, that luminous clarity that is the essence of the mind is never obscured by the samsara of innumerable eons.

The Rangtong school, which is primarily an explanation from the second turning of the wheel of Dharma and is connected with the Prajnaparamita teachings, places great emphasis on emptiness (Skt. *shunyata*) and, in particular, on the fact that all phenomena are inherently empty. The reason for this emphasis on emptiness is that the largest misconceptions that ordinary persons possess are the false belief in and conviction about the apparent reality of outer objects and the false belief that this "self," this "I," is solid and real. When we believe that the self is real and that external objects are also real, we simply fail to understand "the true nature of things" (Skt. *dharmata*). Failing to do so, we will not abandon our obscurations and consequently remain in samsara. To remedy this fixation on solid and real appearances, the concept of emptiness is explained in terms of the sixteen emptinesses, or the fourteen emptinesses.[45] In the same way, presenting outer phenomena as being like the mist in an early morning and so forth is a remedy for this incorrect fixation that our mind has. We normally think, "My mind truly exists. My mind is solid." This incorrect idea must first be remedied by studying emptiness.

Initially, it is appropriate to emphasize only emptiness as a remedy for the fixation on appearances of self and external phenomena. However, if we ask, "Are all things or phenomena merely empty?" the answer would be "No." In the sutra tradition, this is described, for example, when Nagarjuna said, "If someone with intelligence is mistaken about emptiness, they will not achieve spiritual development." In the tantric tradition, Saraha said, "Those who fixate on the solidity of phenomena are like cattle. But those who fixate on an absence of solidity are even dumber." These points emphasize the fact that while it is true that the essential nature of all things is emptiness, the essential nature itself is not just empty—it is natural clarity.

Let's return to verse 6, which presents a metaphor using the sun. This verse states, "It is like the luminous heart of the sun, which could never be obscured even by the darkness of a thousand eons." This means that our mind has an innate luminous clarity or lucidity, and when this lucidity is revealed, then in an instant that lucidity illuminates whatever it encounters. It does not matter how many eons that the mind has been in darkness because in the instant that the lucidity of mind is present, the mind is completely illuminated.

Since the nature of the mind is always luminous clarity, even though we are in samsara and even though we have dwelled in samsara for innumerable eons, when this nature is recognized, the ignorance of the mind is dispelled automatically simply because ignorance is the absence of recognition of that luminous clarity. That inherent lucidity of our mind is always there, and the recognition of it is, therefore, all that is necessary in order to dispel our ignorance. Therefore, when we talk about buddha nature, what we mean is this inherent luminous clarity that is the potential for awakening. Familiarizing ourselves with this inherent luminous clarity allows us to gradually attain buddhahood. The qualities of the mind, with its inherent lucidity, are never lost and never affected. They have always been available to us, to be recognized through the practice of meditation.

Although we refer to the mind as being empty or insubstantial in order to explain and emphasize that the mind is without a true substantial existence, it is actually not true that the mind is just emptiness. And although we refer to the mind as luminosity or clear light because it has the inherent quality of luminous clarity, causing us to say that the mind's nature is wisdom, the mind is not actually a thing. Therefore, the Buddha taught that, on the ultimate level of reality, the true nature of the mind is inexpressible, inconceivable, and indescribable. This means that we cannot accurately say that the mind is either something or nothing. In order to describe the mind's emptiness, we make it sound as though it were nothing. In order to describe the mind's luminous clarity, we make it sound as though it were something. But in fact, the nature of the mind, buddha nature, or Mahamudra is inexpressible because it is inconceivable and can be understood only through direct experience.

It is often harder to recognize the mind's luminous clarity than the mind's essential emptiness. The reason why luminous clarity is more difficult to recognize is not that it is more subtle but rather that it is the basic ground of all experience and has always been there. We are so habituated or used to this clarity that we actually don't trust what we are experiencing as this clarity. When we are told that the nature of the mind is this inherent luminous clarity, we don't believe that this could refer to the basic cognitive clarity that we experience our mind to be all the time. We expect it to be more brilliant, more like an electric light or a flame of a candle. But luminous clarity here refers simply to the inherent capacity of the mind to experience appearances and to be able to think. When this capacity is increased through practice, it develops into the twofold wisdom of a Buddha—the wisdom of understanding the nature of phenomena and the wisdom of understanding the variety of phenomena.

In verse 7 of the *Aspirational Prayer for Mahamudra*, the Third Karmapa, Rangjung Dorje, says:

> The ground of purification is the mind in itself,
> Which is the unity of emptiness and luminous clarity.
> That which purifies is the Vajrayoga of Mahamudra.
> That which is to be purified is the adventitious stains of confusion.

The "ground of purification" refers not to what should be purified but rather to the nature of mind, which is continuous. The "unity of emptiness and luminous clarity" means that the nature of emptiness is luminosity and the nature of luminosity is emptiness. The "Vajrayoga of Mahamudra" is the recognition of that fundamental nature that is the ground, in other words, the recognition that the mind's nature is a unity of emptiness and luminosity. The last line explains what is to be purified, which is the adventitious stains of confusion."[46] This refers to all of the things that arise in the mind—coarse and subtle thoughts and disturbing emotions. They continually arise in our experience but, in fact, they come from nowhere and abide nowhere because they have no solidity. However, if these thoughts and feelings are believed to really exist, they take hold of us and bind us.

The unity of emptiness and luminous clarity is also clearly taught in the sutra tradition. While this tradition uses inferential reasoning to do this, nevertheless, the explanations are of such clarity that they can assist our understanding. For example, Mipham Rinpoche wrote, "This appearance does not lose its vividness as appearance." He meant that we constantly experience things—for example, visible forms such as people, houses, mountains, gardens, and so forth, and yet even though they are very vivid experiences, they are actually without any inherent essence or nature. Then Mipham goes on to say, "This emptiness does not lose its status as being empty. Interdependence arises unimpeded."[47] Normally, when we hear about the unity of appearances and emptiness, we think that these two things are either contradictory to each other or somehow alternate back and forth. We think that emptiness and appearances are two different things, and we tend to imagine one thing being empty and another thing appearing, or as phenomena appearing sometimes and being empty at other times. But, in fact, it is not like this at all. The true nature of phenomena is unchanging, and yet this in no way obstructs the interdependent manifestations of this nature. Of course, this explanation is in the language and style of the sutras, but that does not mean that it is not helpful to our understanding.

When we say that the nature of the mind is empty, this in no way contradicts the fact that we experience the mind as an unimpeded expression of luminous clarity. And although we experience visible images, auditory sounds, and so forth, this in no way obstructs the fact that our mind's nature and the nature of what is experienced are empty. This is what is meant by unity—the aspect of emptiness and the aspect of clarity are neither separate nor mutually obstructive. In this verse, this is communicated using the image of sunlight. Up to this point, these various stanzas have described first the emptiness of the mind's nature and then the luminosity of the mind's nature.

SIXTH METAPHOR: THE INEXPRESSIBILITY OF THE MIND'S NATURE

The seventh verse of the explanation of the view is concerned with the indescribability, or inexpressibility, of the mind's nature:

> 7. For example, just as we apply the term *empty* to space,
> In fact, there is nothing within space that we are accurately
>   describing by that term.
> In the same way, although we call the mind clear light or
>   luminosity,
> Simply calling it so does not make it true that there is actually
>   anything within the mind that is a true basis for that
>   designation.

This first line says, "For example, just as we apply the term *empty* to space," making the point that there is nothing within space that we can accurately describe. In the same way, saying that the mind has "clear light" (Tib. *ösel*) or "luminous clarity" does not make it true that there is actually anything within the mind that is a true basis for that designation. In order to describe the mind in a rough way we use these terms for convenience, but we have to always remember that the terms do not actually describe what the mind really is. That can only be experienced directly through one's own insight. Marpa the Translator described this as "like a mute person tasting sugar." The mute person has a very clear experience of the taste of sugar but is incapable of describing it. In the same way, Marpa said that he had an experience of the nature of his mind in his training under Naropa but was unable to express it in words.

The point of this verse is that we cannot describe this fundamental nature of what the mind is really like. This means that even when a guru tries to communicate this experience to his or her students by saying that the mind's nature is "the unity of emptiness and clarity," this is just an approximate indication and does not really fully describe what the mind's nature really is. When we actually experience the mind's nature, we have nothing to say about it because there is no conceptually graspable quality that we can then describe with words, language, or thought.

> 8a. In the same way, the nature of the mind has from the beginning been like space,
> And there are no dharmas that are not included within that.[48]

To summarize, up to this point the text has been dealing with the first main topic of the view of Mahamudra, which has been explained using six analogies: one of clouds, another of the sun, and four analogies of space—each one used to describe the mind. The four analogies using space each had a distinct meaning.

The Third Gyalwa Karmapa, Rangjung Dorje, wrote an outline of this text. In his outline, he details the intention behind these four uses of space as a metaphor. The first time space is used, he points out that it refers to the insubstantial nature of mind, or Mahamudra. The second time space is used, he points out that when you look directly at your mind, thoughts vanish as though into space. The third time that space is used, he points out that although you may engage in positive and negative activities that create obscurations of the mind, nothing that you do in the way of positive and negative actions can obscure the luminous clarity of the mind's true nature. And the fourth time that space is used, he points out that the nature of the mind is inexpressible.

Verse 8 is a summary of the presentation of the view and is a summary mainly of the six analogies. The text says that the nature of the mind is like space, and therefore everything that you experience is included within that space of the mind. This is an answer to the implicit question, "Even though the mind's nature is as you have explained it, what good does it do me to know that? My problems come from outside. My enemies are not within my mind; my enemies are outside me. Sickness, harm from the elements, and disasters all come from outside. What use is it for me to meditate upon the nature of my mind? The nature of my mind is not the problem."

Although the nature of your mind is not your problem, there is great benefit to meditate on it. While it may appear that disasters and so forth come from outside yourself, in fact, most true disasters start from within. The way that we experience things, which consists basically of intoxicated delight, depressive misery, intense aggression, and addictive desire and attachment—all of these things—comes from our mind. And as soon as we recognize the nature of our mind, all of these afflicted states are pacified. It is not that external disasters need to be avoided and external enemies need to be subdued, rather it is the internal enemies and the internal disasters that need to be subdued.

Shantideva said that if you attempt to avoid suffering by subduing external enemies and other external sources of suffering, you find that, for every one that you subdue, two arise to take its place. He says that the only thing that will actually work in reducing suffering is to subdue the inner enemy, which is your own aggression. And if you subdue your own aggression, then the external enemies will not arise. In *The Way of the Bodhisattva*, Shantideva gives the example of walking barefoot in the forest and discovering that there are thorns and rocks that hurt your feet. If you think that the solution is for you to cover the forest floor with leather to protect you, you are wrong because you can never cover the whole world with leather. On the other hand, if you just cover the bottom of your own feet with leather, it has the same effect as having covered the entire forest floor or the entire world with leather. Similarly, you cannot control the external world completely, so you must instead learn to control your own mind.

Thus, we need to arrive at a correct view of the nature of the mind and moreover we need to experience the nature of our mind. And according to the view of Mahamudra, that is also why we must have direct experience of the mind's nature rather than a mere conceptual understanding.

QUESTIONS

Question: Is the teaching of buddha essence, or buddha nature, a practice that is taught just in the Vajrayana?

Rinpoche: The concept of buddha essence is not particularly part of just the Vajrayana teachings. The Buddha taught two types of doctrines, one called "sutra" and the other called "tantra." The basic difference between these two does not concern the presence of buddha essence but whether the Buddhist path is realized through inferential reasoning of the sutra approach or through direct experience of the Vajrayana approach. The sutra approach can be divided into the Foundation Vehicle and the Mahayana Vehicle. The Mahayana Vehicle can then be divided into "the second turning of the wheel of Dharma," in which the emphasis is on the emptiness aspect of phenomena, and "the third turning of the wheel of Dharma," in which the emphasis is on the luminous clarity of buddha essence. There is no real difference in the importance of these two aspects of the Mahayana presentation because both are necessary for realizing true reality. Neither approach is entirely sufficient to understand the Mahayana because each type of presentation needs to be augmented by the other. For example, some things that are presented in one view will not be entirely clear, while other things will not be clear in the other approach.

However, a distinction can be made between these two phases of the presentation of Mahayana in how they are employed. In the second turning of the wheel of Dharma, we cut through false projections by demonstrating emptiness, which is taught in this vehicle very clearly. But because second turning suggests that emptiness remains after these elaborations have been cut through, it is hard to understand from the second turning how we should practice meditation on emptiness. It is easier to practice meditation on the luminous clarity, which is emphasized more in the third turning.

Question: Rinpoche, Kalu Rinpoche used to speak about the nature of mind as being empty and clear. I was wondering if you could say something about what "unimpeded" (Tib. *mang gakpa*) is. I never really understood that.

Rinpoche: *Mang gakpa*, the unceasing manifestation of the mind, is an aspect of luminous clarity. If you describe the mind in terms of emptiness and luminous clarity, then you would also include the aspect of unceasing manifestation that is unimpeded. In more detail, you can say that the mind is empty of essence, naturally lucid, and of unceasing manifestation. It is easiest to explain this by going back to the emptiness of the mind. As you know, the mind is called "empty" because when you look for it, it is not to be found and has no substantial characteristics. When we try to embrace this concept of not having any substantiality, we develop a concept of nonexistence. However, if the mind were nothing, then you would not be alive. The fundamental meaning of being unimpeded (*mang gakpa*) is that while there is nothing there; it never stops. It never stops in the sense that you continue to think, you continue to remember, you continue to experience. What never stops? If you have to give it a name, it is the luminous clarity. It is the unimpeded or unceasing quality of the lucidity itself. Therefore, it is usually called the "unceasing manifestation."

Question: Rinpoche, when you discussed the quality of our mind's not being impeded or obstructed, I wondered if it would be all right to think of this in terms of impermanence rather than thinking of thoughts or sounds as being followed and so not allowing something else to arise? Being impermanent, they pass on and therefore things arise. Is that all right?

Rinpoche: Actually, the idea of the unceasing variety and display of phenomena refers more to permanence and continuity than it does to impermanence. The connotation of the term *permanence* is something that is unceasing and therefore it is permanent. What *permanence* refers to here is a quality of the mind's nature. The four cardinal doctrines of Buddhism are called the "Four Dharma Seals"[49] and these include the first seal that all composites are impermanent. Therefore, if you accept any composite thing to be permanent, that would be a non-Buddhist view. But what is being asserted when we say that "the nature of the mind has a manifestation that is unceasing" does not indicate the solidity of something that is composite. Rather, because the mind's nature has no true existence, it does not arise and therefore does not cease; therefore it is "unceasing." However, a thought itself is not unceasing because it does arise and then it ceases. For example, thoughts are manifestations of thinking and the manifestation of mental clarity is that a particular thought does arise and it does cease. So a thought would not be considered to be unceasing. But the nature of the mind from which the thought arises is unceasing, in the sense that it transcends the four extremes and elaborations. Therefore, the very emptiness of thoughts is experienced as being an unceasing variety thoughts. So, it (unceasing manifestation) refers more to permanence and continuity and an unchanging quality that nevertheless is totally devoid of any kind of solidity.

Question: Rinpoche, I want to ask about relaxing the mind when you are looking at the mind. What is it exactly that relaxes, and is relaxing the mind somehow connected with merit and having merit to do that.

Rinpoche: The opposite of the type of relaxation that is being suggested here is a tension that is based upon fear with such thoughts as, "I must not think, I will not think. Oh, I stopped that thought. I did not stop this one," and so on. That attitude toward meditation turns the whole thing into a fight. What is meant by relaxation is when thoughts arise, we just let them arise and we look at them directly. It takes less effort and creates a different kind of environment for the practice.

The relationship between the ability to relax in meditation and the accumulation of merit is that the accumulation of merit is helpful in any aspect of meditation, which is why it is recommended that students complete the four preliminary practices (Tib. *ngöndro*) before receiving the instructions on Mahamudra. By doing the first preliminary, the prostrations, we increase our faith and devotion, which enhances our commitment and involvement with the practice. By doing the Vajrasattva practice, we remove some of the tendencies that would cause uncontrolled thoughts to afflict our practice. By doing the mandala offering practice, we gather the accumulations that make it more possible, or workable, for us to do the practice of Mahamudra. By practicing guru yoga, we will receive the guru's blessings, which brings experience and realization. All of these practices, which lead to the accumulations of merit and wisdom, are helpful in many ways in the practice of Mahamudra. However, we should not mistake these words to mean that someone who has not completed these practices cannot do Mahamudra practice. They can. It is just that these preliminary practices are very helpful.

10

The Conduct of Mahamudra

II. The Conduct of Mahamudra

Now we are beginning the second of the seven main sections of the *Ganges Mahamudra*, which is an explanation of the conduct of Mahamudra.

> 8b. Abandoning all physical actions, the practitioner should rest at ease.
> Without any verbal utterance, your speech becomes like an echo, sound inseparable from emptiness.
> Think of nothing whatsoever with the mind and look at the dharmas of the leap.

This verse is concerned with the conduct of actual meditation practice, and the first line that tells us to abandon all physical actions emphasizes that it is necessary to sit in a manner that is physically still but not tense—that is, in a natural and relaxed state. In the narrow sense, this can refer to the posture often called the "seven dharmas of Vairochana."⁵⁰ But whatever sitting posture is used, the key point is to have a posture that leads to naturalness and relaxation. When we meditate, we tend to try to tighten or crank up our awareness and this causes our subtle channels, muscles, and so forth to tighten as well. Because we tend to do this in practice, people complain, "When I meditate, I get exhausted. When I meditate, it simply hurts." All this happens from tightening up the body too much, so in the sitting posture we should be extremely relaxed so that our muscles, joints, and bones actually relax. Otherwise, when we meditate, we may feel as though our heart were being squeezed or bound in some way. This point was explained by Machik Lapdrön who said, "The essential point of physical posture is that the subtle channels and muscles of the limbs are relaxed."

Even though we may consciously relax our entire body while meditating, we may still exert some tension with our eyes and this will cause them to water during practice. Once we have taken the posture—whether the seven dharmas of Vairochana or the fivefold posture of meditation—we should relax while remaining in that posture and not try to maintain it with physical exertion. In a similar way, while meditating, some meditators try to control their breathing. It is important in this practice of Mahamudra to just let our breath be totally natural, breathing the way we always breathe; so if the breath is long, don't try to shorten it; if it is short, don't try to lengthen it. It is important to put some attention into the conscious relaxation of our body, our eyes, and our breathing when we begin to meditate.

The second line of this verse is: "Without any verbal utterance, your speech becomes like an echo, sound inseparable from emptiness." This line refers only to meditation practice because in postmeditation it is fine to speak. But speech during meditation is like an echo, which means that words in the past are now finished, gone, and not to be thought about. So speech in the context of the formal practice of meditation should be seen as irrelevant, of no more consequence than an echo.

This is important because the main cause of distracting thoughts in meditation is not the external images or sounds that we see and hear but the tendency we have to talk to ourselves internally. This internal conversation is usually concerned with what we have said and done in the past or with what we will say and do in the future. It is this internal speech that should be treated as an echo—the unity of sound and emptiness. This line thus refers to outside sounds that might actually disturb our meditation and the internal conversation that arises as a distraction to our meditation.

The main point in this presentation of the conduct of speech is that because Mahamudra is the path of liberation, there is not anything to be chanted or said orally. The practice of speech that is connected with Mahamudra is basically silence. And connected with that is perceiving sound or relating to sound as insubstantial like an echo or, we could say, the unity of sound and emptiness. Whether talking about the body, speech, or mind, the essence of Mahamudra is that there is no special effort involved. This does not mean that if you are practicing Mahamudra, you must abandon the recitation of mantras or that it is forbidden for a Mahamudra practitioner to recite mantras or that if you are a Mahamudra practitioner that in postmeditation you must stop working; rather it means that there is no specific form of physical activity and no specific form of verbal activity that is required for Mahamudra practice.

The phrase "like an echo, sound inseparable from emptiness" explains the approach we should have to speech in Mahamudra. The reason why no particular speech is regarded as necessary or more important than any other is that sound is just one of the expressions of emptiness. And, in that sense, sound is like an echo. It is not anything real; it is just something that we are experiencing. So whatever speech arises in our meditation has that same fundamental quality or that same fundamental nature and therefore does not need to be especially cultivated.

The last line refers to the actual conduct of the mind during meditation. The phrase "think of nothing" could be misinterpreted in many different ways. It does not mean that we should literally try not to think in meditation; rather it means that we should not fixate on, or have an attachment to, whatever thought arises. We should also not become attached to thoughts; we don't try to prolong them. The key term used in this line is *ladawa*, literally "to transverse the pass" or it could be translated as "leap." The concept of "leap" distinguishes the Mahamudra approach of directly experiencing our mind from the sutra approach of reaching a conclusion by using logical reasoning. If we are attempting to use logical reasoning to uncover the ultimate nature of phenomena, there is, figuratively, a slow climb up the pass because the inferential process consists of thinking about all the facts and gradually developing confidence in their ultimate nature. In the Mahamudra approach, however, we are "leaping" past this conceptualization altogether and going into the direct experience of the nature of our mind. So, there is no analysis or labeling of substantiality, insubstantiality, emptiness, and so forth—we are simply looking directly at our mind, directly experiencing it, and thereby directly meditating upon it.

Now, the essence, or nature, of mind is that it is essentially empty, luminous clarity, and this is not impeded by the many appearances or variety of manifestations. While we are looking at the essential emptiness of mind, we are not labeling it or thinking, "Oh, this is empty and that is the clarity," and so forth. Of course, it is emptiness, but we are not labeling it. Rather we just experience the nature of the mind without attempting to draw any inferences from it.

III. THE MEDITATION OF MAHAMUDRA

The third of the seven main topics of the *Ganges Mahamudra* concerns meditation. The next three verses are concerned with meditation involved in our conduct regarding postmeditation—the meditation that we do when we are off the cushion. The first of these verses reads:

> 9. The body is without meaning, empty like a bamboo stalk.
> The mind is like the midst of space. It is inconceivable.
> Rest relaxed within that; do not let it go or force it to rest,
> If mind has no direction, it is Mahamudra.
> With this you will attain unsurpassable awakening.

The view of Mahamudra is the recognition of the ground, which is also the ground of meditation. The conduct of Mahamudra is how to use your body, speech, and mind to practice Dharma in a way that is based upon the recognition of that view. This verse on meditation specifically explains how to familiarize yourself with the view that has been recognized. So, meditation in this context is basically further familiarization with the view. Meditation here has two aspects: the preliminary practices of meditation and the main practice of meditation. Verse 9 of the text begins a description of the preliminary practices.

The first line states, "The body is without meaning, empty like a bamboo stalk." In our everyday experience, we think of ourselves as, first, having a body made of substances such as flesh and blood and, second, as having a mind, which is a nonmaterial entity that is simply cognition. For the duration of our life these two are somewhat interdependent and coexist in the same space. If we think about the nature of our experience, we will easily come to the conclusion that of these two, our mind is the more important and significant entity. Normally, however, we act in a way that regards our body as more important. Because of that, most of what we do day to day is done either directly or indirectly to sustain, cherish, and protect our body. Although the body is really just an agent of the mind, we make the mind a slave or servant of the body. We are constantly agitated and constantly making ourselves miserable mentally with such things as fear that something terrible will happen to our body, and so on. From the long-term point of view, this is meaningless because the body is a very temporary thing. We regard it as somehow intrinsically valuable but, in fact, the body has no value whatsoever.

The actual implementation of this understanding that the body is empty is done by contemplating the four common preliminaries: (1) the difficulty of acquiring the freedoms and resources of our precious human existence, (2) impermanence and death, (3) the result of actions, and (4) the problems of samsara.[51] One of the benefits of contemplating these preliminaries is that our obsession with our physical body will lessen and this will then give us the space to actually practice.

When we contemplate these four common preliminaries, or thoughts that turn the mind (toward the Dharma), the result is usually that we will become inspired to practice meditation, which then naturally leads to diligence in our practice. The actual practice of meditation itself has two stages: Tranquillity (Skt. *shamatha*) and Insight (Skt. *vipashyana*). These can be practiced with a unified approach of Shamatha and Vipashyana from the beginning or they can be practiced in sequence.

The most complete presentation of the meditation would begin with discussing the physical posture of the body and then how to employ mental techniques such as the use of breathing. In this text, the physical posture is not discussed because it is a brief spiritual song and it is assumed that you already understand the seven dharmas of Vairochana.

The Ninth Gyalwa Karmapa, Wangchuk Dorje, in his *Pointing Out the Dharmakaya*, makes the point that while we need to have the meditation posture of the seven dharmas of Vairochana, we must ensure that the way we hold this posture is relaxed. Often when we fix our mind on something or when we concentrate, we automatically generate a state of physical tension along with that. If we become physically tense when practicing meditation, we may experience some kind of heat or discomfort or pain. If these sensations arise, they are not that important because they are just something that comes about from the physical tension of our posture. Nevertheless, in order to avoid them, the Ninth Karmapa makes the following recommendation: "Maintain a posture that is free of tension, too much exertion, or a feeling of being coiled up; in other words, make the posture relaxed and comfortable." These words seem obvious right now, but when we actually practice meditation these instructions become very important and very helpful in developing a stable meditation experience and in preventing unnecessary impediments to our meditation.

While we are greatly attached to our bodies, in fact, our bodies are without essence, which means that they are composites without true existence. That the body lacks essence is conveyed by the metaphor in the text of a hollow bamboo pole. Then the second line says, "The mind is like the midst of space. It is inconceivable." Here again we have the simile of the mind as being like space. If we look at the horizon, we will see many things, but if we look straight up into the center of the sky, we won't see anything. Similarly, if we look at thoughts, there will be no end to the possible contents of those thoughts. But looking at the mind is like looking at the center of the sky—there is nothing to be seen or examined. In verse 11 of *Aspirational Prayer for Mahamudra*, the Third Karmapa, Rangjung Dorje, says:

> It does not exist nor does it not-exist.
> It is not even seen by the victorious ones (the buddhas).
> It is the basis of all samsara and nirvana.
> This is not a contradiction—it is the Middle Way.
> May I realize the dharmata of the mind that is beyond these
>   extremes.

Normally, if we say that something exists, we would conclude that it cannot be nonexistent. And if we say that something does not exist, we would conclude that it cannot be existent. To say that something can exist and not exist at the same time is a logical contradiction. But what Rangjung Dorje says is that we cannot say that the mind's nature exists and we also cannot say that it is nonexistent. But the fourth line of Rangjung Dorje's spiritual song says that, in the case of mind, this is not a contradiction. He then says, "May I realize the dharmata of the mind that is beyond these extremes." "Beyond extremes" here means that the mind's nature does not fall into either the extreme of existence or the extreme of nonexistence. There is a nearly identical verse from the Dzogchen tradition composed by the terton Drime Lingpa, which gives these first three lines exactly and then follows with "It transcends utterance and cannot be described. May this nature of the ground of Dzogchen be realized." The point is that in both traditions, Mahamudra and Dzogchen, the nature of the mind is understood in the same way.

The third line of verse 9 says that we should "not let it go or force it to rest," meaning that it does not matter what is happening within our mind. When we look at the nature of our mind and a thought arises, that is not a problem. If a thought arises, then we look to see the nature of that thought and in that way we will see the nature of our mind. If a thought does not arise, we do not have to regard that as a problem. We do not have to try to cause a thought to arise; we simply look at the nature of that mind in the absence of thought. We do not have to alter the state of our mind in this practice of meditation. We do not have to attempt to force it to have any specific characteristics. If we experience no luminous clarity, we do not have to go looking for it. We just look directly at what we experience and relax our mind, and then we will see the nature of our mind and will be able to remain relaxed within that direct experience of our mind's nature.

This instruction is extraordinarily useful and important because if we lack this instruction, we are liable to think that meditation consists of stopping thoughts and that our goal in meditation is not to think. This is impossible to do because even if we succeed in stopping the emergence of thoughts, that observance will simply become a thought itself. We can never win attempting to conquer thoughts. If, on the other hand, we take the Mahamudra approach and simply look at the nature of whatever arises in our mind, the thoughts become pacified simply by seeing them as they are. To the extent that we get involved in fighting with thoughts in meditation, we become tired and discouraged because it is endless. Simply looking directly at the nature of thoughts is an effortless process because when thoughts are seen as they are, they are self-liberated and pacify themselves.

According to all the teachers in the past, to develop Mahamudra, we need to employ the faculties of mindfulness and alertness. In fact, we need a strong mindfulness as was taught by Tashi Namgyal in *Moonbeams of Mahamudra*, in which he says, "Your mindfulness needs to be sharp and crisp." And in *The Way of the Bodhisattva*, Shantideva says, "To those who wish to grasp hold of their mind, I join my palms together in an attitude of reverence for those who exert themselves in mindfulness."

That is how to rest your mind. Then, within that state of resting the mind, you practice Vipashyana or Insight meditation. The difference between the basic meditation of resting the mind (Shamatha) and the practice of Insight (Vipashyana) is that Shamatha is devoid of Vipashyana because when your mind comes to rest within its own nature, there is no recognition of that nature. In order to develop Vipashyana, some further instruction is necessary and that is given in the last two lines of this verse.

The last two lines of verse 9 of our text say, "If mind has no direction, it is Mahamudra. With this you will attain unsurpassable awakening." The word *direction* here means looking at something. The definition of Vipashyana here is that you are not looking at anything, because there is nothing to look at. If you were looking for direction to your mind, then you would be looking for a certain location where the mind would be and you would be looking for certain substantial characteristics in that location, such as shape and color, and so forth. In fact, the nature of the mind that is recognized is the absence of any such location or any other substantial characteristic. So the nature of mind that is Mahamudra is what you should familiarize yourself with. Familiarization with this nature is the practice of Mahamudra. The Buddha explained this in different ways in different contexts. All of these things are included in this one understanding because this nature of the mind is beyond any location or direction. The nature of a mind that is "free of direction" is the selflessness of persons and the selflessness of phenomena. It is emptiness. It is buddha nature. If you familiarize yourself with this, then that will lead you to unsurpassable awakening.

All kinds of things constantly arise in your mind. You become sad, you become fearful, you become angry, you experience doubt, you experience guilt. Most experiences are unpleasant, and whatever they are, you want them to stop. But you do not know how to make them stop. The more you identify these unpleasant mental states as being real and solid, the more upset and the more angry you will become, the more guilt you will feel, the bigger grudge you will have. Finally, if you maintain this thinking strongly enough, you will become so unhappy that you will become physically ill. The solution is to see right through these thoughts because as long as you are attempting to flee from an unpleasant mental state, it will seem to be very powerful and threatening. But when you look right at it, there is nothing there. For example, if you become intensely sad and you look right at the sadness, you find that there is nothing there that you can really call "sadness." Conventionally, anger is regarded as a very powerful and dangerous emotion, and often it is. But that is true only so long as you ignore looking at it. If you look right at your anger, there is nothing there. And this is true of any other disturbing emotion or unpleasant mental state. If you recognize its nature, whatever it is, it will no longer harm you. So this point is important not only for the ultimate attainment of buddhahood but also for the immediate or short-term ability to live happily.

QUESTIONS

Question: You said that we must keep working on experiencing the direct experience of mind both in our meditation and postmeditation until we become used to it. Is that cultivation of the experience of leap in meditation practice and recognition in postmeditation practice more about cultivating recognition in practice?

Rinpoche: The distinction made between the experience of the leap or the even-placement stage in meditation and the use of recognition in postmeditation is that meditation or even placement being just that, there isn't a great deal of thoughts that arise so it is not a practice concerned with the recognition of thought but rather a practice of simply experiencing this fundamental nature. However, in postmeditation, because we are actively engaged in the world, thoughts do arise and therefore the practice of recognition manifests more in postmeditation when we attempt to experience what arises within a continued recognition of this fundamental nature of Mahamudra. We are trying to continue the experience of this nature in postmeditation, but it is distinct from our meditation practice because there is activity and thought in postmeditation. So these two aspects of practice assist each other: meditation enhances postmeditation and postmeditation enhances meditation.

Question: When you talk about the nature of the mind, are you also referring to the essence of the mind?

Translator: Well, I have used *essence* for the Tibetan *ngowo* and *nature* for *namjen* and *manner of abiding* for *ney luk*, and these three terms can be used distinctly in this context, but they are really referring to the same thing, which we can call the mind's "essence, nature, or manner of abiding."

Rinpoche: I have been referring to "the essence" or "the nature" of the mind, which has also been called "the direct" or "naked" nature of the mind. One way this can be explained is that, in our ordinary (unenlightened) confused state, we believe in the apparent solidity of experiences in our mind because we have one thought and then we jump to the next thought that is just about to begin. So we end up jumping from thought to thought, experiencing this apparent reality or solidity of thoughts because of the continuity of these thoughts. But if we just rest in the present moment—that moment in between what has just finished and what has not yet begun—we can experience that true nature or essence of mind. Thoughts may arise and cease but the mind itself has not come from anywhere, it isn't resting anywhere right now, and it isn't going anywhere. In that sense, the nature of mind is like space, except that it isn't like empty space because, at the same time that nothing is there, the mind has a cognitive clarity, luminous clarity. However, when we try to figure this out and say, "It really is like this," then we run into the problem that I already explained of using words for things that are indescribable, which in turn, "obscures this nature." On the other hand, if we meditate and experience this in our meditation, we can experience this directly. This is more or less what we mean when we talk about the essence or nature of the mind.

Question: You said that we should embrace the view of Mahamudra in every action. What about the boundaries and rules given by society? Do we get rid of them?

Rinpoche: There is absolutely no reason why embracing all actions with the view of Mahamudra should cause them to be in conflict with the customs of the world. In fact, we should act in accordance with the customs of society. There are three aspects to conduct: what you do with your body, what you do with your speech, and what you do with your mind. What you do with your body and speech is simply to behave properly, which means to act in accordance with the way of the world. In this context, in accordance with the ways of the world means to be harmonious with others, not to be in conflict with others, not to be constantly arguing and fighting with others. With speech, it means not to be impulsive but to speak carefully and with consideration of the effect our speech will have on others. Now, sometimes we can't do this, and we act improperly. The reason why we act improperly with body and speech is that our mind is under the control of the disturbing emotions. If our mind is not under the control of disturbing emotions, then our mind is in a state of relaxation and tranquillity and improper actions of body and speech will be less likely to occur. So the mind aspect of conduct is to always experience the nature of the mind. And if we experience the nature of the mind, we will not be overpowered by attachment, aggression, and ignorance.

In the beginning, of course, this is difficult. So we can, right from the start, cultivate the attitude, "I own my mind. My mind doesn't own me and run my life. I am going to control and train my mind." This attitude, and the practice that ensues from this, will bring about the pacification of the mind that will cause the actions of our body and speech to be in accordance with the needs of everyone.

11

THE COMMITMENTS OF MAHAMUDRA

The *Ganges Mahamudra* teachings of Tilopa are divided into seven topics. We have already discussed the first three topics. In this chapter, we will discuss the fourth topic, which is the vows or commitments (Skt. *samaya*) of Mahamudra.

Samaya, or Vajrayana commitments, refers to a pledge or promise or commitment—something you undertake. The way samaya is explained in the tantras and in traditional texts makes it sound extremely dangerous, like some kind of horrific control, a complete lack of personal freedom, and that if you make any attempt to assert personal freedom, you will be cast immediately into the depths of the lowest hell. It is explained this way for a reason, which is that in order to accomplish anything, you need to maintain a certain consistent direction and diligence. This is obvious and true of anything that we attempt to do. It is not true that if you attempt to assert personal freedom or if you impair samaya, you immediately throw yourself into the depths of the lowest hell, but it is true that it is very important to keep samaya.

IV. THE COMMITMENTS OF MAHAMUDRA

10. Those who follow tantra and the vehicle of the paramitas,
The Vinaya, the sutras, and the various teachings of the Buddha with an attachment for their individual textual traditions and their individual philosophy
Will not come to see luminous Mahamudra,
Because the seeing of that luminosity is obscured by their intention and attitude.

Verse 10 is an explanation of what the practice of Mahamudra isn't, in other words, how attachment to a particular conceptual view will not lead to Mahamudra. This is true regardless of the sophistication of the view.

On the face of it, this verse seems a little odd. It seems that Tilopa is saying that none of these aspects of Buddhism are of much use. But he is *not* saying that. He is not saying that these various traditions, vehicles, or aspects of training are useless. Rather he is pointing out that since these different practices are all ultimately methods for realizing Mahamudra, if they are practiced in the absence of that view, they will not lead to that realization that is their true purpose.

For example, he first mentions that those who follow the tantra, or secret Mantrayana, or Vajrayana will obscure Mahamudra. He means that if you attempt to practice the Vajrayana without the view of Mahamudra or without the intention of realizing Mahamudra, then no matter how much you practice, it will not lead you to the realization of Mahamudra. The same is true of the practice of the paramitas, or the perfections. If you practice the six perfections, of course, this will lead to the realization of Mahamudra, provided that the understanding of Mahamudra is there from the beginning. But if you simply practice the perfections in the absence of the Mahamudra view, then you will not realize it. You cannot simply hope that by practicing something other than Mahamudra that you will realize Mahamudra, and this is true of every aspect of Dharma because all these various aspects of the Buddhist tradition are methods for the realization of Mahamudra. But they cannot be effective unless the view of Mahamudra is there from the beginning.

The main point here is that whatever you practice—the Vajrayana, the paramitas, the Vinaya—it should be combined with the practice of Mahamudra. The connection between this and the topic of samaya is that ultimately the true samaya is the commitment to recognize the mind's nature through transcending or pacifying the agitation of thoughts.

> 11. The conceptualized maintenance of vows actually causes you to
> impair the meaning of samaya.
> Without mental activity or direction, be free of all intentionality.
> Thoughts are self-arisen and self-pacified like designs on the surface
> of water.
> If you do not pass beyond the meaning that is not abiding and not
> conceptualizing or focusing,

Then through not passing beyond that, you do not transgress samaya.
This is the torch that dispels all obscurity or darkness.

The Sanskrit word *samaya* was translated by Tibetan translators as
damzik. The first syllable, *dam*, means "a promise, a commitment, an undertaking," such as the acknowledgment "I will do such and such." The second
syllable, *zik*, which is often taken to mean "word," here actually means "a
joint, border, or boundary," like a joint in a bamboo stalk, which is called
a *zik*. What *zik* means in this context is "that which is not to be passed
beyond"—in other words, it is a limit or a boundary.

Sometimes samaya is misunderstood by students as a vow that you make
at an empowerment. For example, students often think that they are under
the constraint of a samaya or vow to recite a certain number of mantras each
day, which is associated with an empowerment they may have received, and
that if they miss a day, then their samaya will be broken and something
terrible will happen to them. Of course, it is good if you commit yourself
to doing a certain Dharma practice, but not doing the practice is not what
is meant by breaking samaya. Some students may also think that samaya is
something that is terribly delicate and dangerous and that if you make the
slightest mistake with regard to your commitments, you will plunge headlong into the lower realms. This is not exactly true. However, if you believe
that samaya is unimportant and can be ignored, this is absolutely not true
either. What you need in this life is to be liberated, and liberation can come
only from practice, and practice can come only from diligence and exertion. So a personal commitment to practice is essential, and if you have the
thought, "I will do this much practice and follow the instructions or commands of my root guru," it is very important. If these commitments are made
and you are committed to practice on the path, then the practice will produce a great result, which is eventual liberation. And if you don't fulfill your
commitment, then obviously having promised that you would do a practice
is utterly meaningless. You must understand that a failure to fulfill these
commitments immediately places you in the category of a samaya breaker,
but you will not be plunged headlong into the lower realms. Nevertheless, it
is important to fulfill or follow up on the commitments made to practice.

The first line of verse 11 discusses the samaya specific to Mahamudra:
"The conceptualized maintenance of vows actually causes you to impair
the meaning of samaya." On the conventional level, it is obviously necessary to behave properly and not allow ourselves to become involved with

conduct that is harmful or unvirtuous and to try to always engage in positive actions. Having this level of mindfulness and attentiveness is, of course, also important. But, at the same time, thinking, "I am keeping these rules. I am doing this. I will not do that," and so forth can become a fixation upon that concept, which will obstruct our Shamatha of Mahamudra because it is a fiercely held concept. So in this sense, if there is a conceptual fixation on, or pride in, our moral choices, it is contradictory to the samaya of ultimate truth, which is the samaya of Mahamudra.

The samaya of Mahamudra is not a matter of not doing something; this samaya is not kept by thinking, "I will do this, and I will not do that." Rather this samaya is described in the next line: "Without mental activity or direction." When the verse says, "without mental direction," it means without any conceptual fixation on solidity or nonsolidity, on existence or the absence of existence. The samaya of Mahamudra fosters the experience of the mind's nature by allowing us to experience it rather than by attempting to create or fabricate a conceptualized experience.

While we are practicing this way in our meditation, thoughts will, of course, arise; dealing with these thoughts is explained in the third line: "Thoughts are self-arisen and self-pacified like designs on the surface of water." This means that thoughts that seem to us to just arise of themselves and disappear in the same way do not need to be chased out or intentionally gotten rid of. The image given is that of drawing a design with a stick in calm water, which will surely vanish, perhaps even before the design is finished. Because thoughts are nothing other than the unimpeded and unceasing display of the mind, there is no need to try to eliminate them and there is no need to view them as obstacles. So, thoughts are not to be considered something that we need to intentionally abandon.

The last lines of verse 11, "If you do not pass beyond the meaning that is not abiding and not conceptualizing or focusing, then through not passing beyond that, you do not transgress samaya." These lines refer to how to practice within the samaya of Mahamudra. Generally, we think that meditation consists of the mind staying still. Although we can experience this stillness, nevertheless, the mind is not actually at rest because the mind does not abide anywhere and the mind itself isn't a substantial thing that can abide or rest. If there is no abider, there cannot be any abiding. If we have had an experience of the mind abiding somewhere, then that idea was not obtained from direct experience of looking at the mind and was therefore a conceptual thought.

Meditation here simply refers to looking directly at the nature of our mind and the nature of whatever arises in our mind. So we are not looking in a certain place to rest our mind. There is no place to rest our mind while looking at the nature of mind. We are not focusing on anything in particular because the mind is empty. The way we keep samaya, the way we look at our mind's nature, is by being free of the idea of a place or focus of the mind.

There are three main points in this verse. The first is that even though the nature of our mind is beyond location, nevertheless it can be experienced. Looking at the nature of mind is not a state of vacant stupidity. There is an actual clarity and an actual experience of mind. It is not a state of distraction. Distraction and mental blankness are different things than the recognition of the mind. Recognition of the mind is not stupidity or distraction. If we remain in that direct looking at our mind's nature without becoming blank or distracted, we will then remain within true samaya because this samaya is experiencing our mind's nature. In fact, by resting in the recognition of our mind's nature, we are doing more than simply keeping samaya because as the verse says, "This is the torch that dispels all obscurity or darkness." It is like lighting a torch that in an instant dispels the obsority or darkness of innumerable eons. So we are removing all our suffering that comes from ignorance. The point of all of this is that we need to keep samaya by resting in the recognition of our mind's nature.

The second point is we look at mind without a reference (Tib. *mikpa mepa*), which means that in the practice of Mahamudra there is no object or objective reference to the meditation and there is no truly existent cognition that could perceive such an object, so there is no reference point whatsoever.

The third point in looking at mind is "not departing from the meaning." We might think that because the mind is not anywhere and without any reference point, it must just be a voidness. This, however, is not true. If we recognize the mind's nature, then "not passing beyond that" means that we do not stray from the recognition of the mind's nature. This also means that although we are not intentionally attempting to get rid of thoughts, we don't do this by letting our thoughts run wild; rather we maintain awareness of the mind's nature.

These three points are the samayas that we should achieve and the previous vows about not trying to get rid of thoughts and so forth are the samayas that we should not follow. So, if these points are kept, then we will be keeping the pure and genuine samaya without violation.

The Benefits of Practicing Mahamudra

V. The Benefits of Practicing Mahamudra

Now we are beginning the fifth main topic of the seven topics of the *Ganges Mahamudra*, which is an explanation of the benefits of practicing Mahamudra.

> 12. If free of all intention you do not abide in extremes,
> You will see without exception the meaning of all the Buddha's
> teachings from all the sections of the Buddha's Dharma.

The *Uttaratantra* and some of the tantras describe being "free of extremes" as meaning that there is nothing we have to remove and nothing we have to add. By looking at the genuine or perfect Dharma, we will become genuinely or perfectly enlightened. On a conventional level of reality, we can say that there are a great number of negative behaviors to be removed and positive behaviors to be added. But this verse says that there is nothing to be removed and nothing to be added to the nature of the mind. In other words, the correct way to experience the nature of mind is to make no attempt to conceptualize it as being existent or nonexistent. If we remain without an investment in this conceptual view, then we will see the essence of all dharmas of the three baskets. By simply remaining in this state, we will not fall into the extreme of existence or the extreme of nonexistence, which we can call "pure samaya."

The Three Baskets are all the teachings given by the Buddha: the Vinaya-pitaka ("the basket of discipline"), which presents the superior training in discipline; the Sutra-pitaka ("the basket of discourses"), which presents the training in samadhi (meditative absorption); and the Abhidharma-pitaka ("the basket of abhidharma"), which presents how to train in knowledge or understanding. Generally speaking, it is said that the Buddha gave twenty-one thousand teachings on discipline connected with the Vinaya as a remedy for the disturbing emotion of attachment, twenty-one thousand teachings on meditation presented in the sutras as a remedy for aggression, twenty-one thousand teachings of the Abhidharma as a remedy for mental dullness, and twenty-one thousand teachings aimed at dealing with all three disturbing emotions at once, which probably refers to the tantras.

Thus, it is said that there are eighty-four thousand different teachings given by the Buddha. Obviously, we cannot learn all of these eighty-four thousand teachings. However, the way that Dharma functions is that fully understanding any one aspect of the Dharma teachings leads to a complete understanding of the meaning of all of these teachings. In this verse, it says that if there is a general understanding of the nature of the mind that transcends the extremes of existence and nonexistence, then one will experience the essence of all the teachings of the Buddha.

13. If you rest in this, you will be liberated from the prison of
    samsara.
    If you rest evenly within this, all of your wrongdoing and
    obscurations will be burned.
    For these reasons, this is called the torch of the doctrine.

Normally, whatever happens to us—whether we are suffering or we are happy or even if we are residing in a lower or a higher realm—all this occurs within samsara. Regardless of how pleasant or unpleasant it may be, samsara's fundamental nature is the same; it is like being in a prison from which we cannot escape. Because our minds are driven by thought and because we have so many shackles on our thoughts, we believe that something that does not exist actually does exist and that something that exists does not actually exist.[52] This mistaken belief prevents us from letting go of our obscurations, which keeps us from developing our good qualities. Of course, within this prison of samsara, we may be able to perform virtuous actions that will certainly lead to states of happiness, but doing virtuous actions cannot by itself lead to liberation. Only the realization of Mahamudra can lead to liberation. This means that any virtuous action that we perform should be embraced by this view of Mahamudra. If we practice the creation stage of tantric meditation and join that practice with Mahamudra, it will become the cause for our liberation. Also, if we engage in the slightest action of generosity and embrace that act with the view of Mahamudra, it too will become a cause for our liberation. Any practice of any of the six perfections[53] combined with the view of Mahamudra becomes a cause for liberation. In sum, any action that is free of conceptualizing the three circles of action (the act, the person performing it, and the recipient) will enable us to escape from the jail of samsara and obtain liberation.

The first line of the thirteenth verse deals with the removal of the effect, which is samsara, and the following line deals with the removal of the cause of samsara, which is doing negative activities. These lines say that if we realize the view of Mahamudra, practice this meditation, and abide within this conduct by observing these samayas, then we will be liberated from the cyclic existence of samsara.

The second line uses the metaphor of fire to describe Mahamudra. Just as a fire can burn up an entire forest, Mahamudra can burn away all of the wrongdoing and obscurations that we have accrued from beginningless time. Because of this, it is the supreme form of purification. Generally speaking, of course, if a negative action such as one of the ten unvirtuous actions or the more serious five actions of immediate result is committed,[54] and this action is not admitted to or confessed, it will lead to suffering and obstacles. But Mahamudra practice itself can burn through the imprints or traces of these actions.[55] The root of all negative behavior is the obscuration of the disturbing emotions and the obscuration to our wisdom. When our mind is totally overpowered by strong disturbing emotions, we cannot rest in meditation or engage in active virtue. Also, the cognitive obscuration of not perceiving things as they actually are is the disturbing emotion of ignorance, and this is also a powerful obstacle for us. When we are influenced by a strong incorrect belief, it obstructs our practice of meditation. On the other hand, if we rest in Mahamudra, we can burn through these obscurations.

The third line mentions that "the torch of the doctrine" eliminates these obscurations, which means that Mahamudra illuminates or makes all the other aspects of the Dharma effective. This is not to say that other practices are not necessary—if only Mahamudra were of any value, then the other eighty-four thousand types of teachings given by the Buddha would be meaningless. In fact, in the practice of Mahamudra, we begin with many other kinds of practice, such as the four common and the four uncommon preliminaries, various forms of guru yoga, yidam practice, and so forth. The point of this verse is not that these practices are worthless; rather they must be embraced by the view of Mahamudra in order to work. For example, if we do refuge practice or the preliminary prostration practice within the view of Mahamudra, it becomes a very powerful method for the removal of the traces of wrongdoing and obscurations. This is also true for doing the second preliminary practice of Vajrasattva practice and so on. Because Mahamudra makes the teachings of the Buddha effective, it is called "the torch of the doctrine."

Sometimes people who have been practicing for some time say that although they have done such and such practices, they have achieved nothing by doing them—the practices seem to be totally ineffective. The defect in their practice is the absence of the view or understanding of Mahamudra. So, if we practice without this understanding, we will not achieve any positive qualities of the practice.

13

The Defects of Not Practicing
Mahamudra

VI. The Defects of Not Practicing Mahamudra

Now we are beginning the sixth of the seven main sections of the *Ganges Mahamudra*, which is an explanation of the problems or defects of not practicing Mahamudra.

> 14. Foolish people who have no interest in this will only be
> continually carried off by the river of samsara.
> Those foolish people experiencing intolerable sufferings in lower
> states of existence are worthy of compassion.

The first line of the fourteenth verse, which begins "Foolish people who have no interest in this," means that whatever else we do—no matter how virtuous it is—if we are without the experience of the mind's nature, we will not attain liberation. Regardless of how pleasant the circumstances that we may experience as a result of having engaged in virtuous actions, we have not transcended the cycle of samsara and therefore will be continually carried off by the river of samsara. We will be thrown about from one type of existence to another without any control because the basic root of samsara has not been cut. Persons who are not interested in realizing the nature of the mind are referred to as "fools" because they lack full knowledge (*prajna*).

In the sutras, the Prajnaparamita is referred to as "the mother who gives birth to the four types of superior beings," which are shravakas and pratyeka-buddhas (the two types of arhats), bodhisattvas, and buddhas. Thus prajna is required not only for the realization of a buddha but also for the partial realization of an arhat, who realizes the selflessness or egolessness of self, and for the realization of a bodhisattva, who realizes the selflessness of phenomena connected with the Middle Way school.[56] This same fundamental prajna, which is the recognition to some extent of the absolute nature of things, must be present. Therefore prajna itself is a deciding factor in liberation. And this is true whether it is a Foundation school realization, a Mahayana school realization, or even the practice of Mahamudra.

In spite of the fact that Mahamudra is extremely easy and convenient to practice and vastly beneficial, people generally have no interest in it. Even though it is a way to effectively accomplish all positive qualities and free oneself from all defects, people can be extremely foolish, having no interest in something that is exactly what they need. The problem with not being interested in recognizing the nature of our mind is that we will instead be continually carried off by samsara.

Another problem with being carried off by samsara is that we continue to experience uncontrolled rebirth. We might be reborn in the lower realms of existence as an animal, a hungry ghost, or a hell being. And regardless of where we are reborn, a great deal of what happens to us in samsara is pretty miserable. As a result, we will continue to experience unpredictable rebirth, and will undergo a great deal of intolerable mental and physical suffering of all kinds, with unpleasant circumstances affecting us, our friends, and our family. All sorts of things will continue to happen to us as long as we reject this single point of allowing what arises in our mind to be pacified. As long as we reject the technique of Mahamudra, our suffering will never end. In the last line, Tilopa expresses great and sincere compassion for those who, having no wish to suffer, reject the only thing that can really end their suffering.

We have now completed the sixth section, which deals with the defects of not practicing Mahamudra. The seventh and final section, which is quite long and detailed, concerns how to practice Mahamudra.

QUESTIONS

Question: In terms of letting go of thoughts, it seems that emotional situations create situations where the thoughts just keep coming up again and again.

Rinpoche: Sometimes there is a strong disturbing emotion or a strong and persistent thought that arises. When we fail to recognize the root of it—where it starts and comes from—then we become very confused. The image we can use here is that of a tree. When a tree and its branches start to grow, its branches start to cover the trunk so much that you cannot see the trunk; all you can see are the branches of the tree. If the branches fall off or die, then you start to see the trunk more and more clearly whether you recognize the root of it or not. In this analogy, if you want to know where this thought, sensation, or emotion is coming from, you must meditate on whatever the thought is, whatever form it takes, and then look directly at its nature and this will cause it to be self-pacified. In other words, if you look directly at the trunk of a thought, it will vanish or subside.

14

How to Practice the Preliminaries

VII. The Manner of Practicing Mahamudra

Of the seven topics of the *Ganges Mahamudra*, we are now concerned with the last one, which is how to practice. We have studied the nature of Mahamudra; the realization of which has many benefits and the absence of which has many defects. We have also studied the view, meditation, and conduct of Mahamudra. But simply knowing these things is of no benefit to us because it is necessary to put Mahamudra into practice. To put Mahamudra into practice, we have to understand this practice. This is why this section is so extensive. If it is properly practiced, we will develop an extraordinary view and realization; if it is not properly practiced, then we will not. There are two aspects to this practice: how to practice the preliminaries and how to practice the main body of Mahamudra. The first section on how to practice the preliminaries has four parts.

Relying on a Guru

15. Wishing to attain liberation from intolerable suffering, rely upon a wise guru.
When the guru's blessings enter your heart, your mind will be liberated.
These phenomena of samsara are pointless and are the causes of suffering.
And since all of these things we have been doing are pointless, look at that which is meaningful.

By properly relying on a teacher, we can develop a stable renunciation of samsara. The correct reliance on a teacher and the subsequent generation of a stable renunciation of samsara allows us to enter the door of Mahamudra. The first thing required at the beginning of our practice is to properly rely on a teacher. This is discussed in the first two lines of verse 15.

Our life is that we are in samsara, which sometimes is pleasant and sometimes extremely unpleasant. When it is unpleasant and we are suffering, we cannot tolerate this suffering. When we are happy, everything seems good. This is good except that the happiness never lasts; the circumstances that produced the happiness will change, and because of this contrast to our happiness, the happiness itself becomes a cause of more suffering for us. This type of suffering is called "the suffering of change." Furthermore, the very essence of every situation in samsara is unstable and in constant change, and this type of suffering is called "all-pervasive suffering." The basis for Buddhist practice must therefore begin with the recognition that the nature of samsara is suffering. This recognition inspires us with a genuine desire to be liberated from samsara.

There are two possible motivations we might have for practicing. One might be the desire for short-term happiness and protection, which refers to the desire to accomplish states of temporary happiness by doing virtuous actions. Although this is a good intention, this motivation is not based on a complete realization of the pervasiveness of suffering. We should begin with the attitude of wishing for a final and complete liberation from samsara altogether. This means recognizing that the basic nature of samsara is ordinary suffering, the suffering of change, and all-pervasive suffering. This renunciation itself is inspired by relying on a proper guru.

We might ask why it is necessary to rely on a guru. The reason for relying on a guru is that accomplishing ultimate liberation is quite different from engaging in mundane activities. When we attempt to learn something on the conventional level, we need a teacher. In other ordinary situations, we may need only a book or video. However, when practicing Mahamudra, which in its very nature transcends the conceptual mind, the only resource that is available to us in practicing Mahamudra is an experienced guru who has practiced Mahamudra himself or herself and who has received the transmission of Mahamudra from a lineage. Experience here means that the guru has to have had an actual experience of dharmata—the true nature of phenomena—that transcends the intellect and the teacher has to be able to point this out to the student.

The first line says, "rely upon a wise guru." "Wise" here could mean either learned in words or learned in the meaning. In this case, a guru who is merely learned in the words of Mahamudra will not be of much benefit. We need a teacher who is experienced in the meaning, which means having actual experience of Mahamudra. An example of this is found in the biography of Naropa. Naropa, who was already a great scholar and pandita at Nalanda University, was sitting outside the temple reading and studying. He was approached by a wisdom dakini in the form of an old woman who asked him if he understood the meaning or merely the words of the teachings. When Naropa said he understood the words, she was joyous; when he said that he also understood the meaning, she became very angry and said that he needed to take Tilopa as a guru because Tilopa indeed understood the meaning.

The second line of this verse says, "When the guru's blessings enter your heart, your mind will be liberated." A successful practice of the path depends upon receiving the instructions and practicing under the guidance of a wise guru. Exactly how does this benefit of a successful practice occur? All of the benefits of working with an authentic guru are included in the concept of blessings. The word *blessing* normally conveys the idea of some kind of power or energy that is transmitted to us by our teacher. The Tibetan word for *blessing* is *jinlap*, and the first syllable, *jin*, is the past tense of the verb "to give." It means that which has been given or transmitted to you by your teacher. The second syllable, *lap*, means "waves." Waves are a metaphor for the actual power or energy of the teacher's blessing that engulfs you. How is this blessing transmitted? It really consists of two related processes, both of which can be called "blessing."

The first of these is the *natural blessing*, or the automatic result of someone's faith and devotion. If we have strong faith and devotion, somehow just through having them, we will experience change, especially a change in our mind. And the mind can possibly change quite radically. For example, if someone whose mind has no stability or tranquillity were to develop this kind of faith and devotion, they would develop a quality of tranquillity at the same time. If someone already has some degree of tranquillity, with an increase of devotion, that tranquillity will increase accordingly. This is also true of mental clarity. With an increase in devotion, there will be an increase in luminous clarity. This natural result of devotion is true of any kind of meditation experience or realization.

The other aspect of blessing is the result of hearing the teachings of the guru. When you hear the guru's teachings, you are benefited by them directly. Through that instruction, you come to recognize your own nature. You come to understand Dharma and, therefore, you develop confidence in it. That confidence in the Dharma automatically leads to diligence, which leads to meditation, which, if it was not there before, will be there, and if it was there before, meditation will increase. So in a sense, this whole process is the blessing of the guru's speech; it takes place through the power of the guru's speech. So the guru's speech can also be called a blessing.

Normally, our mind is so bound up with concepts of existence and nonexistence that we do not allow ourselves to become liberated. The process that we usually go through is one of constantly developing fixations and attachments to external things and situations, and this constantly increases our disturbing emotions. If, on the other hand, we develop both stable renunciation and devotion for an authentic root guru, then these conditions free our mind from this net of conceptuality that impedes our liberation. When the text says, "When the guru's blessings enter your heart, your mind will become liberated," it means that the nature of your mind will manifest. Saraha made the famous statement: "Homage to the mind that is like a wish-fulfilling jewel," which means that the mind is intrinsically free of defects and possesses all possible qualities in completeness and abundance. In other words, the potential to benefit not only yourself but all other beings is innately present in your mind already. For example, all of the qualities and activities of Buddha Shakyamuni—starting from his attainment of unsurpassable awakening, to his turning of the wheel of Dharma and his subsequent helping of innumerable beings in various states of liberation— came from the qualities that were always innate within his mind and that manifested when he attained buddhahood. Buddha Shakyamuni is not the only one who possesses these qualities. We all possess these qualities. The difference between a buddha and ourselves is that our qualities are dormant because they are obscured by what the mahasiddhas of our lineage have called "the cocoon of conceptuality." We create a cocoon with our thoughts that completely covers all of the qualities that are innate in us and have always been present within the mind. We waste the nature of our mind—in the sense that it is so hidden that it is effectively dormant. Liberation refers to bringing the mind out from this obscuration or cocoon.

By relying upon a wise guru, the guru's blessings enter our heart and this produces extraordinary experience and realization and "your own mind will be liberated." So, having first relied upon an authentic guru, the second thing we must do is meditate on renunciation, which is described in the last two lines of verse 15: "These phenomena of samsara are pointless and are the causes of suffering. And since all of these things we have been doing are pointless, look at that which is meaningful." We have been wandering throughout the three realms of samsara, and our mind has been very immature, easily deceived and distracted because we have been enthralled with very interesting and very vivid external appearances. We have become extremely distracted, and, as a result, from the time we are born until the time we die our lives have been confused and agitated. Our mind is based on this confusion, and we engage in a great deal of work and effort that is totally involved with this confusion that we have about appearances. All of this leads to a situation in which there is nothing really gained from these situations that can never free us from suffering.

Superficially, samsara may appear to produce short-term happiness and benefit, but even that is not true. If we analyze the actual results of our actions, we see that these activities are of no benefit to ourselves and often actually make us miserable. Focusing on our experiences and these external appearances actually leads us into a more or less constant state of worry and anxiety. The speech that we engage in almost invariably leads to attachment or anger, which causes us more mental and physical suffering. And the physical activity that we engage in is mostly a cause of our physical pain. Furthermore, anything material that we have accumulated will eventually be lost; any family or companionship that we have will end in separation; and any birth will end in death. This verse says we should rather "look at that which is meaningful." This is to strive for realization of the ultimate truth and Mahamudra, which brings liberation. We should pursue what is meaningful because the practice of Mahamudra—as opposed to worldly activities—produces long-term happiness and final liberation. Mahamudra also produces short-term happiness because it produces a tranquil and happy state. But more importantly, it produces ultimate liberation or full buddhahood, which is the final end of all suffering.

Thus the actual cultivation of meditation is definitely necessary. We have to begin by relying upon an authentic guru, and when we are engulfed by the guru's blessings, then we have to actually meditate and keep on practicing. When we have begun to practice meditation, it is then necessary to foster, stabilize, and make our experience genuine.

We begin with the four common preliminaries, or four thoughts that turn the mind to develop the correct reliance upon an authentic guru and the cultivation of renunciation. The practice of relying on the guru is the fourth "uncommon" or "special" preliminary practice (Tib. *ngöndro*) of guru yoga. The function of guru yoga is explained in *The Mahamudra Lineage Supplication*:

> Devotion is the head of meditation, as is taught.
> The guru opens the treasury gate to the treasury of oral instruction.
> To the meditator who continually supplicates you,
> Grant your blessing that genuine devotion is born within.

Thus the first preliminary practice of Mahamudra is guru yoga, which includes what we normally think of as "the four common preliminaries," or "the four thoughts that turn the mind," and the four uncommon preliminaries of the ngöndro. We could also say that all of these practices are branches of guru yoga.

> 16. If you are beyond all grasping at an object and grasping at a
>   subject, that is the monarch among all views.
> If there is no distraction, that is the monarch among all meditations.
> If there is no effort, that is the monarch among all conduct.
> When there is no hope and no fear, that is the final result and the
>   fruition has been attained.

Tilopa explains the correct ascertainment of the view of Mahamudra in verse 16. He begins by discussing "grasping," which refers to fixating on external objects and conditions and fixating or obsessing on what appears in our mind. If our view totally transcends these two types of fixating (fixating upon objects and subject), then it is called "the king, or monarch, of views." This refers not to the inferential view of the sutras but to the experiential view of the tantras.

The second line of the verse discusses meditation: "If there is no distraction, that is the monarch among all meditations." Normally, when we think of meditation, we regard it as deliberately forcing the mind into a state of strong concentration, but Tilopa points out here that this is not at all what meditation is. Meditation is simply not straying or being distracted from awareness of our mind as being empty and having cognitive lucidity. "Not being distracted" from this means keeping our faculty of mindfulness and alertness. Practically speaking, this means that when a thought or a disturbing emotion arises, we simply look directly at it, and that maintains our awareness of the mind's nature beyond distraction.

The next line is "If there is no effort, that is the monarch among all conduct," which means that within this experience of the mind's nature, our actions are without any contrived intention and therefore are spontaneous. Then this uncontrived activity will cause our experience and realization to flourish and this is what is appropriate—the king of actions.

The last line says that what obstructs the accomplishment of these practices is the hope that we will achieve some result in the future and the strong anxiety that it may not happen. If we can transcend this hope and fear with regard to some future experience of fruition, then it will manifest. With regard to the fruition, Tilopa says, "When there is no hope and no fear, that is the final result and the fruition has been attained." The point here is that hope and fear are unnecessary and inappropriate with regard to our mind. Maitreya said, "There is nothing in this that needs to be removed and there is nothing at all that needs to be added to this." This is the same idea that was expressed in the statement by Saraha: "Homage to the mind that is like a wish-fulfilling jewel." The mind's essential nature is emptiness, and its defining characteristic is luminous clarity, which makes it perfect just as it is. It does not need to be altered or improved upon or to have anything removed from it in any way. Therefore, hope of improving the mind or fear of its not improving is unnecessary and off the track. Through experiencing our mind's nature, we no longer have such hope or fear—that is the fruition.

THE GROUND, PATH, AND FRUITION OF MAHAMUDRA

> 17. It is beyond being an object of conceptual focus, and the mind's nature is lucidity.
> There is no path to be traversed and yet, in that way, you enter the path of buddhahood.
> There is no object of meditation, but if you become accustomed to this, you will attain unsurpassable awakening.

Having presented the ascertainment of the view, meditation, conduct, and fruition, the text then goes on to explain the three stages of Mahamudra in terms of the ground (the foundation), the path that must be taken, and the result of this undertaking. The first line of this verse presents the ground, meaning that the mind cannot be said to exist, not exist, both exist and not exist, or neither exist nor not exist; it is beyond any form of conceptual designation. And yet, at the same time, it is luminous clarity and its nature is referred to as "the unity of emptiness and clarity."

The second line presents the path. Usually, we conceptualize the nature of the path by thinking, "I am in samsara, and I must get out of it. I must therefore engage in the Buddhist path to get out of samsara." We then try to follow what are traditionally called the "five paths," or the "ten bodhisattva stages." But this verse says that, in fact, there is no special path that we have to traverse: "There is no path to be traversed and yet, in that way, you enter the path of buddhahood." The path we should follow is simply the correct recognition of the ground. It is said in a well-known quotation, "To genuinely view that which is genuine will create genuine liberation." The point is that the nature of the ground is itself perfect or pure, and aside from a correct recognition of this ground, there is simply no other path. On the one hand, there is no path to be traversed because the mind's nature is what it is. The nature of mind does not need to be changed or improved upon, and in fact it cannot be. So, in that sense there is no process to be gone through. On the other hand, the recognition of this nature, which is beyond process, is the path that produces awakening.

The third line discusses the fruition of this process. It says that there is nothing to be meditated upon and that becoming used to this process of not meditating upon anything actually is the meditation that will produce a positive result. There is a saying attributed to Gampopa that says, "In meditation do not attempt to remove the two defects of lethargy or excitement. If you try to remove them, you will become like a frog trying to jump into the sky." There is nothing in the practice of Mahamudra that one focuses on as an object of meditation, such as something that might be visualized. There is no object of meditation in that sense. But the process of getting used to, or becoming more familiar with, your own nature is what is called "meditation" in the Mahamudra tradition. And that familiarization with your own nature is what will lead to buddhahood.[57]

How to Abandon Distraction and Rely upon Isolation

18. Thoroughly examine mundane things of the world.
If you do, you will see that none of them persist,
None of them are capable of permanence,

And that they are all like dreams and magical illusions.
Dreams and magical illusions are meaningless.
Therefore, generate renunciation and abandon mundane concerns.

"Thoroughly examine mundane things of the world." If you do, you will see that none of them persist, none are capable of permanence, and in that sense, they are all like dreams and magical illusions. Dreams and magical illusions are meaningless. Therefore, generate renunciation and give up mundane concerns. The point of these lines is that there is no reason to be obsessed with mundane concerns because all of these things that we allow ourselves to become so obsessed with, or attached to, are in their very nature unfit for attachment since they are constantly changing. They cannot, as much as we may want them to, remain the same. Therefore, it is inappropriate to make an emotional investment in their remaining the same. In fact, this obsession, this attachment to things and the resulting aversion toward other things, produces all kinds of problems, impediments, suffering, and so forth.

All the connections that we have with objects of our ordinary perception are usually of one of two types: they are based on either our attachment or our aggression. It is said that our attachment is like boiling water and our aggression is like a blazing fire. Attachment occurs whenever we identify with someone or something as "mine," such as "my friend," "my family," or "someone who will help me." The disturbing emotion of aggression or aversion occurs whenever we identify with someone or something who we think will hurt us and we think, "I dislike this situation or this is my enemy." Most of the connections we make with others and situations around us are not beneficial to us because any form of attachment (even though we think it will make us happy) is in its nature a cause for worry, fear, and agitation, and the nature of aggression or anger also causes misery. Not only does anger cause us to suffer but the actions we engage in based upon anger produce suffering for others as well. So, we are advised in these lines to sever all these connections to the world.

19. Cut through the bonds of attachment and aversion toward those around you and your surroundings.
Meditate in isolated retreats, forests, and so forth, living alone.
Remain in that state without meditation.
When you attain that which is without attainment, you have attained Mahamudra.

The next two verses are concerned with the importance of practice in solitude or isolation. Verse 18 had pointed out that all the phenomena of this world are neither stable nor permanent but rather are like what is perceived in a dream or a magical illusion. Besides being impermanent, external phenomena are also meaningless, being empty of any real substance. So, we are advised to live without craving and attachment for things in this world, to cultivate contentment, and to abandon mundane activities. Then the first two lines of verse 19 suggest that if you want to practice, you have to become independent from what is around you. What is being especially extolled here is the virtue of practicing in an isolated situation. The last two lines say, "Remain in that state without meditation. When you attain that which is without attainment, you have attained Mahamudra." The meditation practice that is to be conducted in solitude is, in a sense, to be free from meditation because there is no object of meditation. And what is attained through meditation in solitude in this way is the attainment of nothing new. It is an attainment that is beyond what we would usually call attainment. But when you realize that there is nothing to be changed, nothing to be attained, that is the attainment of Mahamudra.

This verse gives us the instruction of what we should do. We should sever all connections, and having severed all samsaric connections, we are instructed to remain in solitude. Normally, when we think of meditation in a solitary retreat, we assume that it involves thinking or meditating upon something, but the meditation that is being suggested here is simply to transcend our confused projections by allowing ourselves to rest in the experience of the nature of our mind. There is no process of practice other than this one, so it says, "Remain in that state without meditation," meaning that we should cultivate the one-pointed meditation or samadhi of Mahamudra. The benefit of practicing in a solitary retreat is that we will develop the clarity and tranquillity of samadhi, which can be easier to accomplish under these circumstances.

We should also realize that it is not correct to think that Mahamudra can be practiced only in retreat. In the biographies of the eighty-four mahasiddhas of India, we can see that each mahasiddha had their own particular lifestyle and style of practice.[58] For example, Nagarjuna was a great scholar who composed a vast number of profound treatises while ruling over a large community of ordained sangha. While fulfilling his responsibilities as a leader in the sangha and composing many treatises on previously unknown areas of knowledge, he was still able to practice Mahamudra and obtain supreme siddhi (enlightenment). Another example is King Indrabhuti, who reigned over a considerable region and consequently lived in the midst of great luxury, with a magnificent palace, a wonderful retinue, and so forth. Yet in the midst of all this luxury, he had no attachment to anything around him and was able to practice Mahamudra and attain supreme siddhi. A third example is, of course, Tilopa, who was poor and penniless and at one point devoted himself to the lowly job of grinding sesame seeds to produce sesame oil to be sold. While in the midst of this work, he was able to meditate on Mahamudra and obtain supreme siddhi. So regardless of their different lifestyles, all the mahasiddhas fostered this recognition of the mind's fundamental nature and maintained a mental discipline that prevented their minds from running wild.

We can also see a similar diversity of lifestyles in the practitioners who lived in Tibet, when the doctrine of Mahamudra spread to that country. Naropa's student Marpa, his student Milarepa, and Milarepa's student Gampopa are referred to as "the three forefathers" of the Kagyu teachings. These three teachers had three quite different lifestyles. Marpa was quite wealthy and had a family with seven sons and was engaged in a variety of mundane activities necessary to maintain family and farm, yet at the same time he was able to practice Mahamudra and was able to attain supreme siddhi in one lifetime. On the conventional level of reality, one can say that he was quite attached to his family. There was one occasion in India when Naropa prophesied to Marpa, "Your dharma lineage will flourish like the current of a vast river, but your family line will disappear like a sky flower." Marpa responded, "Thank you very much for the first prophecy. Is there anything we can do to change the second? I have seven sons. Surely at least one of them will be able to produce a family lineage." Naropa responded, "Never mind your seven sons. Even if you were to have a thousand sons, you wouldn't be able to change this." So although on the conventional level he appeared to have been attached to his family, he was still able to practice and achieve Mahamudra. Marpa's student Milarepa, on the other hand, lived his whole life in circumstances of utmost simplicity, asceticism, and freedom from unnecessary activity. Milarepa's student Gampopa exemplified yet another lifestyle; he was an ordained monk who lived in a monastery and ruled over an ordained sangha. The point of these three examples is, again, that there is no one lifestyle that is required for practicing Mahamudra and there is no one lifestyle that is necessary for the realization of Mahamudra. What is necessary is the cultivation of the samadhi of Mahamudra.

If we practice the samadhi of Mahamudra, we will be able to achieve the realization of Mahamudra. The last line of this verse says, "When you attain that which is without attainment, you have attained Mahamudra." This means that what is attained when you attain Mahamudra is not something original or new. All that happens is that the previously unrevealed, unrecognized true nature of phenomena is revealed. Normally, we don't recognize this true nature and are therefore very confused. By receiving and applying the instructions of our guru, we become free of confusion and false projections. These are then replaced by unconfused experience, and this unconfused experience is referred to here as the attainment that is "without attainment."

> 20. For example, if the single taproot of a tree with many branches,
>   leaves, flowers, and fruit is cut,
> Then all will automatically die.
> In the same way, if the root of mind is cut through,
> Then all the branches and leaves of samsara will dry up.

While Mahamudra is essentially one path and one practice, nevertheless, by practicing this one path, we attain freedom from all the various types of suffering that exist. There are many types of suffering in samsara. There are the sufferings of the hell realms (extreme heat and cold), the sufferings of the hungry ghost realms (hunger and thirst), and so forth; these are called the "sufferings of the six realms."[59] Then, there are different causes of these various types of suffering; each type is caused by different disturbing emotions. We might think that, in order to free ourselves from each of these sufferings and each causal disturbing emotion, we need to apply a specific remedy for each. But this is not the case. While it is true that the Buddha did teach eighty-four thousand different types of Dharma to serve as remedies for eighty-four thousand different types of disturbing emotions and their resultant sufferings, nevertheless, in this approach of following the oral instructions (Tib. *men ngak*), instead of resorting to different antidotes or remedies, we resort to one remedy, which is to recognize the nature of mind and the nature of all external phenomena. When this nature is recognized, then through the power of this realization, all the various disturbing emotions are abandoned, which causes all the various types of suffering to be alleviated, or we could say, transcended.

Tilopa speaks further about the benefits of the practice of Mahamudra. He gives the example that if the single taproot of a tree with many branches and leaves is cut, all the leaves and branches will automatically die. The meaning of this verse is that the practice of the Vajrayana, especially the practice of Mahamudra or Dzogchen, consists most fundamentally of looking directly at the nature of our own mind. The function of this practice in both traditions is to cut through our confused mind and recognize that nature once and for all. These two traditions are distinct, but their fundamental practices are the same. If we want to free ourselves from all of the various sufferings that grow on the tree of samsara and we attempt to free ourselves from these adverse conditions and various sufferings one by one, it is extremely difficult. It is like trying to kill a tree by removing each leaf separately. If we want to free ourselves from the various physical and mental sufferings of samsara, then, if we recognize the nature of our mind, automatically all sufferings are pacified and we are liberated from all of them.

THE BENEFITS OF MEDITATION UPON MAHAMUDRA

21. For example, just as the darkness that has accumulated over a thousand eons is dispelled by the illumination of one lamp,
In the same way, one instant of the wisdom of the clear light of one's mind dispels all the ignorance, wrongdoing, and obscurations accumulated throughout numerous eons.

Imagine a room that has been sealed in total darkness for centuries and has received no sunlight, moonlight, starlight, lamplight, or light of any kind. We would then think that the darkness itself is stable, thick, and substantial. Yet, regardless of how long this room has been without any illumination, as soon as a candle is lit in that room, all the darkness is dispelled in an instant. In the same way, the nature of everyone's mind has always had this clear light, or luminosity, which is referred to as Samantabhadra in the Nyingma tradition and Vajradhara in the Sarma tradition.[60] Although this buddha nature has always been present, it has never been recognized and therefore it is like a darkness that has been present since beginningless time.[61] By not recognizing it, we have become confused. Yet through our guru's instructions, our guru's blessings, and our own practice and devotion, it is possible to recognize this nature for the first time. When full recognition of this nature occurs, then, in that instant, all obscurations are dispelled, much as the darkness in the sealed room is dispelled when a candle is lit.

The realization of Mahamudra is said to be very powerful because if it is complete realization, it removes in one instant three things: ignorance (Tib. *marikpa*), wrongdoing (Tib. *dikpa*), and obscuration (Tib. *drippa*). Ignorance is the opposite of *rikpa* (awareness). The presence of awareness is called "the dharmadhatu" in the Mahayana teachings. In the Foundation school, awareness is expressed as the "selflessness of persons," and in the Vajrayana, it is called the "unity of luminous clarity and emptiness." That awareness is called *rikpa yeshe* (the wisdom that is awareness). Also the failure to recognize this true nature is called by different names in different Buddhist teachings. Whether we talk about the failure to recognize the "selflessness of persons," the failure to recognize the "emptiness of phenomena," or "not recognizing the nature of Mahamudra"—they all refer to ignorance or marikpa (where *ma* means "not" and *rikpa* means "awareness). Fundamentally, both of the main types of obscuration—the obscuration of wisdom and the obscuration of the disturbing emotions—stem from this marikpa. Therefore, awareness (*rikpa*) realizes the egolessness of self, the emptiness of phenomena, and Mahamudra, in the three vehicles of Buddhism—that is, the Foundation Vehicle, Mahayana Vehicle, and Vajrayana Vehicle, respectively.

When we are under the influence of ignorance, our actions, or karma, produces imprints of negative actions, referred to as "obscurations" or "veils." All of this ignorance and the result of negative actions and other forms of obscurations have been with us since beginningless time, yet the wisdom that recognizes dharmata can dispel these obscurations in an instant. Wrongdoing and the karmic accumulation of the imprint of actions are also dispelled by the realization of Mahamudra. This verse illustrates the profundity and power of this realization.

You might doubt this, thinking, for example, that in the sutras the Buddha says that one cannot attain buddhahood without undergoing three periods of innumerable eons in which one accumulates the collections of merit and wisdom; therefore to realize dharmata must take an extremely long time according to the sutras. Yet in the Mahamudra tradition, we are told that we can attain the state of complete awakening, the state of unity or Vajradhara, in one lifetime and one body. Surely if one of these is true, then the other must not be. In fact, this is not a contradiction. If someone possesses the pith, or oral, instructions, then it is possible to attain buddhahood in one lifetime. When someone engages in the path and does not have the oral instructions of the Mahamudra, then essentially they are taking logical analysis as the basis of the path to ascertain the emptiness of phenomena. Using logical analysis, one can develop confidence in the emptiness of phenomena, but that confidence is very difficult to apply in actual meditation practice. To be able to apply that logical certainty to meditation practice, one needs to gather a tremendous amount of merit over a very long period of time. That is why the path of logical inference takes so long.

The tradition according to which we can attain the state of Vajradhara in one lifetime is the tradition that is based upon these oral instructions. The essence of these instructions is that we do not attempt to analyze external objects or appearances but we work with our mind. The reason why we work with our mind in the tradition of these oral instructions is that although other things have to be logically proven to be empty, our mind is obviously empty. We can experience the emptiness or insubstantiality of our own mind at any time. Because we are working with something that is obviously empty, we experience the same emptiness that is arrived at through logical analysis. We do this directly, from the beginning, when we learn to meditate. So, this is taking direct experience (direct valid cognition) as the primary technique of the path. Because of the direct experience of the nature of mind, it is possible to attain full buddhahood in one lifetime.

This statement that it is possible to attain buddhahood in one lifetime is not simply an expression. Many mahasiddhas have actually done it.

QUESTIONS

Question: What is the difference between the experience of being empty and of being spaced out?

Rinpoche: There is a great difference. States of being spaced out, such as being in Shamatha meditation that lacks mental clarity, are characterized by an absence of intelligence, or prajna. Being spaced out or in the state of mental dullness is essentially a state of stupidity characterized by being without critical thought. But this absence of conceptuality is really just a sort of stupidity, whereas a recognition of dharmata—the nature of the mind as empty—is a wisdom that has the characteristic of unshakable certainty. It has been said by siddhas in the past that when you have this recognition, even if one hundred buddhas appeared in the sky in front of you and said, "That's not it," you would say, "Yes it is, because I have seen it directly." For example, I can see the vajra that is on the table in front of me, and having seen it, even if one hundred people were to say to me, "There is no vajra on that table in front of you," I would think their claim was meaningless and it would not shake my conviction because I have actually seen it. So, it's a state of wisdom that is totally without doubt.

Question: Rinpoche, the text said that the practice of Mahamudra involves no focus or mindfulness of the mind with a particular focus. Another teaching from Tilopa's text is that whenever a disturbing emotion arises, you look directly at it. So, it seems as if in the practice of Mahamudra you are going from an unfocused resting of the mind to a focused direct looking at something. Particularly, this movement from nonfocus to focus becomes difficult in postmeditation when there are so many distractions. I experience this when driving during rush hour. I must pay attention to the road, and then to look at the mind undistracted at this time seems very difficult.

Rinpoche: First of all, as you say, there is no object of meditation in Mahamudra, but that is from the point of view of an unconfused or ultimate state. From the point of view of the relative level, there is a focus, which is an object. For example, when a thought arises, then at the initial moment of directing your awareness to looking at the nature of that thought, there is a conceptual focus. Because the thought arising is a relative truth and is confused, you are working in a context of ignorance or bewilderment. When you actually see the nature of that thought, it is not there. So when you look, there is a focus, but when you see, there is no focus.

The essence of postmeditation practice is simply not to be distracted from whatever you are doing. There is far less danger in driving a car if you are not distracted and are mindful and alert, than there is in driving when you are distracted. So, in fact, postmeditation mindfulness and alertness should alleviate the fear of having an accident.

Question: Rinpoche, if the nature of all phenomena is emptiness and if we look at a bubble and it pops, there is nothing there, or if we look at fear, there is nothing there. I'm wondering if it is the same when we look at family or friends. Is it the same emptiness?

Rinpoche: There are many logical demonstrations of the emptiness of phenomena and of persons. But these arguments are not applied in the context of meditation practice because we are concerned with the direct experience of mind. The easiest, most direct experience of emptiness is the direct experience of the nature of mind. So, in the practice of Mahamudra, we do not analyze the existence of external objects or persons but examine only thoughts, which can be experienced directly without recourse to analysis. It is said in our tradition, "Do not attempt to eliminate, create, or alter external appearances. Just leave them as they are because they do you no harm and bring you no benefit." The external appearances are not the issue here; it is the mind and the mind's grasping at them that is the problem. Therefore, we take thought and mind as the basis for meditation.

Something that is important to understand is the question of what does and what does not constitute distraction. Tilopa said, "Child, it is not appearances that fetter you, but craving. Therefore, Naropa, cut through craving." A distinction needs to be made between appearances and our craving for or grasping at them. Appearances themselves are not a problem, but grasping at them is problematic. When you study the Dharma, you are training your intellect through the acquisition of knowledge and you are practicing to learn more efficiently. That training of the intellect, that cultivation of the prajna, is not a problem because you are essentially working with luminous clarity, which is one of the major qualities of your mind (the other quality being emptiness). The problem is with grasping at, or fixating on, the concepts acquired through knowledge. The way to work with this is simply to study in such a way that you cultivate mindfulness within the studying; if you have mindfulness and alertness while you are studying, then your intellectual study will not cause any grasping or attachment. In this way, you can mix your meditation and studying.

Question: Rinpoche, I wonder if you could provide some clarity on the meditation instruction in Mahamudra. I understand that when disturbing emotions arise in meditation, we should feel the context of the disturbing emotion, feel the essence of the distraction without the content. Is this similar to looking directly at the disturbing emotion?

Rinpoche: These two ways of working with disturbing emotions are different. The approach that you described, in which you try to feel the texture of the disturbing emotion and appreciate the origin of it, is based upon maintaining the concept of the disturbing emotion's existence in the first place. Basically, what you are doing in this approach is treating the disturbing emotion as something. What we are doing in Mahamudra is not working with what the disturbing emotion seems to be but with what it really is. Looking directly at it without becoming concerned with its appearance allows you to experience it as being more like nothing than something. The significance of this is that the way that you actually let go of disturbing emotions is through perceiving that they have no substantial existence whatsoever. The technique described in this text is to look directly at the disturbing emotion and in that way see its nature. What you experience was explained earlier in the text as seeing them as ripples or designs drawn on the surface of water. As these waves are emerging, they are already dissolving.

Question: I believe that there are passages by other authors that say that there is no self-awareness and that the mind cannot see itself. Could you please say more on that?

Rinpoche: If you read Shantideva's *The Way of the Bodhisattva*, you will come across the statement, "There is no such thing as self-awareness. The mind cannot see or know itself." Also, if you read Chandrakirti's *Introduction to the Middle Way*, you will find many similar statements such as "There is no self-awareness; the mind cannot see or know itself." I mention this because some of you may have read these texts and when you encountered statements such as these, you might have thought, "Shantideva and Chandrakirti say that the mind cannot know itself, so what I heard about looking at the mind is nonsense." Shantideva and Chandrakirti were making these statements as a refutation of the view that the mind is a substantially existent thing. They are refuting the view that the mind as a substantial thing could experience itself as a substantial thing. The mind, of course, does not experience itself as substance, which means that, when you look at your mind's nature, you do not experience any substantial characteristic. When you do experience the mind, you are not experiencing what Shantideva and Chandrakirti say you cannot experience. There is, in fact, no contradiction here. When you look at thoughts or at the mind itself, what you experience is the nature of those thoughts, the nature of that mind, which is emptiness. You do not experience a substantial presence. You experience something that is beyond elaboration, beyond any kind of conceptualization. But because mind has this innate capacity of cognition, we characterize it as a unity of emptiness and luminous clarity. So the context of the *Ganges Mahamudra*, which states that the mind can know itself, being self-aware, and the context of Shantideva's and Chandrakirti's texts, which state that the mind cannot know itself, are two contexts that are distinct from each other.

How to Practice the Main Body of Mahamudra

This section of the *Ganges Mahamudra* is the main practice and it is divided into four sections.

The Practice for Those of the Highest Faculties

Kye ho!

The explanation of the practice from the point of view of those of the highest faculties begins with Tilopa's expression of delight in Mahamudra itself, with *Kye ho.* Through the practice of Mahamudra, we need not go through three periods of innumerable eons of gathering accumulations in order to achieve enlightenment. Rather, we can go through this practice of Vajradhara in one body and in one lifetime. The Mahamudra path is easy and, not only easy, it is also extraordinarily powerful in dispelling all the obscurations of ignorance. Tilopa is also expressing his delight in the possibility of actually transmitting Mahamudra to someone else, in this case, to Naropa.

This is in contrast to the Buddha's exclamation that he made after reaching enlightenment under the bodhi tree when he said, "I have found a profound, tranquil Dharma that transcends all elaborations, and it is like healing nectar. Yet no matter to whom I would explain this Dharma, no one would be able to understand it. It is better that I remain silent." This expression of sadness by the Buddha is understood as a way of expressing the profundity of the Dharma. In any case, in this instance, Tilopa is not expressing himself in that way but is sharing his genuine delight because there is someone he can transmit Mahamudra to and so someone else will also directly benefit from this practice.

> 22. The intellect cannot see that which is beyond conceptual mind.
> You will never realize that which is uncreated through created dharmas.
> If you wish to realize that which is beyond the intellect and is uncreated,
> Then scrutinize your mind, and strip awareness naked.

This verse begins by explaining that the conceptual mind cannot experience something that is nonconceptual in nature; it cannot see what is beyond it. Next it says that you will never realize that which "is uncreated through created dharmas," where "dharmas" are any facts or truths. This means that any attempt to fabricate realization—through inferential reasoning or fabricated meditations—cannot truly help us discover the fundamental nature. In other words, through conceptual fabrication, we fail to realize the nature of the mind. The mistakes that can occur through the tendency to intellectualize are pointed out in many subsequent meditation instructions of the Kagyu lineage. These are traditionally explained in terms of the mistakes that we can make with regard to emptiness, which are called "turning emptiness into an antidote," "turning it into a seal," or more literally, "getting lost in emptiness of the ground of all that is knowable."

The expression "Getting lost in emptiness as a seal" means that when a disturbing emotion arises, we begin to think, "Oh, this is no problem because its nature is empty." But this is not a true experience; it is just an intellectual attitude. The "seal," in this case, means trying to seal your experience with an intellectual idea of emptiness. "Getting lost in emptiness of the ground of all that is knowable" again means trying to conceptually develop a certainty that emptiness is the nature of all things. While from one point of view, having such certainty is good, nevertheless, because it is just an intellectual concept, it is not appropriate for the practice of Mahamudra and is therefore a deviation. The deviation called "getting lost in emptiness as an antidote" is the belief that if you conceptually meditate on emptiness, the disturbing emotions will disappear when they arise. What these three types of errors have in common is that they are all conceptual and are attempts to produce something through the application of concepts.

The alternative to these deviations is the direct experience of dharmata, or "the nature of phenomena," which transcends concept and transcends intellect and is not constructed by any kind of conceptualization. The last line explains how to do this: "Scrutinize your mind, and strip awareness naked." *Scrutinize* can be taken in two different ways. We might understand *scrutinize* to mean to analyze the mind, but that is not what it means here. Analyzing the mind is trying to determine through logic exactly what the mind must be like. When we try to think about the mind, the process is endless because there are endless thoughts or concepts that can be generated about the mind. The mind generates thoughts, and we think that because we experience thoughts, they must exist too. And we experience disturbing emotions, so we think they too must exist. In this way, we end up with an endless procession of things that appear to exist. Here *scrutinize* means to look directly at the mind and to try to experience directly whether it is something or nothing. If it is something, what is it? What is it like? If it is nothing, what is that like? By looking directly at the mind, we begin to have a direct experience of the mind that is beyond any concept that you might logically generate. By scrutinizing the mind in a direct way, in effect, we strip the mind of conceptualizations about it, and that is called "stripping awareness naked." The kernel or essence of mind is awareness, which is revealed when we stop conceptualizing what the mind is like. If we rest in that direct experience of our mind's nature, then we will come to realize that it is meaning that is beyond the intellect and beyond any attempt to create anything.

Again, there are two possible ways to understand "to scrutinize the mind." We might consider scrutinizing the mind to be watching it and thinking, "Now I am thinking. Now I am happy. Now such and such disturbing emotion is arising," and so forth. Except during the beginning of practicing Shamatha, this approach has no benefit and is not what is meant by scrutinizing the mind. In this verse, it means to look directly at the mind without saying that it is one thing or another, to experience its nature just as it is. This nature of the mind can be observed as being empty, or as being luminous clarity, or it can be observed as being both these qualities. It is this nature that we have not yet recognized. To recognize this nature is then to rest in this "naked awareness." The term *naked* here means "direct, without anything in-between"—without any kind of veil between that which is looking at the mind and that which is being looked at. Normally, we process everything we experience through a veil of intellectualization. As long as we do not abandon looking though this veil, we will never experience the direct nature of mind.

There are many different instructions on meditation, and as Patrul Rinpoche has said, "Some are better than others." We can use "the guidance of the words of a pandita" or "the guidance of the experience of a meditator." A pandita is a scholar who tends to elaborate with a lot of references to texts and their philosophical underpinning. While this type of approach is elegant, it is not profound; that is, it is not practical. The guidance of an experienced meditator is less elegant and certainly less complicated but it is practical because it is easy to understand and therefore easy to use. So, we are advised to abandon the guidance of a pandita and to make use of the experiential guidance of a meditator.

The main emphasis in this section of the text is to let go of intellectual contrivances such as inferential reasoning. Yet, to let go of all intellectualization may make it possible to go astray in a different manner—by becoming too attached to experiences in meditation. There is a certain type of experience that can arise in our meditation that can be deceptive, and this deceptive experience can veil our naked awareness and prevent us from experiencing mind directly. These deceptions are called "temporary experiences" (Tib. *nyam*) that can veil our awareness. The first deception is the *nyam* of bliss, which is traditionally called "being stuck to the glue of the disturbing emotions." This is an experience in meditation where there is comfort, bliss, and joy. Being so delighted with this feeling, we identify with this bliss. But this bliss is not awareness (Tib. *rikpa*). A second temporary experience is an experience of intense luminous clarity. We then identify with this very clear thinking, with an experience of brilliant lucid insight, and that can obscure our direct experience of awareness. The third temporary experience is the distinct experience of nonconceptuality—the experience of not having any thoughts.

These three temporary experiences are much different from the true experience of realization. Although the nature of actual realization can be blissful and lucid, nevertheless, the qualities of these temporary experiences are very different from the quality of true realization. The siddhas of the past have said that these temporary experiences do not last—they are here today and gone tomorrow—and we should not get caught up in them by believing that they are signs of true realization. Temporary experiences are created by the process of meditation and are just a veil over our awareness.

23. Allow the cloudy water of thought to clarify itself.
Do not attempt to stop or create appearances.
Leave them as they are.
If you are without acceptance and rejection of external appearances,
All that appears and exists will be liberated as Mahamudra.

This verse is concerned with resting in the state of Mahamudra, which is called the "even placement of Mahamudra." We can do this even placement as ordinary individuals. If we have gone through the process of scrutinizing the mind by looking for the mind in a very precise manner, we will be able to rest in naked awareness. Nevertheless, from time to time, when we are engaged in the even placement of Mahamudra, thoughts will arise as concepts. Now the nature of thought is conceptual, and the nature of the even placement of Mahamudra is nonconceptual transcending the conceptual mind. From this point of view, we could regard thoughts as a problem or defect. However, we must regard thoughts as being like silt that has been stirred up in a body of water. Just as we can allow the water to be clarified by simply leaving it alone so that the silt will naturally settle to the bottom, in a similar way, if we allow our mind to rest without being agitated, then the silt of thought will settle down naturally. Also, because we don't have to do anything to eliminate thoughts, our thoughts should not be regarded as harmful.

Similarly, we should treat external appearances—what we hear, see, smell, feel, and so on—as not being a problem either. Previously, we had pointed out that Tilopa said to Naropa, "Child, it is not appearances that are the problem, but it is the clinging to appearances that is the problem. Therefore abandon clinging, Naropa." The same point is expressed in the last line of this verse. Because appearances themselves are just like reflections in a mirror and cannot do us any harm, we don't have to do anything to appearances themselves or how we experience them. So, we don't have to try to stop appearances, such as reducing the vividness of appearances, nor do we have to try to turn them into anything other than what they are—we just let them be as they are.

All Buddhism can be divided into three vehicles: the Foundation, the Mahayana, and the Vajrayana teachings. All of these vehicles are alike in the sense that they were all taught to benefit beings and to tame their disturbing emotions. So all the vehicles have the nature of the path. However, these vehicles have three different methods for dealing with the disturbing emotions. The approach of the Foundation Vehicle is to abandon the disturbing emotions because they are identified as being bad or problematic. These Foundation practitioners, through cultivating an intense desire to be free of the disturbing emotions, seek to abandon them.

The approach of dealing with disturbing emotions taken in the Mahayana Vehicle is one of transformation. Although the disturbing emotions continue to arise naturally, by embracing them with an enlightened heart (Skt. *bodhichitta*), they are slowly and gradually transformed. For example, our tendency to divide the world into friends and enemies and to be attached to the people we like and to have aversion toward those we don't like is gradually transformed by the development of our loving-kindness and compassion into an all-pervasive bodhichitta that embraces all beings.

The Vajrayana Vehicle takes another approach to dealing with disturbing emotions by actually taking the disturbing emotions as the path. Bringing disturbing emotions onto the path means, for example, that we look directly at the disturbing emotion of anger, and by looking at it directly, we discover that the anger's nature has no true existence. Realizing that our disturbing emotions are not solid things and recognizing their fundamental nature, we bring them onto the path. In this approach, we must not develop the attitude "I must abandon emotion," and we do not get involved with the disturbing emotions in the way an untrained person would. We neither view disturbing emotions as our enemy nor allow ourselves to become attached to, and involved with, them.

When we practice in this way, thoughts will, of course, continue to arise from time to time. The thoughts that arise can be either fully manifest, which we call "coarse thoughts," or an undercurrent of subtle, almost imperceptible, thoughts. Therefore, the text continues, "Allow the cloudy water of thought to clarify itself." When we have a glass of water with sediment in it and we leave it undisturbed, the sediment falls to the bottom and the water becomes clear and is no longer cloudy. In the same way, if we place our mind at rest, the apparently cloudy or obscuring quality of thought will naturally subside and our awareness will not be obscured by thoughts.

The text next says, "Do not attempt to stop or create appearances. Leave them as they are." To not attempt to stop appearances means that we don't try to change them in any way—we don't reject unpleasant appearances or attempt to increase pleasant ones. We continue, of course, to experience these various appearances that we regard as either pleasant or unpleasant. Normally, when we experience an external appearance, our mind places greater importance on determining whether it is pleasant or unpleasant than on seeing the actual characteristics of the apparent thing itself. This means that as long as our mind is not lost in appearances, we will not be particularly affected by them. We become affected by appearances when our mind is attached to them, which is why Tilopa said, "Child, it is not external appearances that bind you but the attachment to them that binds you. Therefore, Naropa, cut through craving." Essentially, this means that whatever we see, hear, or perceive, we do not conceptualize it as good or bad or as inherently pleasant or unpleasant. And we must always remember that the root of pleasure and pain is not external appearances but our own mind. The text makes the point that if you do not accept or reject external appearances, all that appears and exists will be liberated as Mahamudra.

> 24. The all-basis is unborn, and within that unborn all-basis,
>   abandon bad habits, wrongdoing, and obscurations.
> Therefore, do not fixate or reckon, but rest in the essence of the
>   unborn nature.
> In that state, appearances are fully apparent,
> And within that vivid experience, allow concepts to be exhausted or
>   dissolve.

"The all-basis is unborn" in this verse refers to both the primordial all-basis and to the present all-basis, which contains the imprints of habits.[62] Since this is unborn, there is no solidity for habits to rest in. If this nature is directly perceived, then we do not have to intentionally abandon these obscurations because their nature and the nature of what they obscure is seen directly; they do not have to be individually abandoned. The term *all-basis* is used, for example, in the Mind-Only tradition, to refer to the all-basis consciousness (Skt. *alaya*), which is the basis for all of samsara— for all impure phenomena. Here it is being used in a different way, to refer to the ground of everything, the nature of phenomena. And that ground is the absence of true generation; it is the unborn quality, which is emptiness.

The next line, "Therefore, do not fixate or reckon, but rest in the essence of the unborn nature," means that if we perceive this nature directly, then we don't have to worry about whether we will be able to abandon the disturbing emotions. We do not have to engage in thinking, "Well, I can abandon this disturbing emotion but won't be able to abandon that disturbing emotion."

This is because we are working much more directly by seeing the nature, seeing what is beneath all this. So it is unnecessary to worry about abandoning the disturbing emotions. Instead, when disturbing emotions arise, it is fine; when they don't arise, it is also fine because the true nature itself (the dharmata) is unchanging and unaffected by the presence or absence of disturbing emotions. Rather than putting our attention into manipulating disturbing emotions, we are advised to put our attention into just resting within that unborn and unchanging nature.

The last line says, "In that state, appearances are fully apparent, and within that vivid experience, allow concepts to be exhuasted or dissolve." This means, again, to let what is experienced just be without attempting to manipulate what we hear, see, taste, and feel. We should allow these thoughts, which only solidify our experience, to be exhausted. This is much the same as what we said earlier with regard to allowing appearances to be just what they are. When we experience these appearances, they will be extremely vivid because their vividness will not be diminished by the involvement of conceptualization. Because there is no conceptualization in Mahamudra, the projection that is produced by concepts is exhausted. Experiencing our mind is the root of experience; by not conceptualizing the experience, we become free from the fetter that conceptualization produces.

HAVING THE RESULTANT VIEW

> 25. Complete liberation from all conceptual extremes is the supreme
>   monarch of views.
> Boundless vastness is the supreme monarch of meditations.
> Being directionless and utterly impartial is the supreme monarch of
>   conduct.
> Self-liberation beyond expectation is the supreme result.

This verse summarizes the view, meditation, conduct, and fruition of Mahamudra. Previously, in verse 16, we had a four-line explanation that said, "If you are beyond all grasping at an object and grasping at a subject, that is the monarch among all views. If there is no distraction, that it is the monarch among all meditations. If there is no effort, that is the monarch among all conduct. When there is no hope and no fear, that is the final result and the fruition has been attained." Here, in verse 25, it is slightly different. The reason these four lines are mentioned twice in the text is that previously Tilopa explained how to enter into the view, the meditation, and conduct. Here he explains how we actually are when we have become accomplished in this meditation and conduct.

The point of the first line, "Complete liberation from all conceptual extremes is the supreme monarch of views," is that the supreme view is a view without fixation on things as they really exist or don't exist. Then it says, "Boundless vastness is the supreme monarch of meditations," with *boundless* referring to the same quality in our meditation of cultivating the view that is beyond extremes and experiencing this in meditation. The boundless quality in the experience of vastness, of total freedom and a lack of being hemmed in, is similar to the liberation from conceptual extremes. The next line, "Being directionless and utterly impartial is the supreme monarch of conduct," refers to the same idea that our conduct will be totally beyond the expectations of existence and nonexistence. The result is the discovery of what abides within ourselves as distinct from hoping for a particular outcome in the future. The final line is "Self-liberation beyond expectation is the supreme result." What is meant by self-liberation beyond hope or expectation is that self-liberation consists of the direct recognition of the single nature of all things. Therefore, there is no hope for liberation since it is recognized that things are self-liberating.

This is an explanation of the view, meditation, conduct, and result from the point of view of a practitioner of the highest faculties and is an explanation that applies to the practice of someone who is said to have simultaneous realization and liberation. A person with these highest faculties does not really have to pass through different stages of practice. The other two types of practitioners—those of average and those of lesser faculties—have to pass through a certain number of stages of practice to come to this realization.

THE PRACTICE FOR THOSE OF MEDIUM OR LESSER FACULTIES

26. For a beginner, it is like a fast current running through a narrow ravine.
In the middle, or after that, it becomes like the gentle current of the Ganges River.
In the end, it is like the flowing of all rivers into the mother ocean,
Or, it is like the meeting of the mother and child of all the rivers.

This verse explains the practice for the practitioner who hasn't developed high realization. In this verse, Tilopa describes the experiences of practitioners at three levels: those starting to practice meditation, those experienced in meditation practice, and those who have realized meditation practice. The analogies given are applicable to both the practice of Shamatha and Vipashyana and the union of Shamatha and Vipashyana. When we first begin to cultivate samadhi (meditative absorption), there is a great fluctuation in our experience. The text says, "For a beginner, it is like a fast current running through a narrow ravine." This means that when someone starts to practice meditation—whether it is Tranquillity or Insight meditation—there is not much stillness in their mind. They have an experience of a great deal of agitation and a great deal of speed in their meditation. There might be moments of stillness, but these will probably be followed by an even stronger upsurge of thoughts. This is explained in all commentaries on meditation as being an experience in which the beginner will think that there are more thoughts arising in their mind than before they practiced meditation. In fact, what has happened is that the meditation technique provides enough space so that they actually become aware for the first time of how many thoughts have been in their mind all the time. So it is not really that there are more thoughts, but nevertheless it will seem to that person as though there are.

Next, the text says, "In the middle, or after that, it becomes like the gentle current of the Ganges River." The Ganges River in India does not have huge waves or much turbulence, but it does have a current and it is moving. So when someone has become practiced in meditation, their mind is not completely still—they have more or less a constant flow of thought—but these thoughts are experienced without the turbulence and uncontrolled speed that they had earlier.

Finally, the last line, "In the end, it is like the flowing of all rivers into the mother ocean, or it is like the meeting of the mother and child of all the rivers," refers to a point in practice where from the point of view of Shamatha, there is such stillness in the mind that it has become immovable. From the point of view of Vipashyana, there is a clarity that is more or less constant because it is not obscured by any kind of agitation in this stillness.

27. If those of little intelligence find they cannot remain in that state,
They may apply the technique of breathing and emphasize the
essence of awareness.

Through many techniques such as gaze and holding the mind,
Tighten your awareness until it stays put,
Exerting effort until awareness comes to rest in its nature.

Verse 27 begins with "those of little intelligence," which refers to people who are inferior to practitioners of the highest capabilities who do not need any other techniques. When persons of average faculties start to practice meditation, sometimes their mind is clear and sometimes it is not, sometimes it is stable and sometimes it is not. As a result, they have to go through the process of gradually increasing the lucidity and stability of their meditation. The second line refers to instructions that are traditional among the siddhas of our lineage used to cultivate samadhi—the methods of middle breathing, vase breathing, and the threefold gentle breath. The fourth line tells us to tighten our awareness until it stays put. This line suggests that we should put our energy into tightening our awareness. It is true that if a person's awareness is too tightly adjusted and controlled, it needs to be loosened. Generally speaking, this is not a problem; rather, we usually have too little lucidity and too little stability in samadhi and need, therefore, to exert more energy in maintaining awareness so that we have enough attention to notice what is happening in our meditation and correct any defects. Thus, it is necessary to engage in techniques that will allow our mindfulness and attentiveness to become stable. There are various techniques given for the practice of Shamatha and Vipashyana when our mind will not simply remain at rest. If our mind will not remain at rest, then it causes too much fluctuation in the clarity of Vipashyana meditation and we cannot maintain a steady clarity. This is a common experience for beginners who have glimpses of the nature of their mind through meditation practice but find that these glimpses are immediately followed by some kind of distraction. In the case of extraordinary teachers dealing with extraordinary students, it may be sufficient for the teacher to simply point out the nature of the mind directly to the student and then the student will be able to rest within that and progress. But often, even though the student may have had some kind of recognition at the time of the pointing-out instruction, it is likely to be fragile and unstable and dependent upon the teacher's presence. In this case, it may be necessary to use a supportive technique, and these techniques are generally used to increase both the tranquillity of the mind and the luminous clarity of insight.

The first of these are the breathing techniques that we have already mentioned. We can follow the breath by counting the breath, for example, as is taught in the Ninth Karmapa's *Pointing Out the Dharmakaya*, where we count each breath as it passes out of our nostrils. Or we can hold the breath in the technique called "vajra repetition," in which we even the length of the breath so that the period of inhalation, the period of retention, and the period of exhalation are all of the same duration. We can also accompany the inhalation with the sound OM, the retention with the sound AH, and the exhalation with the sound HUNG. These can be coordinated in other ways because the actual coordination varies with each tradition. Or we can use a more forceful technique called "vase breathing," in which the air that has been inhaled is forcefully retained below the navel. The function of all of these breathing techniques is to allow the practitioner's mind to come to rest and thereby promote the clarity of insight.

When this verse mentions that we should exert effort "until awareness comes to rest in its nature," *awareness* refers to the dual faculty of mindfulness and alertness, which, as we saw before in the quote from Tashi Namgyal, needs to be sharp and clear for the Mahamudra practitioner. It may be helpful, therefore, to intentionally sharpen our awareness for very brief periods of time, perhaps a minute or two, within a longer meditation session. The reason this may be helpful is that if we can cultivate the faculty of sharp mindfulness and alertness, then we will be free from distraction because whenever we lose mindfulness, we immediately become distracted.

This verse also mentions the use of gaze and ways of holding the mind. There are, of course, many defects that can occur in meditation, and there are different ways to enumerate them, such as the five defects of samadhi, and so on. To help practitioners recognize these defects when they occur and recognize when to apply remedies to them, we can sum up these defects as being of two major types—namely, torpor and agitation. Torpor (Tib. *mukpa*) is a state of mind in which we feel sleepy, dull, or devoid of mental clarity. Agitation (Tib. *göpa*) is a state in which our mind is wild, excited, and all over the place. We need to prevent these two defects. The first remedy is to use the gaze: When torpor arises, we raise our gaze, looking upward and also opening our eyes fairly wide. On the other hand, when we are agitated in our meditation, we lower the gaze and keep our eyes half-closed.

Another technique for steadying the mind is visualization. If we feel torpor, we can visualize a drop, or sphere (Tib. *tigle*), of white light and visualize it rising up through our body to the top of our head and then we hold our attention on this drop. If we are afflicted with excitement in our meditation, we can visualize a drop of black light that descends into our meditation cushion and hold our mind on that. Other ways of dealing with torpor is to recollect the qualities of the Buddha or of bodhisattvas, the benefits of Mahamudra, and so forth. When we are afflicted by agitation, we should recollect the defects of samsara, contemplate impermanence, and so on. All of these techniques are applied as needed at the discretion of the practitioner based upon what is happening in his or her practice. And what we are doing here is, as the text says, exerting tension or effort until awareness comes to rest in that state or in its nature.

> 28. If you rely upon karmamudra, the wisdom of bliss and emptiness will arise.
> Enter into the union, having consecrated the upaya and the prajna.[63]
> Slowly send it down, coil it, turn it back, and lead it to its proper place.
> Finally cause it to pervade your whole body.
> If there is no attachment or craving, the wisdom of bliss and emptiness will appear.

Generally speaking, Karmamudra practice refers to taking desire as the path. Although this can be helpful for one or two very extraordinary individuals in each generation, most people who have attempted to do this practice have merely increased their disturbing emotions.[64] While this practice is taught for exactly the opposite purpose, nevertheless, this seems to be what happens. So in the Kagyu lineage, we tend to replace Karmamudra practice with inner heat (Tib. *tummo*) practice.

Karmamudra describes a method that can be used to enhance the practice of Mahamudra. This practice is for a practitioner who has a stable practice but who has not been able to achieve the intense wisdom of Mahamudra. The text says, "If you rely upon karmamudra, the wisdom of bliss and emptiness will arise." This is a supplementary technique used to enhance or intensify the wisdom of Mahamudra. This technique, called "Karmamudra" or the "Action Seal," has two styles of practice. One is called the "upper door" or "upper gate" and the other is called the "lower door" or "lower gate." The lower door, which involves physical sexual relations, is a very risky way to achieve enlightenment, so only a few great yogis and yogins do it; most do not. What is more commonly practiced is the upper-door style of Karmamudra practice, from which is derived the practice of *tummo*, as found, for example, in the Six Dharmas of Naropa. Essentially, this technique involves using the subtle channels, winds, and drops within the physical body to allow the wisdom of bliss and emptiness to arise. In normal Mahamudra practice, the unity of luminous clarity and emptiness arises. In the Karmamudra practice, that same wisdom arises in a slightly different way. Instead of this wisdom being primarily the unity of lucidity and emptiness, it arises primarily as the unity of bliss and emptiness. Essentially, what occurs is that physical bliss arises in the body, and when the practitioner looks at the nature of that bliss, which is emptiness, he or she will experience, or realize, the unity of bliss and emptiness.

In more detail, through the correct application of the subtle channels, winds, and drops within the subtle body, one can generate a special type of warmth or heat. This warmth produces a sensation of bliss. This bliss becomes the basis for the experience of emptiness. The technique involves visualization, such as visualizing subtle drops dripping down from the syllable HAM, which is visualized in the top of the head, and of the inner heat (*tummo*) blazing up from the AH stroke visualized just below the navel. This is described in Tilopa's song when it says, "Send it down, coil it, turn it back, and lead it to its proper place." The details of how to actually do this particular practice are normally taught in long retreat sessions such as the three-year retreat. What is of utmost importance in either the upper- or the lower-door version of this Karmamudra practice is that there be no craving for the bliss and no attachment to it. The purpose, of course, is to use the bliss as a basis for the realization of emptiness. So if there is no attachment to the bliss, then one will see the emptiness of it, as the text says, "The wisdom of bliss and emptiness will arise."

THE RESULTS OF THE PRACTICE OF MAHAMUDRA

> 29. You will possess longevity without white hair, and you will be as healthy as the waxing moon.
> Your complexion will be lustrous, and you will be as powerful as a lion.
> You will quickly attain the common siddhis, and you will come to attain the supreme siddhi as well.

Generally speaking, there are two results that come from the practice of Mahamudra. The first is called "the uncommon or supreme siddhi" and the second is called "the common or ordinary siddhi." A siddhi is a spiritual attainment. The supreme siddhi is achieved through the samadhi of Mahamudra when all that can be abandoned (the disturbing emotions and so forth) is pacified. The pacification of all that should be abandoned results in the two wisdoms: the wisdom of the variety of phenomena and the wisdom of how phenomena really are. That is the supreme siddhi, also called "the ultimate result."

A common siddhi that results from the practice of Mahamudra is a state of mind that is supremely peaceful and placid. Normally, our mind is anything but peaceful; we are afflicted by our thoughts, afflicted by the fact that although some thoughts are pleasant, most are unpleasant, and this all results in agitation and worry. This agitation and worry can actually get to the point of making us physically uncomfortable and finally physically sick because of their negative influence on the subtle channels and winds. This agitation and worry also makes us age more quickly and makes us more susceptible to becoming ill. The samadhi of Mahamudra produces a state of mental peace, mental bliss, and comfort, and therefore places us in a state of physical comfort and health that will cause us to have a long life "without white hair," a complexion that is "lustrous," and strength "as powerful as a lion."

The actual words in this verse are fairly clear, but we need to understand that there is often a hidden meaning in the sentence, "You will quickly attain the common siddhis, and you will come to attain the supreme siddhi as well." The literal meaning is that, through the realization of Mahamudra, your channels and winds become straightened so the vital energy flows more easily and, as a result, you become healthy, so that you will have a long life with great health. The hidden meaning is that the unchanging longevity that is free of the signs of aging, such as white hair, refers to the unchanging realization of Vajradhara. The phrase "healthy as the waxing moon" refers to the fully expanded wisdom of Mahamudra. Wisdom in this case is intelligence, or prajna, which can be the insight that comes from hearing, contemplating, or meditating but here it refers to the wisdom that comes from meditating—specifically, the realization of the true nature through Mahamudra practice. This wisdom will be stable and luminous or as it says, "You will be as powerful as a lion," meaning that you will possess the uncommon qualities of a buddha, such as the ten powers,[65] the fourfold fearlessness,[66] and so on.

DEDICATION AND ASPIRATION

The text ends with the dedication and aspiration, which consists of only two lines:

> These instructions of the essential point of Mahamudra, may they abide in the hearts of fortunate beings.
> May these essential instructions in Mahamudra abide in the hearts of worthy beings.

These last two lines are an aspiration that all beings will be able to practice this teaching and that they will have access to the Mahamudra instructions and keep these instructions in their hearts. In other words, the aspiration is that these instructions will actually be imbibed and understood by those who are going to practice them. When Tilopa mentions "the essential instructions of Mahamudra," he means that he has presented the central essence and technique of all Mahamudra practice in this doha.

This completes the vajra words of Mahamudra spoken by Tilopa. Naropa underwent what are called the "twelve minor austerities" while looking for Tilopa, and then, after he found him, he underwent twelve even greater hardships or austerities. Tilopa taught this spiritual song to Naropa on the Ganges River after the last of Naropa's twelve greater hardships.

COLOPHON

This was bestowed on the banks of the Ganges River by the great and glorious siddha Tilopa, who had realized Mahamudra, upon the Kashmiri pandit Naropa, who was both learned and realized, after he had engaged in twelve hardships or austerities. This was translated and written down at Pullahari in the north by the great Naropa and the great Tibetan translator, the king among translators, Marpa Chokyi Lodro.

NOTE BY THRANGU RINPOCHE

There are different editions of this text,[67] which differ mostly in the order of the verses. There are two principal editions, and I used the one titled *The*

Collected Works of Lord Pema Karpo. I also used *The Topical Analysis* of Lord Rangjung Dorje, the Third Karmapa, for my commentary.

QUESTIONS

Question: It is taught that we should not fixate on achieving any particular end in Mahamudra. But when the Buddha sat under the bodhi tree, he said that he definitely would not get up until he had achieved enlightenment.

Rinpoche: Generally speaking, any aspect of the view, meditation, and conduct in Buddhism has two aspects. There is the conventional level of reality, which is how things appear to us, and the ultimate level of reality, which is how things really are. These two levels are true for any level of the teaching—the shravaka approach of view, meditation, and conduct; the bodhisattva approach of the Mahayana; and the Vajrayana approach of Mahamudra and Dzogchen. When we say, "Have no hope or fear of an outcome," this is an explanation of how to experience ultimate reality and not relative reality. This is not unique to Vajrayana because even in the Foundation path we have teachings that there is no personal self on the ultimate level and therefore there is nothing to be abandoned, nothing to be realized, and so forth. In the Mahayana, there also is nothing to be abandoned, nothing to be realized, and so forth.

The explanation in the *Ganges Mahamudra* that says that we should not have any particular goal is from the point of view of the mind's nature and this is from the view of ultimate reality. However, in the context of conventional reality, each one of these paths would have their own fruition. For example, in the shravaka path, there is the attainment of an arhat; in the Mahayana path, there is the attainment of the bodhisattva levels and buddhahood; and in the Mahamudra path, there is the attainment of supreme siddhi, or buddhahood.

So, the Buddha, in his realization, sat under the bodhi tree at Bodh Gaya and said, "My body may dry up, my bones and flesh rot, but I shall not move from this seat until I achieve the very essence of awakening."

Question: One of the spiritual songs of Jamgön Kongtrul Lodro Thaye described Mahamudra as "simplicity, one taste." Is that the same as the non-meditation referred to here?

Rinpoche: No, in *The Spiritual Song of Lodro Thaye* to which you are referring, Jamgön Kongtrul is discussing the stages of the practice of Mahamudra meditation. There are four stages of Mahamudra experience and realization that are usually described as: one-pointedness, beyond elaboration, one taste, and nonmeditation. Each of these is a stage along the path. Nonmeditation in this context refers to a certain level of Mahamudra realization. The instruction in the *Ganges Mahamudra* is that one should not intellectualize and conceptualize our meditation. This is an instruction that is to be applied from the very beginning of meditation and is therefore not equivalent to the nonmeditation in the fourth stage of Mahamudra. Our biggest problem in the practice of Mahamudra is that we want things to go well—we want meditation to be very elegant and to know exactly what we want it to be. In trying to program our meditation in this way, we create the circumstances for our own disappointment and it causes us to think, "Oh, it is not going well." These expectations are among what is to be renounced. What is intended by these instructions is to simply rest in direct and naked awareness.

Question: It seems to me that this state of meditation is the ground of Mahamudra and then we have to go on the path. Is it quite reasonable that we can also remember what the path is when we are practicing? For example, when I receive the teachings on the essence of nonmeditation, I can receive it only in a conceptual way and do not have the direct experience of it.

Rinpoche: Concepts can be used right now; all of this can be applied right now. From the point of view of the lower vehicles, of course, there is a long sequential arrangement of practice and the path is seen as very long. But in Mahamudra the path consists of looking at your own mind, and there should be no great difficulty in looking at your own mind because it is your own mind. This means not pretending that something that is not empty is empty, that something that does not appear to be empty is empty, that something that does not appear to be lucid is lucid. It has nothing to do with programming or convincing yourself of anything. Of course, it is true that as beginners we have obscurations that we have to deal with, yet these can definitely be dispelled by our faith and diligence, and there is no real difficulty in this. Whether we consider it the blessing of the Kagyu gurus or our own faith and devotion, if we have trust in the validity of this process, it will definitely occur.

Question: Rinpoche, I wonder if you would talk a little more about Shamatha Mahamudra. It sounds like the enemy of dullness happens without us knowing it is already there. I know that clarity is present, but I am not sure if I know what the distinction is. If someone is sitting and the perception is vivid and there isn't much thought, is that an indication that clarity or dullness is present?

Rinpoche: Luminous clarity is present in Mahamudra meditation, and it is the absence of the defect of torpor and is the unimpeded experience of appearances, but it is also the certainty of a direct recognition of the mind's nature. It refers to the certainty that there is a distinct and clear experience of the mind's nature. In general, what is said to be most necessary for the practice of Mahamudra, for example, in *The Moonbeams of Mahamudra* by Tashi Namgyal, is the two faculties of mindfulness and attentiveness. This text says that there should be as much of these two qualities as possible; the more mindfulness and attentiveness, the better, and we should never be apart from these in our meditation practice for even an instant. In fact, mindfulness and attentiveness have to be so clear that they have almost a hard edge to their lucidity. Without that crisp clarity, it will become vague and dark, which is called "torpor."

Question: Rinpoche explained that the intellectual mind is a direct obstacle to the realization of the true nature of our own mind. Does this mean that if I study Buddhist knowledge, I increase the obstacles?

Rinpoche: No. There are two situations with regard to the use of conceptual thought in the Dharmic sense. When I said that the conceptual or intellectual attitude could be an obstacle, I was referring to one situation and not to the other. Generally speaking, to study Dharma and various areas of knowledge a great deal is not only *not* an obstacle to the practice and realization of Mahamudra but it also *is* of great assistance to us. However, it is an obstacle if you think about all that you have been reading while you are meditating. This becomes an obstacle because you might make the mistake of thinking that you can figure out the nature of mind by using inferential reasoning. Mahamudra is not a practice involving trying to figure this out. Mahamudra is allowing direct experience of this nature to occur. So, aside from that particular mistake in meditation, studying certainly can stabilize and enhance the practice of Mahamudra and definitely will not hurt it.

Afterword

You have all come here out of a great interest in the Dharma and especially out of devotion for the profound Dharma of Mahamudra. With that as your motivation, you have come here and listened to this explanation and asked questions about what was unclear to you, and all of this is delightful to me. I feel very fortunate to have had the opportunity to take part in this. Whereas I myself have no real ability to benefit you under my own power, nevertheless, these words of the mahasiddha Tilopa are utterly reliable and free of error. So I am certain that there is great benefit in this, especially since you are committed practitioners of meditation who have undertaken this practice and are attempting to bring it to its fruition. So I delight in what we have done here and have enjoyed it very much, and I thank you all for making it possible.

APPENDIX A: TILOPA'S SIX POINTS
FOR MAHAMUDRA

(Tib. *gNad kyi gzer drug*, pronounced *Nākyi zerdruk*)
Tilopa's famous six instructions on what to do in Mahamudra meditation were taken from a spiritual song that he sang to Naropa. The full text of that song is given below, following Thrangu Rinpoche's commentary on the six instructions.

mi no	Don't recall [the past].
mi säm	Don't anticipate [the future].
mi sem	Don't think [about the present].
mi gom	Don't meditate [on something].
mi jö	Don't analyze [your actions].
rangsar zhag	Just rest naturally.

THRANGU RINPOCHE'S COMMENTARY

"Don't recall" means that we don't make any attempt to think about what went on in the past. "Don't anticipate" means that we don't reflect on what may happen in the future. "Don't think" means that we don't reflect on what is happening now. In short, we completely let go of thoughts that have anything to do with the past, present, and future. "Don't meditate" may seem like a contradiction. Here we are, sitting down and trying to develop an understanding of Mahamudra, and Tilopa says, "Don't meditate." What he means in this context is that if we approach the meditation session thinking "Now I'm going to meditate on this, and I'm going to work at it," this determined approach won't work or produce very good results. We have to make sure that this instruction "Don't meditate" is not interpreted to mean that we don't have to do any meditation and just be. Rather these instructions are for when we are already in a meditation session, actually cultivating the understanding of Mahamudra, and these instructions tell us to place the mind in such a way that we are not trying to do anything. This is the actual practice of meditation; this is the cultivation of the understanding of Mahamudra. "Don't examine or act" means don't examine your meditation session by trying to see if meditation is just like this or that and try to get into the inner workings of meditation.

So these are the first five instructions. Instead [of doing any of these things], we should just rest naturally in our meditation, and that's the sixth point. Tilopa's instructions on how to maintain meditation in the understanding of Mahamudra were taken from a spiritual song that he sang to Naropa. This is what songs of realization are like; they don't go into long explanations but just go straight to the point. Don't recall, don't anticipate, don't think, don't meditate, don't examine, rest naturally. That's it.

THE DOHA TREASURE

In Sanskrit: *Doha-kosha-nama*
In Tibetan: *Do ha mdzod ces bya-ba*

I pay homage to Shri Vajrasattva.
I pay homage to unchanging self-knowing Mahamudra.

The skandhas, dhatus and ayatanas,[68]
Without exception, appear from and merge back into the nature of
    Mahamudra.

Freedom from the conceptualization of things and nothing,
Nonactivity in the mind, should not be mistaken as the meaning.
Within the nature of everything being unreal,
Beginning is eliminated and end is eliminated.
Whatever becomes the perception of the mind is not the true nature;
It is a subjective naming.

The true nature is not created by the guru or by the pupil;
Without realizing it as mind or nonmind,

Know it to be the one that eliminates the many;
If there is attachment to the one, that alone will cause bondage.

I, Telo, have nothing to teach.
The place is not solitary; it isn't not solitary.
The eyes are not open; they are not closed.
The mind is not contrived, it is not uncontrived.
Know that there is nothing to be done in the natural mind,

Realize that incidental experiences, memories, and knowledge are unreal,
And let them go where they like.
In the dharmata, which is free from conceptualization,
There is no decrease or increase, attainment or loss, whatsoever.

Do not rely on earnest asceticism in the forest!
Through washing and cleanliness, you will not find happiness!
Even though you make offerings to deities, you will not attain liberation!
Know the free openness that has no adoption or rejection!

One's own true nature is the result.
Simultaneous realization and attainment do not depend on a path.
The ignorant world searches elsewhere;
But bliss is having cut through dependence on hope and fear.

Whenever the mind's grasping to a self ceases,
The appearances of dualism completely cease.

Don't think! Don't contemplate!
Don't examine and analyze!
Don't meditate! Don't act! Don't have hope and fear!
Spontaneously liberate the composite mind that grasps at that.
By this, come to the primordial dharmata.

This completes *The Doha Treasure* composed by the lord of yogins Tailopa
[Tilopa].
It was translated on his own by the Indian Pandita Vairochana[rakshita].[69]

Appendix B: The Five Buddha Families

The five buddha families are basic types of energies that can be experienced in meditation and they are referred to in many tantric practices. These energies are not simply cultural representations because anyone, whether Buddhist or not, can, for example, train in the Nyingma practice of sky gazing and will see these families in a mandala.

Buddha Vairochana is of the *buddha* family, and he is white in color and resides in the center of the mandala. He represents the element space and the purification of the disturbing emotion of ignorance, which, when purified, becomes the dharmadhatu wisdom. The disturbing emotion of ignorance is failing to recognize what is wholesome and unwholesome, failing to know the ultimate and conventional truth, and failing to realize the true nature of phenomena. For example, it is only out of ignorance that we become angry and act aggressively toward others because we are ignorant that anger will bring only pain and suffering to ourselves and others. Elimination of the darkness of ignorance is the realization of the wisdom of Buddha Vairochana; when our ignorance is overcome, it is the wisdom of dharmata. Purification of ignorance engenders realization of the wisdom that sees the true nature of phenomena.

Buddha Akshobhya is of the *vajra* family, and he is blue in color and resides in the east of the mandala. He represents the element water and the purification of the disturbing emotion of anger, which, when purified, becomes the mirrorlike wisdom. With the mirrorlike wisdom, there is no distinction between self and outer phenomena so everything is experienced in unity and harmony. It is called "the mirrorlike wisdom" because phenomena then appear to the mind in the same way that things appear in a clean mirror—completely accurately and with no distortion. Understanding and realizing mirrorlike wisdom can take place only with the elimination of the negative emotion of anger.

Buddha Ratnasambhava is of the *jewel* family, and he is yellow in color and resides in the south of the mandala. He represents the element earth and the purification of the disturbing emotion of pride, which, when purified, becomes the wisdom of equality. As soon as we are born, we develop a belief in self or ego, and we think, "I am separate from others." This feeling of separation leads to pride because we begin to think that we are superior to others. As long as we hold on to this belief, we will never be able to learn from others. To purify our pride and develop the wisdom of equality, we must give up our ego-clinging. When we are free from pride, the wisdom of equality that is associated with Buddha Ratnasambhava begins to arise.

Buddha Amitabha is of the *lotus* family, and he is red in color and resides in the west of the mandala. He represents the element fire and the purification of the disturbing emotion of desire, which, when purified, becomes the discriminating wisdom. With the discriminating wisdom, or the realization of Buddha Amitabha, there is no attachment and desire and thus no dissatisfaction or craving for more and better things. This realization is so powerful that all things are naturally magnetized as our own, creating no energy or force, as in a state of desire.

Buddha Amoghasiddhi is of the *karma* family, and he is green in color and resides in the north of the mandala. He represents the element air and the purification of the disturbing emotion of jealousy, which, when purified, becomes the all-accomplishing wisdom. Jealousy prevents us from accomplishing our own well-being, and as a result we experience more suffering and continue to develop further jealousy toward those who have more. This is the reason why the all-accomplishing wisdom is experienced in the absence of jealousy, and when jealousy is removed, all our wishes are naturally and effortlessly accomplished. As long as jealousy determines our attitude, we are bound to experience more obstacles in achieving personal success and in accomplishing positive goals. This is why Buddha Amoghasiddhi's activity is wrathful. It is by decisively cutting them off that he removes all obstacles and hindrances preventing spiritual maturation and success. He is green in color, the same color as growing plants, symbolizing the numerous activities that he employs to remove hindrances.

Appendix C: The Eight Consciousnesses

The Five Sensory Consciousnesses

The five sensory consciousnesses perceive the five sense objects of visual forms, sounds, tastes, smells, and bodily sensations. The five sense objects are neither good nor bad, but some are perceived as being good and are accepted, and some are perceived as bad and are rejected. These perceptions of pleasure and displeasure give rise to the afflictions or disturbing emotions (Skt. *kleshas*), which then cause all the suffering and illusory appearances of samsara.

The visual consciousness is in the brain and sees visual information from the eye and turns it into images. The auditory consciousness is in the brain and processes sounds heard by the ears. The smell consciousness relates to the nose organ and differentiates smells. When you taste something, it is not the tongue that distinguishes a taste, rather it is the taste consciousness. The fifth consciousness relates to the tactile organs of the body and perceives touch.

Each consciousness has its own function. For example, the visual consciousness perceives an image of an object, the ear consciousness perceives a sound, and so forth. Since each sensory organ and its respective consciousness has a different function, they are not one but distinctly different consciousnesses. The Buddha explained that the five sense organs and their corresponding sensory consciousnesses are "without thought," which means that they do not discriminate and make judgments about the perception. The eye consciousness merely sees a visual form, and the nose only smells without the ability to distinguish, for example, between two different smells. It is the mental consciousness that differentiates and identifies perceptions and therefore the mental consciousness is said to be "with thought."

The Sixth Consciousness, the Mental Consciousness

The sixth consciousness, the mental consciousness, is internal and refers to the individual's experience of happiness, suffering, excitement, and frustration. Some people think that all mental events—thoughts, memories, and anticipations of the future— take place in the brain. The brain is involved, but recollecting the past, reflecting on the present, and planning for the future, with all their emotions of happiness, sadness, and frustration, take place in the mental consciousness.

The Seventh Consciousness, the Afflicted Consciousness

The seventh consciousness is known as "the afflicted (klesha) consciousness." Whether we are awake or asleep, happy or sad, the mind clings to the feeling of the existence of "I," of a self, and we are very attached to this regardless of what experiences we encounter or what time of day it is. This afflicted consciousness is the feeling of ego and is like a bridge between the sixth consciousness and the eighth consciousness. It experiences the material coming from the eighth consciousness and assumes that it is a real self.

The Eighth Consciousness, the All-Basis Consciousness

The eighth consciousness is called the "ground" (Skt. *alaya*) or "all-basis" consciousness. It is the basis out of which all the other consciousnesses arise. The eighth consciousness has two functions: (1) to know everything taking place in the mind in the moment (the immediate function) and (2) to record all habitual patterns accumulated through mental and physical activities (the storehouse function).[70]

Upon realization, these eight consciousnesses are transformed into the five wisdoms of the five buddha families (see appendix B).

GLOSSARY

Abhidharma. Buddhist teachings classifying phenomena into types and categories. One of the Three Baskets (Tripitaka), the other two being the Sutras (teachings of the Buddha) and the Vinaya (teachings on conduct). Also it is an authoritative set of scriptures on Buddhist metaphysics, according to the Foundation tradition.

Akshobhya. A sambhogakaya buddha of the *vajra* family. He is blue in color and resides in the east of the mandala. See also **five buddha families.**

all-basis consciousness (Skt. *alaya*). The eighth consciousness, according to the Mind-Only school. It is often called the "ground consciousness" or "storehouse consciousness" because it is the container or foundation for all the other consciousnesses and stores all the latent imprints of the sixth consciousness.

Amitabha. Known as the "buddha of boundless light." A sambhogakaya buddha of the *lotus* family. He is red in color and resides in the west of the mandala. See also **five buddha families.**

Amoghasiddhi. A sambhogakaya buddha of the *karma* family. He is green in color and resides in the north of the mandala and represents accomplishment in Dharma. See also **five buddha families.**

amrita. See **healing nectar.**

arhat. The highest level of practitioner on the Foundation path, one who is free from the four maras: the mara of conflicting emotions, the mara of the deva, the mara of death, and the mara of the aggregates (Skt. *skandhas*).

bardo. The intermediate state between the end of one life and rebirth into another. The bardo can also be divided into six different levels: the bardo of birth, dreams, meditation, the moment before death, dharmata, and becoming.

bhikshu. A fully ordained Buddhist monk.

bindus. Subtle drops, or spheres of energy, that are often visualized in Vajrayana practice. They travel in the subtle channels of the subtle body. See also **subtle channels.**

blessings (Tib. *jinlap*). Energy created by the buddhas and bodhisattvas that an individual who has great devotion can "tap into" or receive. The blessings of the lineage are always present but can be received only if one is receptive to them. They are not something bestowed externally by more enlightened beings.

bodhi tree. A pipal tree (a kind of fig tree) with heart-shaped leaves. The Buddha achieved enlightenment under one of these trees in Bodh Gaya.

bodhichitta. Literally, "the mind of enlightenment." There are two kinds of bodhichitta: absolute bodhichitta, which is the completely awakened mind that realizes the emptiness of phenomena, and relative bodhichitta, which is the aspiration to practice the six paramitas and free all beings from the suffering of samsara.

bodhisattva. Literally, "one who exhibits the mind of enlightenment." An individual who is committed to the Mahayana path of practicing compassion and the six paramitas in order to achieve buddhahood and free all beings from samsara.

buddha nature or **buddha essence** (Skt. *tathagatagarbha*). The original nature present in all sentient beings that, when realized, leads to enlightenment. Although it is called "buddha nature," it is common to all sentient beings, not just Buddhists.

chakras. Literally, "wheels." Centers of energy along the central channel at the forehead, throat, heart, solar plexus, and the tip of the sexual organ, where there is a broadening of channels.

Chakrasamvara. One of the five main deities of the Kagyu lineage. He belongs to the *lotus* family and Chakrasamvara practice plays an important part in the Six Yogas of Naropa. The other four main deities of the Kagyu lineage are Mahamaya, Vajrayogini (who is the consort of Chakrasamvara), Guhyasamaja, and Hevajra.

Chenrezik (Skt. Avalokiteshvara). A deity representing compassion.

Chittamatra school. See **Mind-Only school.**

coemergent wisdom. The advanced realization of the inseparability of samsara and nirvana and how these arise together simultaneously.

completion stage. A method of tantric meditation in which one attains bliss, clarity, and nonthought by means of working with the subtle channels and energies within the body. See also **creation stage.**

Consequence school (Skt. *prasangika*). One of the two major schools of the Middle Way Mahayana school, which is associated with Chandrakirti. The other tradition is associated with Kamalashila.

conventional truth or reality (Tib. *kunsop*). The perception of an ordinary (unenlightened) person who sees the world veiled by his or her projections that are based on the false belief in a solid self.

creation stage. Also known as the generation stage. A method of meditation that involves visualizing and contemplating deities for the purpose of realizing the purity of all phenomena. In this stage, visualization of the deity is established and maintained.

cyclic existence. See **samsara.**

daka. The male counterpart to a dakini. See also **dakini.**

dakini. Literally, "sky goer." A yogini who has attained high realization. She may be a human being who has achieved such an attainment or a nonhuman manifestation of the enlightened mind of a meditational deity.

Dark Retreat. A practice in which one goes into a cabin or place that is completely dark and meditates there for a week or longer.

Dharma. The teachings of the Buddha (also called "Buddhadharma"). See also **dharmas.**

dharmadhatu. The all-encompassing space, unoriginated and without beginning, out of which all phenomena arise. The Sanskrit term means "the essence of phenomena," and the Tibetan equivalent means "the expanse of phenomena," but it usually refers to emptiness, which is the essence of phenomena.

dharmakaya. One of the three bodies of the buddha. It is enlightenment itself, the wisdom that is beyond reference points. See also **three kayas.**

dharmas. Phenomena or truths. See also **Dharma.**

dharmata. Phenomena as they really are or as perceived by a completely enlightened being who is without any distortion or obscuration. *Dharmata* is often translated as "suchness," "the true nature of things," or "things as they are."

disturbing emotions (Skt. *kleshas*). Emotional obscurations (in contrast to intellectual obscurations), also called "afflictions" or "poisons." The three main disturbing emotions are attachment, anger, and ignorance or delusion. The five disturbing emotions are the three above plus pride and jealousy.

doha. A spiritual song spontaneously composed by a Vajrayana practitioner. They were originally composed in the Apabhramsha language in the seventh to twelfth centuries in northeastern India in the form of rhyming couplets (*do* means "two").

Drime Lingpa (1700–1775). An incarnation of Padmasambhava's disciple Gyalwa Chöyang. He is known as a terton who revealed some of Padmasambhava's hidden teachings.

dullness, or **torpor** (Tib. *mukpa*). One of the two main obstacles to meditation. Dullness refers to a sinking, lethargic feeling that often leads to sleep. See also **excitement.**

Dzogchen. Also known as "Great Perfection." This is one of the main practices of the Nyingma tradition and, like Mahamudra, involves directly examining the mind.

eight consciousnesses. The five sensory consciousnesses of sight, hearing, smell, taste, touch, and bodily sensation; the mental consciousness (sixth), which is our ordinary thinking; the afflicted (klesha) consciousness (seventh), which is the ever-present feeling of "I"; and the ground (*alaya*) consciousness (eighth), which holds the other consciousnesses together and also stores karmic latencies.

eight forms of leisure. Eight conditions favorable to practicing Dharma. They are (1) not being born into one of the hell realms, (2) not being born as a hungry ghost (Skt. *preta*), (3) not being born as an animal, (4) not being born in the god realm (which is part of samsara), (5) not being born in a country without the Buddhist Dharma,

(6) not possessing wrong views such as denying that there is such thing as karma, (7) not being born where a buddha has not appeared, and (8) not being too mentally or physically handicapped to practice the Dharma.

eighty-four thousand teachings. The twenty-one thousand teachings of the Buddha on each of the Vinaya, Sutra, Abhidharma, and their combination. Their purpose is to eliminate the eighty-four thousand different types of disturbing emotions latent in one's mind. This is a symbolic number indicating a vast number of teachings.

empowerment (Skt. *abhisheka*). A ceremony in which a qualified lama gives the student permission to begin the practice. To do a particular Vajrayana practice, one should receive permission from a qualified lama, and one should also receive the practice instruction (Tib. *tri*) and the textual reading (Tib. *lung*).

excitement (Tib. *göpa*). One of the two main obstacles to meditation. When the mind is in a state of excitement, it is wild, jumping from thought to thought, so that one cannot meditate properly. See also **dullness**.

father tantra. One of the three kinds of tantras. The father tantra is concerned with transforming aggression. See also **mother tantra**.

feast offering (Skt. *ganachakra*). An offering of food and other delights that is given in important practices, which is a way of showing respect to the deities. The food is later eaten by the attendees as well as offered to the animals outside.

five actions of immediate consequence. Actions that will cause one's very next rebirth to be in a lower realm. These are (1) killing one's father, (2) killing one's mother, (3) killing an arhat, (4) intentionally wounding a buddha and causing him or her to bleed, and (5) creating a schism in the sangha.

five aggregates (Skt. *skandhas*). The five collections that compose sentient beings. In the *Surangama Sutra*, the Buddha said that a person was made up of five aggregates or heaps. The first aggregate is form, which is material and is what one perceives in the outside world. The second through fifth aggregates are not material, but mental. The second aggregate is sensation, which can be positive, negative, or neutral. The third aggregate is identification or perception, which labels and categorizes the sensation. The fourth aggregate is formation, which combines the perception with past experience. The fifth aggregate is consciousness, which is ordinary consciousness with all its discursive thoughts.

five buddha families. The five families to which the five sambhogakaya buddhas belong. Each sambhogakaya buddha embodies one of the five enlightened wisdoms. Vairochana of the *buddha* family represents the dharmadhatu wisdom, Akshobhya of the *vajra* family represents the mirrorlike wisdom, Ratnasambhava of the *jewel* family represents the wisdom of equality, Amitabha of the *lotus* family represents the discriminating wisdom, and Amoghasiddhi of the *karma* family represents the all-accomplishing wisdom. See also appendix B.

five paths. Five stages, or paths, to enlightenment: (1) the path of accumulation, which emphasizes purifying one's obscurations and accumulating merit; (2) the path of junction, or application, in which the meditator develops profound understanding of the four noble truths and cuts the root to the desire realm; (3) the path of insight, or seeing, in which the meditator develops greater insight and enters the first bodhisattva level; (4) the path of meditation, in which the meditator cultivates insight on the second through tenth bodhisattva levels; and (5) the path of fulfillment, which is the complete attainment of buddhahood.

Foundation Vehicle. Also called the "shravaka" path. It focuses on contemplation of the four noble truths, the twelve links of dependent origination, and the selflessness of persons for the sake of one's individual liberation.

four common preliminaries. Four points to be contemplated before beginning any Vajrayana practice: precious human birth; impermanence and the inevitability of death; karma and its effects; and the faults of samsara. They are also called "the four thoughts that turn the mind." See also **four special preliminaries**.

four extremes. Four conceptions that are inadequate to describe the nature of phenomena, according to Middle Way Buddhist philosophy. These are (1) the extreme of existence, (2) of nonexistence, (3) of both existence and nonexistence and (4) neither existence nor nonexistence.

four seals. The four main principles of Buddhism: all compounded phenomena are impermanent, everything defiled (with ego-clinging) is suffering, all phenomena are empty and devoid of a self-entity, and nirvana is perfect peace.

four special preliminaries. (Tib. *ngöndro*). Practices that should be completed at the beginning of the Vajrayana path: one hundred thousand refuge prayers and prostrations, one hundred thousand Vajrasattva mantras, one hundred thousand mandala offerings, and one hundred thousand guru yoga practices. See also **four common preliminaries**.

Gampopa (1079–1153). One of the main lineage holders of the Karma Kagyu lineage in Tibet. A student of Milarepa, he established the first Kagyu monastic monastery and is best known for writing the *Jewel Ornament of Liberation*.

gandharvas. A class of deities that are nourished by smells. They are also the celestial musicians.

garuda. A mythical bird that hatches fully grown.

Gelug school. One of the four main schools of Tibetan Buddhism, founded by Tsongkhapa (1357–1419) and presently headed by His Holiness the Fourteenth Dalai Lama.

geshe. A scholar who has attained a doctorate in Buddhist studies. This usually takes seven to twelve years to attain.

Guhyasamaja tantra. A father tantra of the Anuttarayoga Tantra, which is the highest of the four tantras. Guhyasamaja is the central deity of the *vajra* family.

Guru Rinpoche. See **Padmasambhava.**

guru yoga. A practice of devotion to the guru that culminates in receiving his blessing and blending indivisibly with his mind. Also the fourth practice of the four special preliminaries (Tib. *ngöndro*).

healing nectar (Skt. *amrita*, Tib. *dutsi*). A blessed liquid substance that can cause spiritual and physical healing.

heruka. In Indian culture, a spirit originally associated with cremation grounds. In Buddhism, the name for a male deity in a wrathful form. Can also be used to refer to the deities Chakrasamvara and Hevajra.

Hevajra tantra. A mother tantra of the Anuttarayoga Tantra, which is the highest of the four tantras. Hevajra is one of the main yidams of Vajrayana Buddhism. The Hevajra tantra was taught to Tilopa, who taught Naropa, who passed it on to Marpa. Marpa also received instructions on this tantra from Maitripa.

inner heat (Tib. *tummo*). An advanced Vajrayana practice for combining bliss and emptiness, which produces heat as a byproduct. One of the Six Dharmas (or Yogas) of Naropa.

interdependent origination. The principle that nothing exists independently but comes into existence only in dependence on various previous causes and conditions. There are twelve successive phases of this process that begin with ignorance and end with old age and death.

Jamgön Kongtrul (1813–1899). Also known as Lodro Thaye. A prolific writer of ninety volumes of Tibetan Buddhist works. He is best known for founding the Rimé movement, which was a nonsectarian, eclectic movement that preserved the various practice lineages that were on the verge of extinction.

Kagyu. One of the four major schools of Tibetan Buddhism, founded by Marpa. The other three are the Nyingma, the Sakya, and the Gelugpa schools.

karma. Literally "action." Karma is a universal law that when one performs a wholesome action, one's circumstances will eventually improve, and when one performs an unwholesome action, negative results will eventually occur.

Karma Kagyu. One of the four greater Kagyu lineages, headed by His Holiness the Karmapa. Also called the "Kamtsang Kagyu."

Karmamudra. A practice that involves using the energies of sexual union to reach higher levels of meditation. There is an "upper-door practice," in which one visualizes union with a consort, and there is the "lower-door practice," in which one actually engages in sexual union with one's consort.

karmic latencies or imprints (Tib. *bakchak*). Impressions left on our mind by what we think, say, and do that are stored in the eighth consciousness. These latencies ripen into various kinds of experiences when they leave the eighth consciousness and enter the sixth consciousness upon being stimulated by external experience. See also **eight consciousnesses.**

Khenpo Gangshar Wangpo (1925–?). A teacher from Shechen Monastery who was a lama to Thrangu Rinpoche, Chögyam Trungpa, and Dezhung Rinpoche. His teachings can be found in Thrangu Rinpoche's book *Vivid Awareness*.

kleshas. See **disturbing emotions**.

Lavapa. Also known as Kambala. A tenth-century mahasiddha who is known for teaching dream yoga, which he taught to Tilopa.

Leap (Tib. *tögal*). Literally, "leap over." One of the two basic methods of Dzogchen meditation. Leap Over is a series of yogic practices that affect the subtle winds and channels of the body.

life-supporting wind (Skt. *prana*, Tib. *lung*). The subtle energy that gives the inanimate body the energy to be a living system. It flows in the body's subtle channels (Skt. *nadis*). See also **subtle channels**.

Luipa. Literally, "fish eater." One of the eighty-four mahasiddhas. He lived in eastern India in the eighth century and wrote a number of texts. He is especially associated with one of the three Chakrasamvara lineages.

luminous clarity (Tib. *salwa*). The knowing that is characteristic of the insubstantial mind. In the third turning of the wheel of Dharma, it is said that everything is empty or insubstantial but that this emptiness is not completely void because it has the quality of knowing, which is called "lucidity," "luminosity," or "luminous clarity." Lucidity or luminous clarity allows all phenomena to appear.

Machik Lapdrön (1031–1129). A famous female saint who developed the Chöd practice of "cutting off" (one's attachment to one's body), which is said to be the only practice developed in Tibet that was actually taken back to India and also practiced there.

Madhyamaka. The Middle Way school, the highest of the four Buddhist schools of philosophy. To practice the Middle Way means not to hold any extreme views, especially those of eternalism and nihilism. See also **Rangtong Madhyamaka, Shentong Madhyamaka**.

Mahamudra (Tib. *chak gya chen po*). Literally, "Great Seal" or "Great Symbol." A meditation practice that emphasizes perceiving the nature of mind directly rather than understanding it through inferential reasoning.

mahasiddha. A practitioner who has a great deal of realization. Many practiced outside the normal religious establishment in places such as cemeteries and engaged in fairly outrageous behavior.

Mahayana. Literally, the "Great Vehicle." This term was first used in the *Lotus Sutra*. In India, this was not a separate school, but a set of teachings found within various Buddhist schools. The Mahayana emphasizes compassion and the bodhisattva path of practicing the six paramitas. It is particularly associated with the Mind-Only and Middle Way schools. See also **six paramitas**.

Maitreya. A buddha who resides in the Tushita pure realm until he becomes the next buddha of this eon. He is known for transmitting the five treatises of Maitreya to Asanga, of which the *Uttaratantra* is best known.

mandala. A diagram used in Vajrayana practices. It usually represents the three-dimensional palace of the central deity with other deities placed in the four directions.

Mantrayana. See **Vajrayana.**

Marpa Chokyi Lodro (1012–1097). A Tibetan who made three trips to India and brought back many tantric texts that he translated into Tibetan including the Six Dharmas of Naropa, the Guhyasamaja, and the Chakrasamvara practices. A student of Naropa, Marpa founded the Kagyu lineage in Tibet.

meditational deity. See **yidam.**

Middle Way school. See **Madhyamaka.**

Milarepa (1040–1123). A student of Marpa who attained enlightenment in one life-time. His student Gampopa founded the Dagpo Kagyu lineage.

Mind-Only school (Skt. *Chittamatra*). One of the four major schools in the Mahayana tradition, founded by Asanga in the fourth century. Its main tenet (to greatly simplify) is that all phenomena (internal and external) are mental events.

Mipham Rinpoche (1846–1912). A very influential philosopher and teacher in the Nyingma school of Tibetan Buddhism. He wrote over thirty-two volumes on many subjects and is one of the major founders of the Rimé nonsectarian movement.

mother tantra. One of the three kinds of tantras. The mother tantra is concerned with transforming passion. See also **father tantra.**

mudra. A "hand seal," or gesture, that is performed in specific tantric ritual practices to symbolize certain aspects of the practice.

nadis (Tib. *tsa*). See **subtle channels.**

Nagarjuna. An Indian scholar in the second century who founded the Madhyamaka philosophical school that emphasizes emptiness. See also **Madhyamaka.**

nagas. Water spirits that may take the form of serpents. They are often the custodian of treasures—either texts or material treasures—that they keep underground.

Nalanda. A famous Buddhist university that flourished from the fifth to the tenth centuries, located near modern Rajgir, in the Indian state of Bihar. It was the seat of the Mahayana teachings, and many great Buddhist scholars studied there.

Naropa (956–1040). An Indian master who is best known for transmitting many Vajrayana teachings to Marpa, who took them back to Tibet, where many became important practices in the Kagyu lineage.

nine formless dakinis. Teachings received by Tilopa from the wisdom dakinis at the Gandhola Temple. These teachings were then transmitted to Naropa, and then, in part, to Marpa, Milarepa, and his disciples.

nirmanakaya (Tib. *tulku*). One of the three bodies of the Buddha. The nirmanakaya, or "emanation body," manifests in the world and is perceptible to ordinary people. For example, Shakyamuni Buddha was a nirmanakaya. See also **three kayas.**

Nyingma school. The oldest school of Tibetan Buddhism. It is based on the teachings of Padmasambhava and others in the eighth and ninth centuries.

oral instructions (Tib. *men ngak*). Instructions given directly by a guru to his or her students concerning meditation on the nature of mind. While some of these are written down, many are passed on only orally. Sometimes they are called "quintessential instructions" or "pith instructions."

Padmasambhava (Tib. Guru Rinpoche). Founder of the Nyingma school of Tibetan Buddhism. He was invited to Tibet in the eighth century and is known for pacifying the non-Buddhist forces. He taught many tantras and Vajrayana practices and concealed many texts that were to be revealed later by his disciples.

pandita. A great scholar.

parinirvana. The event of Buddha's death. It is called "parinirvana" because it was the end of all rebirth since he had achieved complete enlightenment.

Patrul Rinpoche (1808–1887). A famous Nyingma teacher who wrote *The Words of My Perfect Teacher.*

pith instructions. See **oral instructions.**

prajna (Tib. *sherab*). A term with multiple meanings: perfect knowledge, wisdom, understanding, or discrimination. Usually it means the wisdom of seeing things from a nondualistic point of view.

Prajnaparamita. Sanskrit for "perfection of wisdom." The transcendent perfect wisdom (*prajna*) of the Mahayana path regarding emptiness. It also refers to a collection of about forty Mahayana sutras that deal with the perfection of wisdom.

prana. See **life-supporting wind.**

pratyekabuddhas. "Solitary awakened ones." Foundation-level practitioners who practice alone and have attained awakening on their own with no teacher guiding them. Generally placed on a higher level than an arhat, they have attained the fruition of the second level of the Foundation path through contemplation of the twelve interdependent links.

Rangjung Dorje (1284–1339). The Third Gyalwa Karmapa, known for writing a series of texts widely used in the Karma Kagyu school. His text *Buddha Nature,* which is on Mahamudra meditation, and *The Distinction between Consciousness and Wisdom* introduced the Shentong Madhyamaka view into the Karma Kagyu lineage. See also **Shentong Madhyamaka.**

Rangtong Madhyamaka. A subschool of Madhyamaka that is based on the second turning of the wheel of Dharma and teaches that reality is empty of self (Tib. *rangtong*) and beyond concepts.

samadhi. A state of meditation that is nondualistic—there is an absence of discrimination between self and other. Also called "meditative absorption" or "one-pointed meditation," this is the highest form of meditation.

Samantabhadra (Tib. Kuntuzangpo). The primordial dharmakaya buddha, according to the Nyingma school. Samantabhadra is also the name of one of the eight main bodhisattvas who attended the historical Buddha.

samaya. The vows or commitments made in the Vajrayana to a teacher or practice. These often include maintaining a harmonious relationship with the vajra master and one's Dharma friends and not straying from the continuity of the practice.

sambhogakaya. One of the three bodies of the Buddha. It is also called the "enjoyment body." To make it possible for high practitioners or bodhisattvas to contact the dharmakaya, the dharmakaya displays itself in the form of the sambhogakaya. See also **three kayas.**

samsara. The conditioned existence of ordinary life in which suffering occurs because one still possesses attachment, aggression, and ignorance; that is, "cyclic existence." It is contrasted to nirvana.

sangha. Companions on the path to awakening. It may include all the persons on the path or just the noble sangha, which are the realized ones.

Saraha. A mahasiddha and yogi who lived in India in the eighth century and was taught Mahamudra by a female arrow maker. He wrote three dohas, which are considered the first written descriptions of Mahamudra meditation.

seed syllable. A Tibetan letter, or syllable, that symbolizes the essence of a deity or an element. Tantric practices often involve visualizing seed syllables, which then transform into the deity or element it represents. For example, HRI is the seed syllable for Chenrezik, so one would first visualize empty space, and then a HRI arising from it, which then would transform into Chenrezik.

selflessness (Tib. *dak me*). Also called "egolessness." The absence of an inherently existing self. In two of the Foundation schools (Vaibhashika and Sautrantika), this refers exclusively to the fact that a person lacks a real permanent self, being just a collection of thoughts and feelings. In two of the Mahayana schools (Chittamatra and Madhyamaka), this was extended to mean that outside phenomena also lack inherent existence.

Shakyamuni Buddha (563–483 BCE). The historical Buddha, often called "Gautama Buddha."

Shentong Madhyamaka. A subschool of Madhyamaka that is based on the third turning of the wheel of Dharma and teaches that reality is emptiness inseparable from luminosity, where emptiness means "empty of other" (Tib. *shentong*) rather than "empty of self," as in Rangtong Madhyamaka.

shravakas. Literally, "those who hear." It refers to realized Foundation practitioners (arhats) who have achieved the realization of the nonexistence of a personal self.

siddhas. Accomplished Buddhist practitioners.

siddhis. Spiritual accomplishments of advanced practitioners. The "supreme siddhi" refers to complete enlightenment, whereas the "common siddhis" refer to the eight mundane accomplishments, which are powers such as being able to visit the celestial realms, having fast legs able to travel great distances with many obstacles in a very short time, and having blessing pills that make you invisible.

six paramitas. A Sanskrit term meaning "perfections." The Tibetan translation literally means "gone to the other side." These are the six practices of the Mahayana path: transcendent generosity, transcendent discipline, transcendent patience, transcendent exertion, transcendent meditation, and transcendent knowledge (Skt. *prajna*). When listed as tenfold, they consist of these six plus skillful means, aspirational prayer, power, and pure wisdom (Tib. *yeshe*).

skillful means (Skt. *upaya*). The skillful methods used by enlightened beings to present the Dharma by taking a person's capabilities and propensities into account.

subtle channels (Skt. *nadis*). Subtle pathways that are not anatomical but more like acupuncture meridians, through which subtle energy (Skt. *prana*) travels in the form of subtle drops (Skt. *bindus*). These energies are utilized in advanced tantric practices through special physical exercises (Tib. *trul khor*) and visualization techniques. See also **bindus, life-supporting wind, vajra body.**

sutras. Foundation and Mahayana texts that were recorded as being the words of the Buddha. These are often contrasted with the tantras, which are the Buddha's Vajrayana teachings, and the shastras, which are the commentaries on the words of the Buddha by great scholars (panditas).

tathagatagarbha. Literally, "the nature of the ones thus gone," usually translated into English as "buddha nature" or "buddha essence." It is the seed, or essence, of the tathagatas, which is the essence of enlightenment possessed by all sentient beings and that gives them the potential to attain enlightenment.

ten bodhisattva levels (Skt. *bhumis*). Literally, "ground." The levels, or stages, a bodhisattva goes through to reach enlightenment. There are ten levels in the sutra tradition and thirteen in the tantra tradition. The first level is the direct realization of emptiness, and the final level is buddhahood.

ten endowments. The ten qualities a person must possess that will enable them to practice the Dharma. These are (1) to be born a human, (2) to reside in a land where the Dharma is practiced, (3) to possess all of the mental and physical faculties needed to practice the Dharma, (4) to not experience great negative karma that inclines one not to practice the Dharma, (5) to have faith in the Dharma, (6) to have a buddha who has appeared in the world where one is born, (7) to have this buddha teach the Dharma, (8) to have been born at a time where the Dharma still exists, (9) to be in a place where the Dharma is still practiced, and (10) to have a spiritual master who has accepted one as a student.

ten nonvirtuous actions. A list of nonvirtuous deeds compiled at the request of the Dharma King Trisong Detsen that could be used by his subjects: killing, stealing, sexual misconduct, lying, slander, abusive words, idle gossip, covetousness, ill will, and wrong views. These acts result in undesirable karmic effects that will express themselves later in one's life or even in future lifetimes. The first three are actions of body, the next four of speech, and the last three of mind. The ten virtuous actions are the opposites of the above ten nonvirtuous actions.

Tengyur. Shastras, or commentaries, on the sutras in the Tibetan Buddhist canon, called the "Kangyur."

three kayas. The three bodies of the Buddha: the nirmanakaya, sambhogakaya, and dharmakaya. The dharmakaya, also called the "truth body," is the complete enlightenment, or the complete wisdom, of the Buddha, which is unoriginated wisdom beyond form. It manifests in the sambhogakaya and the nirmanakaya. The sambhogakaya, also called the "enjoyment body," appears only to bodhisattvas, usually when they reside in one of the pure lands. The nirmanakaya, also called the "emanation body," manifests in our world and can be seen by ordinary beings with impure perception. For example, Shakyamuni Buddha was a nirmanakaya.

three realms. Three categories of samsara: the desire, form, and formless realms. In the desire realm, beings are reborn in solid bodies, due to their karma. They can be reborn in circumstances that range from the god paradises to the hell realms. In the form realm, beings are reborn in a subtle form, due to the power of meditation. These are the meditation paradises. In the formless realm, beings enter a state of meditation after death, due to their meditation (samadhi), in which the processes of thought and perception have ceased.

Tilopa (988–1069). One of the eighty-four mahasiddhas. He was the guru of Naropa, who transmitted Tilopa's teachings to Marpa, who then brought these teachings to Tibet, where they became the foundation of the Kagyu lineage's teachings.

tsakali. A visual image or symbol. It can also refer to a small card on which is a painted image of a deity, offerings, and so on, used during rites and initiations.

twelve ayatanas. The twelve sensory constituents of cognition. These are the five sensory objects of sights, sounds, smells, tastes, and bodily textures, plus mental objects, and the five sense faculties of eyes, ears, nose, tongue, and body, plus the mind.

vajra (Tib. *dorje*). Usually translated as "diamond." It can refer to an implement held in the hand during certain Vajrayana ceremonies, or it can refer to a quality that is so pure and enduring that it is like a diamond.

vajra body. The subtle body, which is not anatomical in nature, that contains chakras, subtle channels, and subtle drops of energy (Skt. *bindus*). It is often visualized in advanced tantric practices. See also **bindus, chakras, subtle channels.**

Vajradhara (Tib. Dorje Chang). The dharmakaya Buddha. Vajradhara symbolizes the primordial wisdom of the dharmakaya and is depicted holding a bell and vajra in his hands, with his arms crossed in front of him, and wearing the ornaments of a sambhogakaya Buddha, symbolizing his richness.

Vajrayana. "Diamond Vehicle." One of the three major traditions of Buddhism (Foundation, Mahayana, and Vajrayana). The Vajrayana is based on the tantras and emphasizes the clarity aspect of phenomena. It is practiced mainly in Tibet.

Vajrayogini (Tib. Dorje Palmo). A semiwrathful meditational deity (Tib. *yidam*), also known as Vajravarahi, who is a consort of Chakrasamvara. She is a principal deity within the Karma Kagyu tradition.

whispered lineage. Also called the "oral lineage." The Kagyu lineage.

wisdom of the nature of phenomena. Transcendent knowledge (Skt. *jnana*) of a realized practitioner who perceives phenomena as they really are (Skt. *dharmata*).

wisdom of the variety of phenomena. Transcendent knowledge (Skt. *jnana*) of a realized practitioner who understands the vast variety of phenomena.

yidam. A tantric deity who embodies the qualities of buddhahood and is used as a meditational deity in Vajrayana practice. For example, Chenrezik is a yidam who represents true compassion, and he is visualized in the Chenrezik practice.

Yonge Mingyur Dorje (1641–1708). A treasure revealer (Tib. *terton*) whose appearance was predicted by Padmasambhava. He traveled throughout Tibet practicing a yogic lifestyle and is known for developing a physical antidote, based on a vision, to the Han plague that was decimating Tibet's yak population.

GLOSSARY OF TIBETAN TERMS

PRONOUNCED	SPELLED	MEANING
bakchak	bag chags	karmic latencies
bardo	bar do	intermediate state
chak gya	phyag rgya	mudra
chak gya chen po	phyag rgya chen po	Mahamudra
Chenrezik	spyan ras gzigs	Avalokiteshvara
Chö druk gi men ngak	chos drug gi man ngag	Six Dharmas of Tilopa
chö nyi	chos nyid	innate luminosity
chongwa	mchong ba	leap
dak me	bdag med	no self
damzik	dam tshig	commitment
de shin nyi	de bzhin nyid	suchness, reality
dikpa	sdig pa	wrongdoing
döndam	don dam	ultimate reality
dorje	rdo rje	vajra
Dorje Chang	rdo rje 'chang	Vajradhara
drippa	sgrib pa	obscuration
drol lam	grol lam	path of liberation
dutsi	bdud rtsi	healing nectar
dzok rim	rdzogs rim	completion stage
geshe	dge bshes	accomplished scholar
göpa	rgod pa	mental excitement
gur	mgur	spiritual song
gyü	rgyud	tantra
gyü lü	sgyu lus	illusory body

PRONOUNCED	SPELLED	MEANING
jinlap	byin rlabs	blessing
Kagyu	bka' brgyud	Kagyu
khom	goms	habituation
kunsop	kun rdzob	relative reality
Kuntuzangpo	kun tu bzang po	Samantabhadra
ladawa	la zla ba	cross over, leap
lama	bla ma	guru
lhenchik kyepa	lhan cig skyes pa	coemergence
lung	lung	reading transmission
lung ten	lung bstan	prophecy
mang gakpa	ma 'gags pa	unimpeded
marikpa	ma rig pa	ignorance
men ngak	man ngag	oral, or pith, instructions
mikpa mepa	dmigs pa med pa	without reference
mukpa	rmugs pa	dullness
namtar	rnam thar	spiritual biography
naro chö druk	na ro'i chos drug	Six Dharmas of Naropa
ney luk	gnas lugs	true nature, manner of abiding
ngowo	ngo bo	essence
nyam	nyams	temporary existence
nyen gyü	snyan brgyud	whispered lineage
nyön mong	nyon mongs	affliction
nyük ma	gnyug ma	natural (innate)
rangtong	rang stong	empty of self
rikpa	rig pa	awareness
rikpa yeshe	rig pa ye shes	awareness wisdom
sarma	gsar ma	new translation school
sem nyi	sems nyid	mind's true nature
shentong	gzhan stong	empty of other
te so	gtad so	reference point
thamel gyi shepa	tha mal gyi shes pa	original mind
thap	thabs	skillful means

Pronounced	Spelled	Meaning
thap lam	thabs lam	path of ripening
thukdam	thugs dam	death practice
tögal	thod rgal	leap over
tri	'khrid	practice instruction
trul khor	'khrul 'khor	yantra yoga postures
tsakali	tsa ka li	physical representation
tül shuk	brtul zhugs	vanquishing behavior
tummo	gtum mo	inner heat
wang	dbang	empowerment
yidam	yi dam	meditational deity

Notes

1. *Mahāmudrā and Related Instructions: Core Teachings of the Kagyü Schools*, trans. Peter Alan Roberts (Somerville, MA: Wisdom Publications, 2011), 13.
2. The website of the Dharma Fellowship of His Holiness the Gyalwa Karmapa, www .dharmafellowship.org/biographies/historicalsaints/mahasiddha-sri-tilopa.htm.
3. *The Life of Tilopa*, in *Religions of Tibet in Practice*, ed. Donald Lopez (Princeton, NJ: Princeton University Press, 2004), 137–56.
4. Tibetan words are given as they are pronounced, not as they are spelled in Tibetan. The correct transliterated spelling of these words may be found in the glossary of Tibetan terms.
5. The Six Yogas of Naropa are six special yogic practices that originated with Tilopa and were transmitted to Naropa, who then taught them to Marpa. They consist of the subtle heat, illusory body, dream yoga, luminosity, the ejection of consciousness, and the bardo practice.
6. Pith instructions (Tib. *men ngak*), also called "oral instructions" or "quintessential instructions," are practice instructions given directly by the guru to the student concerning meditation on the nature of mind. While some of these are written down, many are passed on only orally.
7. Fully enlightened beings, buddhas, may manifest in three ways: through the dharmakaya, which can be perceived only by other enlightened beings; through the sambhogakaya, which can be perceived only by advanced bodhisattvas in the pure lands; and through the nirmanakaya, which can be perceived by ordinary beings, for example, those who perceived the historical Buddha in our world.
8. When we look for the mind and its characteristics, we find nothing. Yet the mind has awareness and cognition, and we call this quality "luminous clarity" (Tib. *salwa*), or "luminosity," or "clarity."
9. Buddha nature (Skt. *sugatagarbha*) is a quality that is possessed by all sentient beings, and it is this quality that allows these beings (not just human beings) to eventually reach buddhahood.
10. In the Vajrayana there are two stages of meditation: the creation and the completion stage. The creation stage is a method of tantric meditation that involves visualization and contemplating deities for the purpose of realizing the purity of all phenomena. In this stage, visualization of the deity is established and maintained. The

completion stage has two meanings: first, it can refer to the dissolving of everything visualized in the creation stage, leaving the meditator with just his or her mind. It can also refer to working with the subtle winds, channels, drops, and the chakras during the practice.

11. It is generally accepted that Nagarjuna, who is the founder of the Madhyamaka school, lived in the second century and Tilopa lived in the eleventh century. Some have explained this anomaly by saying that the Nagarjuna who met Tilopa was a different person from the founder of the Madhyamaka school. On the other hand, Rinpoche has also said that mahasiddhas, unlike ordinary beings, have the power to appear at different times and places.

12. The display of miracles such as trees becoming warriors arises from the samadhi recognizing that all phenomena are uncreated and, in fact, illusory. Whatever is required to benefit beings can be magically manifested out of the samadhi of realizing this emptiness.—Thrangu Rinpoche

13. A spontaneous arisen form usually means that the form of a deity gradually appears on a rock, for example, without anyone ever touching it. A heruka indicates that the form was of Chakrasamvara.

14. The "secret Mantrayana" is another name for tantric teachings in the Vajrayana.

15. Also, see appendix B for the disturbing emotion that is purified and the wisdom that results when it is purified that is associated with each of the five buddha families.

16. In the actual empowerment that is still performed to this day, the guru puts a teaspoon of liquor or juice in the palm of the recipient and then it is consumed.

17. The subtle energy travels in the form of subtle drops through subtle channels, which are not anatomical structures but more like acupuncture meridians. These are all part of what is called the "vajra body," and in advanced tantric practices, these subtle channels and energies are purified through special physical exercises and visualization techniques.

18. In the creation stage of a tantric practice, we visualize the deity and his or her surrounding retinue. Then after the main practice, we engage in the completion stage, where we dissolve everything that we have visualized into emptiness and rest our mind in that emptiness. Luminous clarity creates the visualization, and the dissolving of it emphasizes the emptiness aspect of all phenomena.

19. The three heart spheres is actually the title of a tantra called the *Mahamudra Subtle Drop* tantra.

20. The account that Thrangu Rinpoche used was from Pema Karpo. Sangyes Nyenpa says that Pema Karpo's biography states that Tilopa met Nagarjuna's female disciple Matangi when he tried to find Nagarjuna. Matangi later sent Tilopa to her friend Dharima who was prostitute who helped Tilopa reach the last part of his path to enlightenment. The other accounts of this event imply that Matangi was a man, not a woman.

21. Mahabrahma, or the "Great Brahma," is the same as the Hindu god Indra who is mentioned in many Buddhist works.

22. Thrangu Rinpoche's teaching in 1994 on the "marketplace doha" uses a translation of

this doha by the Nālandā Translation Committee, published in *The Rain of Wisdom* (Boston: Shambhala Publications, 1980).

23. "Nakedly" here means without any preconception or conceptualization, like a baby looking at a shrine for the first time.

24. Tibetans divided the Madhyamaka, or Middle Way, school into two major schools. The Rangtong school follows the teachings of Nagarjuna fairly closely and maintains that everything is empty of itself, whereas the Shentong school maintains that although the nature of mind lacks substantiality, its emptiness is indivisible from luminous clarity and that all sentient beings possess this buddha essence.

25. Being "unborn" means that it has always been there since beginningless time.

26. The word "nature," also called "essence," has a technical meaning in Buddhism. For example, solid ice, a flowing stream, and steam have entirely different appearances and characteristics, but they all have the same "nature" as water, or in scientific terms, H_2O. Similarly, all the different thoughts, feelings, and memories are various appearances, or events, of the mind, while the actual essence or "nature" of the mind is emptiness, without any of these appearances clouding it.

27. The whispered lineage is the pith instructions given by a teacher to the student on how to do a practice that are not usually found in the practice texts.

28. The first quality is having perfect samaya, the second is having received a prophecy of one's future enlightenment, and the third is having developed a deep level of realization. Tilopa, being an emanation of Chakrasamvara, has automatically fulfilled the second and third prophecies.

29. In the Vajrayana, there are two paths—the path of liberation (Tib. *drol lam*) and the path of ripening (Tib. *thap lam*)—that are generally followed either simultaneously or alternately by the practitioner. The path of liberation is sometimes referred to as "formless meditation" and includes Mahamudra. In this approach to meditation, one relates to the mind in terms of the awareness aspect of mind.

30. Tilopa passed these teachings, called "the nine formless dakinis," to Naropa, who lived in India. Naropa then passed them to Marpa, who took them to Tibet. According to Tsangnyön Heruka, who wrote Milarepa's spiritual biography, Marpa passed on only four of them to his student Milarepa. Rechungpa, Milarepa's disciple, then received the other five teachings from Bharima in Nepal and from Tiphupa in India and transmitted them to Milarepa.

31. For example, at one point Tilopa staked out a cloth that was soiled. He then lit it, and the cloth burned up, leaving only the carbon threads of the warp and woof behind. He then asked Naropa what this meant, and Naropa said, "I understand that the Guru's illuminating understanding and instructions, which are like fire, and this fire burns the disciple's emotional instability, which is like cotton cloth. Thereby the belief in the solid reality of an external object is destroyed, and since this sort of belief about reality is no longer effective, there is no return to worldliness."

32. At that time, when taking refuge in the Buddha, the disciple's hair was completely shaved off. Today, those receiving ordination shave their hair but householders usually have just a few strands of hair cut off.

33. There are many different translations of the *Ganges Mahamudra*, and while they all have the same material, some versions have the verses in a different order. The numbering of the verses may also be different—for example, David Molk's translation of the root text in Sangye Nyenpa's commentary on the *Ganges Mahamudra* combines our verses 8a, 8b and 9 into just verse 8. See Sangye Nyenpa, *Tilopa's Mahamudra Upadesha: The Gangama Instructions with Commentary*, trans. David Molk (Boston: Snow Lion, 2014).

34. There are two English translations: *Mahamudra: The Quintessence of Mind and Meditation*, trans. Lobsang P. Lhalungpa (Boston: Shambhala Publications, 1986) and *Moonbeams of Mahāmudrā*, trans. Elizabeth M. Callahan (Boulder, CO: Snow Lion, 2019).

35. Thrangu Rinpoche has given an extensive commentary on this work in his *Essentials of Mahamudra: Looking Directly at the Mind* (Boston: Wisdom Publications, 2004).

36. The ten bodhisattva levels are ten stages that a bodhisattva goes through on the path to enlightenment. It begins with the first level called "Joy," which is the first realization of emptiness, and through this, he or she achieves the perfection of generosity. He or she then continues up to the tenth level, which is complete enlightenment.

37. In fact, these teachings were originally translated from the Bengali language of Apabhramsha, not Sanskrit.

38. Ignorance as used in Buddhist texts is one of the three main disturbing emotions. It does not mean "not knowing something" in general but rather it refers specifically to not realizing the empty nature of phenomena.

39. These are explained in detail in Naropa's biography. See Herbert Guenther, *The Life and Teachings of Naropa* (Oxford: Oxford University Press, 1963) and Khenchen Thrangu, *Naropa's Wisdom: His Life and Teachings on Mahamudra* (Boulder, CO: Snow Lion, forthcoming).

40. This definition of "space" is actually a description of "ether," which has been part of philosophy and physics in Asia, and also in Western civilization since Aristotle. Western philosophy and science abandoned the concept of ether because of an experiment performed by Albert Michelson and Edward Morley in 1887.

41. There is a distinction between thoughts and feelings and the mind's original nature (Tib. *sem nyi*), which is how the mind has always been without all its thoughts, confusion, and disturbing emotions. Usually, this distinction is described in terms of thoughts being like waves on the surface of a great ocean and the original mind as being the ocean.

42. The word "nature" (Skt. *svabhava*, Tib. *ngowo*) is also translated as "essence." See n. 26.

43. In Indian mythology, a wish-fulfilling jewel has the power to grant a person anything that they want. In Buddhism, it is used as a metaphor for the fact that once one has achieved complete enlightenment, one has achieved everything that there is to achieve.

44. These eighteen characteristics are the eight forms of leisure and the ten endowments. These are described more fully in the glossary; see under "eight forms of leisure" and "ten endowments."

45. There are sixteen kinds are emptiness (Skt. *shunyata*, Tib. *tongpa nyi*): (1) Emptiness of internal phenomena. This is the emptiness of the body, which is constantly changing and renewing. (2) Emptiness of external phenomena. Outer phenomena are constantly changing and have no substantial reality. (3) Emptiness of both internal and external phenomena. External objects are perceived and become internal images, and the relationship between the two is not a solid, unchanging connection. (4) Emptiness of emptiness. This is the emptiness of everything, what is normally referred to as emptiness in Buddhist texts. (5) Emptiness of the great. This is the emptiness that pervades in all directions. (6) Emptiness of the ultimate. This is emptiness of nirvana, which is ultimate reality. (7). Emptiness of composite phenomena. Everything that is compounded, that can be broken into smaller parts, is a composite phenomenon, and these are also empty. (8) Emptiness of noncomposite phenomena. Noncomposite phenomena are things that don't arise or cease; they are also empty. (9) Emptiness of that which is beyond extremes. The emptiness of the two extremes, or limitations, of externalism and nihilism, or samsara and nirvana. (10) Emptiness of that which has no beginning or end. Samsara is said to have no beginning (we cannot discover when it began) and no end (there is no time when it will end). (11) Emptiness of that which is not to be abandoned. The Dharma and the path to enlightenment should never be abandoned, yet they are empty too. (12) Emptiness of true nature. The true nature of reality is also empty. The Rangtong school uses this emptiness to refute the Shentong position. (13) Emptiness of all phenomena. All external phenomena, the contact with the sense organs, the sense organs themselves, and the sensory consciousness are also empty. (14) Emptiness of defining characteristics. All composite and noncomposite phenomena have characteristics, but these characteristics themselves are also empty. (15) Emptiness of the imperceptible. The past and the future don't exist, and the present is only a minute, fleeting moment so nothing is apprehendable. (16) Emptiness that is the absence of entities. Since everything arises from cause and effect, there cannot be anything that arises as a composite.

46. "Adventitious" means that it is not an inherent part of mind. The example given to illustrate this is that if gold is buried under a lot of dirt, the dirt does not become part of the gold. Therefore the dirt is adventitious, "not part of" the gold.

47. The Buddha rejected the idea that the world and everything that happens in it is due to the influence of God or gods, rather he said that everything is created and changed due to cause and effect. This is called "interdependent origination" (Tib. *tendril*). One event causes another event, that causes another event, without there being any interference of a creator.

48. The second part of this verse (verse 8b) concerns conduct and is discussed in the next chapter.

49. The Four Dharma Seals are (1) all compounded things are impermanent, (2) all emotions are painful, (3) all phenomena are without inherent existence, and (4) nirvana is beyond description.

50. The seven dharmas of Vairochana are (1) straighten the upper body and the spinal column, (2) look slightly downward into space straight across from the tip of the nose while keeping the chin and neck straight, (3) straighten the shoulder blades in the manner of a vulture flexing its wings, (4) keep the lips touching gently, (5) let the tip of the tongue touch the upper palate, (6), form the legs into either the full lotus or the diamond posture, and (7) keep the back of the right hand flat on the left open palm with the inside of the tips of the thumbs gently touching.

51. The four common preliminaries are explained in detail in Thrangu Rinpoche, *Four Foundations of Buddhist Practice* (Boulder, CO: Namo Buddha Publications, 2018).

52. This refers primarily to believing that our mind, external phenomena, and our self exist as real, solid objects, whereas they are actually empty, and believing that the emptiness, or the insubstantiality, of mind and phenomena do not exist, when they actually do exist.

53. The six perfections (Skt. *paramitas*) are transcendent generosity, transcendent discipline, transcendent patience, transcendent exertion, transcendent meditation, and transcendent knowledge (*prajna*). Each perfection is "transcendent" because it goes far beyond, or transcends, our ordinary generosity, discipline, patience, exertion, meditation, and knowledge.

54. The ten virtuous deeds are (1) not destroying life, (2) not taking what has not been given, (3) refraining from improper sexual conduct, (4) not telling a falsehood, (5) not using abusive language, (6) not slandering others, (7) not indulging in irrelevant talk, (8) not being covetous of other's property or power, (9) not being malicious, and (10) not holding false or destructive beliefs. The ten unvirtuous deeds are violating any of the ten virtuous deeds.

The five actions of immediate result are (1) intentionally killing one's father, (2) intentionally killing one's mother, (3) killing an enlightened being, (4) shedding the blood of a bodhisattva, and (5) creating a schism within the sangha (the community of Buddhist practitioners). These five actions are deeds that lead to one going directly to the lower realms upon death. These come from *The Sutra Preached by the Buddha on the Total Extinction of the Dharma.*

55. Every action that a person does creates karmic imprints or latencies (Tib. *bakchak*) that are stored in the eighth consciousness. Later, when stimulated by the appropriate external experience, the karma of these latencies express themselves, leaving the eighth consciousness and entering the sixth consciousness.

56. The selflessness of persons is the fact that persons are not solid entities because they are constantly changing. This was taught mainly by the Buddha. The selflessness of phenomena, or simply emptiness, is that all external objects are also insubstantial, and this is emphasized mostly in the Mahayana teachings. Thrangu Rinpoche explains this in detail in *The Open Door to Emptiness* (Glastonbury, CT: Namo Buddha Publications, 2012).

57. In many other texts, Thrangu Rinpoche points out that the Tibetan word for "meditation" is *sgom* (pronounced "gom") and the word for "getting used to" or "habituated" is *goms* (pronounced "khom"), making these words sound very similar.

58. For English translations of the compilation of the lives of the eighty-four mahasiddhas by Abhayadatta, see the entries under Abhayadatta in the bibliography.

59. The six realms are traditionally said to be the three higher realms—god, jealous god, and human realms—and the three lower realms—animal, hungry ghost, and hell realms. There are many more different realms than these that are invisible to ordinary persons.

60. Indian Buddhist texts were brought to Tibet and translated into Tibetan during two different periods. The first was during the seventh century, when Guru Rinpoche brought texts from India and had them translated into Tibetan. The second wave of translations, referred to as the "new translation tradition" (Tib. *sarma*), introduced new teachings and translations into Tibet in the eleventh century.

61. Beginningless time refers to the fact that one can go back to one's previous incarnation, and then back to the next earliest incarnation, and back and back without any beginning.

62. Thrangu Rinpoche follows the Third Karmapa, who divided the eighth (alaya) consciousness into the storehouse consciousness, which stores all of one's karma, and the all-basis consciousness, which holds the other seven consciousnesses together.

63. Upaya (skillful means) here refers to the various tantric techniques to develop bliss in union with wisdom (Skt. *prajna*), which is the wisdom developed using these techniques.

64. Karmamudra is the use of sexual activity between a man and woman to generate bliss and emptiness. The bliss and emptiness generated in this practice is much more than an orgasm and lasts for a much longer period of time. The danger with engaging in this practice is that the partners might become attached to each other and then the practice would no longer be a meditational practice.

65. The ten powers are knowing (1) what is and isn't possible, (2) the results of actions, (3) the aspirations of human beings, (4) the elements, (5) the powers of human beings, (6) the path that leads everywhere, (7) the origin of disturbing emotions, (8) previous lives, (9) transference and death, and (10) that one's defilements are exhausted.

66. The four fearlessnesses are that one is not afraid to (1) assert one's perfect realization, (2) assert one's having abandoned all faults, (3) reveal the path to liberation, and (4) reveal obstacles on the path.

67. Karl Brunnhölzl explains in his *Straight from the Heart: Buddhist Pith Instructions* (Ithaca, NY: Snow Lion Publications, 2007), 508n359, that one edition is from the Tibetan Tengyur and the other, the one that Thrangu Rinpoche used, is from a collection of Kagyu works that was published by the Sixteenth Karmapa in Rumtek.

68. Tib. *phung po, kham, kye che*. The five psychophysical "aggregates," the eighteen "elements" of sensory perception, and the twelve "bases" of sensory perception.

69. This translation is available at www.dharmasanctuary.org/pdf/Doha_Treasures.pdf, last accessed March 22, 2019.

70. This description of the eight consciousnesses is taken from Thrangu Rinpoche, *The Five Buddha Families and the Eight Consciousnesses* (Glastonbury, CT: Namo Buddha Publications, 2013). Used with permission.

Annotated Bibliography

Tantras

Mahamudra Subtle Drop Tantra (Skt. *Mahamudratilaka*, Tib. *Phyag chen thig le*)
This tantra has not been translated into English.

Other Works

Abhayadatta
Buddha's Lions: The Lives of the Eighty-Four Siddhas. Translated by James B. Robinson. Berkeley, CA: Dharma Publishing, 1979. Also translated as *Masters of Enchantment: The Lives and Legends of the Mahasiddhas.* Translated by Keith Dowman. Rochester, VT: Inner Traditions, 1989.

   Translations of the original text on the eighty-four siddhas collected by Abhayadatta, an Indian scholar in the twelfth century. The translation by Dowman also includes a large amount of additional information on the mahasiddhas.

Brunnhölzl, Karl
Straight from the Heart: Buddhist Pith Instructions. Ithaca, NY: Snow Lion Publications, 2007.

   Translations of various pith instructions of the Kagyu lineage, including a translation of Tilopa's *Ganges Mahamudra* that includes a comparison of the two major Tibetan versions of this doha—one in the Tibetan Kangyur and the other in the Kagyu lineage.

Chandrakirti
Introduction to the Middle Way (Skt. *Madhyamakavatara*). Translated by the Padmakara Translation Group. Boston: Shambhala Publications, 2004.

   One of most celebrated Indian works on the study of emptiness. It is written in verse and has ten chapters describing each of the bodhisattva levels. Tibetan Buddhists regard it as being the most authoritative text of the Madhyamaka Prasangika view. This book has a translation of the root text and a commentary by Mipham Rinpoche.

Dakpo Tashi Namgyal
Phyag chen zla ba' i od zer. English translation: *Mahāmudrā: The Quintessence of Mind and Meditation.* Translated by Lobsang P. Lhalungpa. Boston: Shambhala Publications, 1986. Also *Moonbeams of Mahāmudrā.* Translated by Elizabeth M. Callahan. Boulder, CO: Snow Lion, 2019.
A classic book covering all aspects of Mahamudra meditation in great detail.

Dorje Dze Öd
The Great Kagyu Masters. Translated by Khenpo Könchog Gyaltsen. Ithaca, NY: Snow Lion Publications, 1990.
A compilation of the lives of the Kagyu masters from the Drikung Kagyu tradition. The retelling of Tilopa's life included here is mostly in accord with the biography used by Thrangu Rinpoche.

Gendun Choephel (1903–1951)
The White Annals. Translated by Samten Norboo. Dharamsala, India: Library of Tibetan Works and Archives, 1978.
An unfinished history of Tibet by a brilliant Tibetan writer who often took a view contrary to the traditional Tibetan Buddhist view.

Guenther, Herbert
The Life and Teaching of Nāropa. Oxford: Oxford University Press, 1963.
One of the few translations of the biography of Tilopa's student Naropa. It also contains information on Tilopa as well.

Hoffman, Helmut
The Religions of Tibet. Translated by Edward Fitzgerald. Westport, CT: Greenwood Press, 1961.

Jackson, Roger
Tantric Treasures. Oxford: Oxford University Press, 2004.
Contains a translation of three dohas, including Tilopa's *Doha Kosha*, translated from the original Apabhramsha language of Bengal.

Khenchen Thrangu Rinpoche
Essentials of Mahamudra: Looking Directly at the Mind. Boston: Wisdom Publications, 2004.
An extremely detailed description of Mahamudra meditation—Thrangu Rinpoche's commentary on Dakpo Tashi Namgyal's *Moonbeams of Mahamudra*, which Rinpoche gave over five summers in Big Bear, California.

The Five Buddha Families and the Eight Consciousnesses. Glastonbury, CT: Namo Buddha Publications, 2013.

Explanations of the five buddha families in terms of their connections with the five aggregates, five types of disturbing emotion, and five buddha wisdoms

Four Foundations of Buddhist Practice. Boulder, CO: Namo Buddha Publications, 2018.
An extensive explanation of the four common preliminaries, also called the "four turnings of the mind," which are four contemplations one should engage in before beginning any Dharma practice.

Naropa's Wisdom: His Life and Teachings on Mahamudra. Boulder, CO: Snow Lion, forthcoming.
Teachings on Naropa's life and on some of his dohas on Mahamudra.

The Open Door to Emptiness. Glastonbury, CT: Namo Buddha Publications, 2012.
A careful examination of emptiness, one of the more difficult concepts in Buddhism, which uses simple, straightforward examples and explanations.

Pointing Out the Dharmakaya: Teachings on the Ninth Karmapa's Text. Ithaca, NY: Snow Lion Publications, 2003.
One of the Ninth Karmapa's three major works on Mahamudra meditation. The commentary is by Thrangu Rinpoche and was orally translated by Lama Yeshe Gyamtso.

The Spiritual Song of Lodro Thaye. Auckland, New Zealand: Zhyisil Chokyi Ghatsal, 2008.
A translation of Jamgön Kongtrul's 273-verse spiritual song on the ground, path, and fruition of Mahamudra with Thrangu Rinpoche's line-by-line commentary. It was translated by Sarah Harding and Cornelia Weishaar-Gunter.

Maitreya
The Uttaratantra (Skt. *Mahayana Uttaratantra-shastra*; also known as *Ratnagotravibhaga*)
One of five transmissions from the Buddha Maitreya received by Asanga in the fourth century CE. This text consists of 404 verses mainly on the subject of buddha nature and the development of the realization of the nature of phenomena through the purification of the disturbing emotions. The root text and a commentary by Thrangu Rinpoche can be found in *The Uttaratantra: A Treatise on Buddha-Essence* (Auckland, New Zealand: Zhyisil Chokyi Ghatsal, 2003).

Marpa, Chokyi Lodro
The Life of the Mahāsiddha Tilopa. Translated by Fabrizio Torricelli and Sangye Naga. Dharamsala, India: Library of Tibetan Works and Archives, 1995.
A translation of the earliest known biography of Tilopa, which was composed by

Marpa. This book also includes the Tibetan text, extensive notes, and a review of eight different spiritual biographies written about Tilopa.

Michelson, A., and E. Morley
"On the Relative Motion of the Earth and the Luminiferous Ether." *American Journal of Science* 34, no. 203 (1887): 333–45.
The findings of an experiment that ended almost two thousand years of Western scientists and philosophers believing in the existence of the ether.

Nālandā Translation Committee, trans.
The Rain of Wisdom. Boston: Shambhala Publications, 1980.
A collection of spiritual songs by the Kagyu lineage masters, which includes the "Marketplace Doha" by Tilopa.

The Life of Tilopa. In *Religions of Tibet in Practice*, edited by Donald Lopez, 137–56. Princeton, NJ: Princeton University Press, 2004.
A summary of Tilopa's life and a translation of Pema Karpo's *Pekar Chöjung* (History of the Dharma).

Patrul Rinpoche
The Words of My Perfect Teacher. Translated by the Padmakara Translation Group. Boston: Shambhala Publications, 1998.
An excellent summary of the Dharma from a Tibetan viewpoint.

Pema Karpo
Pekar Chöjung (History of the Dharma)
The root text that Thrangu Rinpoche used for his commentary on the life of Tilopa. It has been translated into English by the Nālandā Translation Committee as *The Life of Tilopa*. See above under Nālandā Translation Committee.

Rangjung Dorje, The Third Gyalwa Karmapa
Aspirational Prayer for Mahamudra. Translated by John Rockwell. Boulder, CO: Namo Buddha Publications, 2001.
A prayer aspiring to achieve Mahamudra. It also gives a brief outline of the path. This translation includes a commentary by Thrangu Rinpoche.

Roberts, Peter Alan, trans.
Mahāmudrā and Related Instructions: Core Teachings of the Kagyü Schools. Somerville, MA: Wisdom Publications, 2011.

Sangyes Nyenpa
Tilopa's Mahamudra Upadesha: The Gangama Instructions with Commentary. Translated by David Molk. Boston: Snow Lion, 2014.

A translation of the root verses of Tilopa's *Ganges Mahamudra* with a commentary by Sangyes Nyenpa. Also includes a translation of *The Golden Garland of the Kagyu* by Rangjung Dorje, which is a commentary on the *Ganges Mahamudra,* and *A Brief Account of Tilopa and Naropa* by Gampopa.

Saraha
A Song for the King: Saraha on Mahamudra Meditation. Edited by Michele Martin. Boston: Wisdom Publications, 2006.
  The shortest of the three doha cycles on Mahamudra by Saraha. This volume has an extensive commentary by Thrangu Rinpoche, edited by Michele Martin from oral translation by Peter O'Hearn (Lama Yeshe Gyamtso).

Shantideva
The Way of the Bodhisattva (Skt. *Bodhicharyavatara*). 2nd rev. ed. Boulder, CO: Shambhala Publications, 2006.
  One of the most widely read Mahayana texts describing how to conduct oneself as a bodhisattva. See Thrangu Rinpoche, *Shantideva's "A Guide to the Bodhisattva's Way of Life"* (Dharamsala, India: Library of Tibetan Works and Archives, 2016) for a commentary on this text along with a translation of Shantideva's root text.

Tilopa
The Oral Instructions of the Six Yogas (*Saddharmo Padesha*). In *The Practice of the Six Yogas of Naropa*, translated by Glenn Mullin, 23–30. Ithaca, NY: Snow Lion Publications, 1997.
  Contains a translation of this work by Tilopa, as well as the *Six Dharmas of Naropa* and several commentaries on Naropa's text.

"The Tanjur Text of Tilopa's *Dohākoṣa*." Translated by Fabrizio Torricelli. *The Tibet Journal* 22, no. 1 (1997): 35–57.
  Contains a translation of "Tilopa's Treasure of Songs," a thirty-seven-verse doha by Tilopa.

Torricelli, Fabrizio
"Chos drug and bKa'-babs bzhi Material for a Biography of the Siddha Tilopa." *East and West* 43, no. 1/4 (1993): 185–98.
  Provides extensive materials on the different transmissions that Tilopa received and also information on the Six Dharmas of Tilopa.

Tsangnyön Heruka
The Hundred Thousand Songs of Milarepa: A New Translation. Translated by Christopher Stagg. Boulder, CO: Shambhala Publications, 2016.
  An excellent translation of many of Milarepa's spiritual songs. Milarepa was one of the greatest Buddhist saints to live in Tibet, and his incredible story of

accomplishing enlightenment is one of the truly inspirational stories in Buddhism. He taught almost all his profound teachings in the form of spiritual songs.

The Life of Milarepa. Translated by Lobsang P. Lhalungpa. New York: Penguin Books, 1977.
    Many of Milarepa's songs are collected and beautifully translated in this book.

Vasubandhu
The Treasury of Abhidharma (Skt. *Abhidharmakosha)*
    A summary of the Abhidharma that is studied in many Tibetan Buddhist monasteries. Available in English as *Abhidharmakośabhāṣyam.* Translated by Louis de La Vallée Poussin. English translation by Leo M. Pruden. Berkeley, CA: Asian Humanities Press, 1991.

Wangchuk Gyaltsen (b. 1317)
"The Life of Tilopa." Unpublished manuscript. Translated by Ives Waldo.
    An English translation of one of the three important biographies of Tilopa.

INDEX

Abhayadatta, x, 189n58
Abhidharmakosha, 76
Abhidharma-pitaka, 108
accumulation of merit and wisdom, 22, 87
Action Seal, 147
Adzom Rinpoche, xi
afflicted (seventh) consciousness, 164
aggression
  cutting the bonds of, 123–24
  teachings on remedies for, 108
agitation
  calming with luminous clarity, 73–74
  common siddhi for easing, 149
  in meditation, 144, 146–47
Akshobhya, 13, 161
alertness, importance of, 61, 95, 120, 130, 146
all-accomplishing wisdom, 162
all-basis, as unborn, 141
all-basis (eighth) consciousness, 77, 141,
  164, 188n55, 189n62
all-pervasive suffering, 116
Amitabha, 13, 162
Amoghasiddhi, 13, 162
anger
  looking directly at, 71, 140
  wisdom nature of, 161
antidote, turning emptiness into, 136
appearances
  emptiness as remedy for fixation on, 79
  ignorance of being enthralled with, 119
  leaving as they are, 131, 139, 140–41, 142
  luminous clarity and, 153
  unity with emptiness, 81
  See also external objects
arhat, 112, 151
Aspirational Prayer for Mahamudra
  (Rangjung Dorje), 70, 80, 94

attachment
  to a conceptual view, 102
  cutting the bonds of, 123–24
  teachings on remedies for, 108
attentiveness, mindfulness and, 104, 145,
  153
austerities and hardships, understanding,
  63–65
awakening
  attainment of unsurpassable, 72, 92,
  95–96, 121
  in one lifetime, 22, 28, 58, 128–29
  two different methods for, x
awareness (*rikpa*)
  not being distracted from, 120–21
  as opposite of ignorance, 128
  resting in naked, 137–39
  techniques for increasing, 145–47
  temporary experiences that veil, 138

benefiting beings
  compassion and, 5, 59
  supreme nirmanakaya for, 59
Bhagavati, 32–34
Biography of Milarepa, 22
blessings
  devotion and, 63
  of guru, 117–18, 119
bliss
  nature of mind and, 77
  as veil of awareness, 138
bliss-emptiness
  attainment of, 14
  Karmamudra and, 147–48
bodhisattvas
  realization of, 112
  ten levels of, 60, 122, 151, 186n36

body. *See* physical body; physical posture
breath
  applying techniques of, 144, 145–46
  in meditation, 90, 93
buddha family, 161
buddha nature
  buddhahood and, 5, 78, 118, 183n9
  full recognition of, 127–28
  luminous clarity and, 79–80, 85
  Mahamudra view of, 24–27
  sesame oil metaphor for, 20–24
Buddha Shakyamuni
  brief history of, 59
  buddha nature and, 118
  commentaries on teachings of, 58
  enlightenment of, 135, 151
  as supreme nirmanakaya, 4, 59, 183n7
  teachings of, ix, 4, 84–85, 107–8, 126
buddhahood
  austerities and, 64
  familiarization with mind's nature and, 122
  as meaningful pursuit, 119
  in one lifetime, 22, 28, 58, 125, 128–29, 135
  recognizing luminous clarity and, 79–80
  relying on a guru for, 116, 118

cause and effect
  Buddha's teachings on, ix
  realization of wisdom and, 20
Chakrasamvara, 4–5, 30, 32, 34, 184n13, 185n28
Chakrasamvara tantra, 6, 14, 15
Chandrakirti, 132
Chenrezik, 5
clear light, 80, 82. *See also* luminous clarity
commitments (samaya), of Mahamudra
  as being free of location or focus of mind, 104–5
  as free of extremes, 107
  of maintaining awareness of mind's nature, 105
  meaning of, 101, 103
  to specific practices, 103
  view of Mahamudra and, 101–2
  without conceptualization, 103–4
compassion
  benefiting beings and, 5, 59
  buddha bodies and, 4

conceptual fabrications, of emptiness, 136
conceptual fixation
  guru's blessings for liberating, 118
  samaya and, 103–4
  samsara and, 108–9
  stripping mind of, 137–38
  transcending, 120, 142, 143
conduct
  acting in accordance to customs, 98–99
  of Mahamudra, 89–91, 92
  monarch of all, 121, 142, 143
confidence
  importance of, 63–64, 118
  in recognition, 129–30
Consequence (Prasangika) school, 21
conventional reality
  fruition of path and, 151
  Heart Sutra on, 78
  Mahamudra view of, 77
  mind and, 76, 77
creation and completion stages, 6, 183n10, 184n18
  joining with Mahamudra, 109
  Tilopa's practice of, 12–13, 14–15

dakinis, Tilopa's teachings from, 12–13, 29–34
Dakpo Tashi Namgyal, 55, 95, 146, 153
dark retreat, 56
De Je Gawa, 40
dedication and aspiration, 150
deities
  creation stage and, 6, 12–13, 183n10
  as dharmata, 5
  spontaneously arisen form of, 12, 184n13
delight, spiritual songs and, 27–28
desire
  taking as the path, 147, 189n64
  wisdom nature of, 162
devotion
  blessings and, 117
  immediate benefit of, 63
  true function of, 63–64
Dharima, xi, 16–17, 19, 184n20
Dharma
  Buddha's expression of profundity of, 135
  power and effectiveness of, 22
  turnings of wheel of, 21, 23, 59, 84–85
  vast teachings of, 4, 108, 126
  of whispered lineage, 30, 32, 185n27

dharmadhatu, 128, 161
dharmakaya, 183n7
  compassion and, 4
  guru pointing out, 20
  instructions from lineage of, 32–33
  Vajradhara as, 59
dharmata
  deities and, 5
  direct experience of, 33, 137
  of mind beyond extremes, 94
  wisdom of, 161
  wisdom that recognizes, 128
diligence
  commitment and, 103
  confidence and, 63, 118
direct experience
  of dharmata, 33, 137
  of emptiness, 21–22, 26, 27, 74, 131
  as "leaping" past intellect, 91
  of nature of mind, 131
  uncommon view and, 62, 67–68, 71
discriminating wisdom, 162
distraction, 105
  how to abandon, 122–27
  maintaining awareness beyond, 120–21, 146
disturbing emotions
  as adventitious stains, 81
  cutting the bonds of, 123–24
  as distinct from original mind, 69–70, 74, 186n41
  emptiness of, 23
  liberation from, 20, 109
  looking directly at nature of, 71–72, 96, 113, 131–32, 137, 140
  mental suffering and, 73
  resting in unborn nature and, 141–42
  self-liberation of, 27
  sense perceptions and, 163
  suffering and, 126
  three vehicles' different approaches to, 139–40
  Vinaya remedies for, 108
Doha Treasure, The (Tilopa), 158–59
dohas (spiritual songs)
  great value of, 27–28, 58
  importance of Tilopa's, 58–61
  spontaneous composition of, xiii, 68
  Tilopa's marketplace doha, 19–28
Dorje Dze Öd, xiii

dreams and magical illusions, mundane
  things as, 123, 124
Drime Lingpa, 94
Dzogchen, 56, 94

echo metaphor, for conduct of speech, 90–91
eight consciousnesses, 163–64, 189n62
Eighty-Four Mahasiddhas (Abhayadatta), x
empowerment of the word, 14
empowerments
  of Karpo Sangmo, 13–14
  samaya and, 103
emptiness
  vs. being spaced out, 129–30
  completion stage and, 15, 184n18
  crystal ladder metaphor for, 31
  difficulties with realizing, 24
  direct experience of, 21–22, 26, 27, 74, 131
  display of miracles and, 184n12
  inferential reasoning and, 21–22, 24, 67, 129
  inseparability of wisdom and, 57
  Mahamudra view of, 24–27
  mistakes made regarding, 136
  of nature of mind, 26–27, 71, 78, 121
  of physical body, 93
  Rangtong vs. Shentong on, 21, 23, 78–79, 185n24
  sixteen kinds of, 79, 187n45
  space as physical, 68
  sunlight as metaphor for mind's, 78–82
  unity with luminous clarity, 27, 74, 78–82, 122, 128, 132–33, 185n24
ether, 186n40
external objects
  difficulties looking directly at, 28
  emptiness as remedy for fixation on, 79, 187n45
  looking at mind that experiences, 26
  transcending fixation on, 120
  See also appearances
external world, as not cause of suffering, 83–84
extremes
  being free from, 107, 108
  of existence and nonexistence, 94
  ground as beyond, 121–22
  view beyond all, 143

fire metaphor, for Mahamudra, 109
five actions of immediate result, 109, 188n54
five aggregates, 13
five buddha families, 13, 161–62, 184n15
Foundation Vehicle, 84
  awareness in, 128
  on disturbing emotions, 140
  realization in, 23, 112
  selflessness of persons in, 71
Four Dharma Seals, 86, 188n49
fourfold fearlessness, 149, 189n66
fruition
  conventional view of, 151
  of Mahamudra, 121, 122, 142, 143,
    148–49
future, not anticipating, 157

Gampopa, 122, 125
gandharvas, 14
Ganges Mahamudra (Mahamudra
    Upadesha, Tilopa)
  benefits of practicing, 50, 107–10,
    127–29
  brief description of text, xiii, xiv, 47–48,
    62–64
  colophon, 53, 150
  commitments of Mahamudra, 49, 101–5
  conduct of Mahamudra, 49, 89–91
  dedication and aspiration, 53, 150
  defects of not practicing, 50, 111–12
  different editions of, 62, 67, 150–51,
    186n33, 189n67
  homage, 47, 62
  importance of, 57–61
  main practice, 51–53, 135–49
  manner of practicing, 50–51, 115–29
  meditation of Mahamudra, 49, 92–96
  results of practice, 148–49
  root text, 47–53
  seven major topics of, 67
  for those of highest faculties, 135–43
  for those of medium or lesser faculties,
    143–48
  title, 47, 57, 60, 61
  view in six metaphors, 47–48, 67–84
garuda, 5
gaze, for steadying the mind, 146
Gendun Choephel, 3
generosity, joining with Mahamudra, 109
god realms, 41–43

grasping
  as source of problem, 131
  transcending, 120
  See also conceptual fixation
Great Kagyu Masters, The, xiii
ground
  getting lost in emptiness of, 136
  of Mahamudra, 121–22
  path as recognition of, 122
  of purification, 80–81
  as unborn all-basis, 141
  view as recognition of, 67, 92
Guhyasamaja tantra, 14
guru
  blessings of, 117–18, 119
  relying on a, 115–21
  showing the truth of reality, 24, 25, 82
guru yoga, 87, 120

hagiography, 3
happiness
  seeking short-term, 116, 119
  virtuous actions and, 42, 77, 108
Heart Sutra, 26, 78
hell realms, 41, 126
Hevajra tantra, 6
higher realms of existence, 42–43
highest faculties, practice for those of,
    135–43
Hindu culture, Buddhism and, ix
Hoffman, Helmut, xii–xiii
homage, 62
hope and fear
  absence of, as fruition, 142, 143, 151
  transcending, 121
human existence, characteristics of, 75, 93,
    187n44
hungry ghost realms, 126

ignorance, 186n38
  dispelling with luminous clarity, 79
  intellect as aspect of, 62
  as marikpa, 128
  pacification of, 128
  wisdom nature of, 161
impermanence and death, 93
  renunciation and, 123, 124
inexpressibility, of nature of mind, 82–84
inferential reasoning
  common view and, 67, 71

emptiness and, 21–22, 24
limitations of, 69, 91, 129, 136, 138
innate coemergent wisdom, 19
    being introduced to, 23–24
    meaning of, 24–25
    path of recognizing, 24–27
    See also wisdom
inner heat (*tummo*) practice, 147–48
Insight meditation. *See* Vipashyana
    (Insight meditation)
Instructions of the Six Yogas (Tilopa), xiv
intellect
    as aspect of ignorance, 62
    conventional reality and, 67–68
    letting go of contrivances of, 138
    study of Dharma and, 153
    See also conceptual fixation
interdependent origination, 81, 187n47
intermediate state, liberation in, 58
isolation, relying upon, 124

Jamgön Kongtrul Lodro Thaye, 151–52
Jangden Kukpa, 41
jealousy, wisdom nature of, 162
jewel family, 162

Kagyu lineage, xiii
    three forefathers of, 125
Kalachakra tantra, 56
Kalu Rinpoche, 85
karma family, 162
Karmamudra practice, 147–48, 189n64
Karmapa, Ninth, Wangchuk Dorje, 93,
    146
Karmapa, Seventeenth, xi
Karmapa, Sixteenth, Rigpe Dorje, 55
Karmapa, Third, Rangjung Dorje, 62, 67,
    70–71, 80, 83, 94
karmic imprints
    results of actions and, 93, 188n55
    wrongdoing and, 77, 128
Karpo Sangmo, 13, 14, 15
Kasuriva, 34
Khenpo Gangshar, 31
Khenpo Könchog Gyaltsen, xiii
King Indrabhuti, 125
knowledge and wisdom empowerment, 14

Lama Norlha, xi
Lavapa, 15

Leap Over (*tögal*) practice, 56
lesser faculties, practice for those of,
    143–48
Life of Mahasiddha Tilopa, The (Marpa),
    xii
logical reasoning. *See* inferential reasoning
lotus family, 162
Luipa, 15
Luje Denma, 42
luminous clarity
    of buddha nature, 79–80, 85
    calming agitation with, 74
    creation stage and, 5, 15, 184n18
    devotion and, 117
    difficulties with recognizing, 80
    nature of mind and, 74, 79–80, 121,
        183n8
    sunlight as metaphor for mind's, 78–82
    third turning's emphasis on, 23
    as unimpeded, 85, 153
    unity with emptiness, 27, 74, 78–82,
        122, 128, 132–33, 185n24
    as veil of awareness, 138

Machik Lapdrön, 90
Madhyamaka. *See* Middle Way
    (Madhyamaka) school
Mahabrahma, 19, 184n21
Mahamudra
    attainment of, 124, 126, 127–29
    benefit of result of, 27–28, 148–49
    brief overview of, 55–57
    direct experience as path in, 21–22, 62
    even placement of, 97, 139
    examples of different styles of practice,
        124–25
    as familiarization with nature of mind,
        92, 96, 122
    far-reaching, unfathomable meaning of,
        27–28
    ground, path, and fruition of, 121–22
    Jamgön Kongtrul on stages of, 152
    no special effort in, 90, 157–58
    practice of path of, 24–27
    relying on a guru in, 115–21
    Saraha's teachings on, xiii
    summary of Tilopa's instruction in, 15
    Tibetan translation of word and
        meaning of, 56–57
    Tilopa's six points for, 157–59

Mahamudra (*continued*)
  as torch of the doctrine, 109–10
  unchanging nature of teachings, xiv–xv
  view of, 20–24, 67–84, 120, 142, 143
  See also *Ganges Mahamudra*
Mahamudra Lineage Supplication, The,
  120
Mahamudra Subtle Drop tantra, 184n19
Mahamudra Upadesha. See *Ganges*
  Mahamudra
mahasiddhas, x–xi
  spiritual biographies of, 3–4, 124–25,
    189n58
  stories about powers of, xi–xii
  three stages of actions of, 11
  Tilopa as king of, 58–60
  unsurpassable attainments of, 72–73
  from Urgyen, 30
Mahayana Vehicle
  awareness in, 128
  on disturbing emotions, 140
  emptiness and, 21–22, 71
  realization in, 112
  two aspects of, 84–85
Maitreya, 121
mandala offering practice, 87
mantra recitation, 90
marketplace doha, xiv
  on benefit of result, 27–28
  on practice of path, 24–27
  root text, 19–20
  on view of Mahamudra, 20–24
Marpa, xi, xii, 22
  on experiencing nature of mind, 82
  Ganges Mahamudra and, 55, 150
  lifestyle of, 4, 125
  Naropa's transmission to, 5, 6, 24,
    185n30
Matangi, xi, 14–16, 184n20
meditation
  beginner experiences in, 144
  conduct for, 89–91
  formless, 185n29
  importance of practicing, 75, 119
  jeweled bridge metaphor for, 31
  of Mahamudra, 92–96, 124, 126
  monarch of all, 120, 142, 143
  with no object, 124, 130
  by not doing anything, 157–58
  physical posture for, 89–90, 93, 188n50

as process of familiarization, 92, 96, 122,
  189n57
  recognizing defects of, 146–47
  relaxation in, 86–87
  scrutinizing the mind, 137, 139
  in solitude, 124
  techniques for stabilizing, 145–47
  temporary experiences that veil, 138
  two stages of, 93
medium faculties, practice for those of,
  143–48
mental (sixth) consciousness, 74, 164
mental dullness, 108, 129–30
mental factors, 74
Middle Way (Madhyamaka) school, 112,
  184n11
  path of inference, 21–22
  Rangtong and Shentong schools, 21, 23,
    77, 185n24
Milarepa
  hardships and austerities of, 64–65
  lifestyle of, 125
  on nature of thoughts, 75
  on power of Dharma, 22
mind
  conduct of, during meditation, 91
  conventional vs. ultimate meaning of,
    76–77
  cutting through confused, 126–27
  as free of direction, 95–96
  as like the midst of space, 94
  looking directly at mind, 70–73
  regarding body as more important than,
    92–93
  scrutinizing, 137, 139
  self-awareness of, 132–33
  unceasing manifestation of, 85–86
  as wish-fulfilling jewel, 69, 74, 118, 121
  See also nature of mind
mindfulness
  gaining stability in, 145
  importance of, 61, 75, 104, 120
  in postmeditation, 130
  as sharp and crisp, 95, 146, 153
Mind-Only school, 23, 141
Mipham Rinpoche, 81
miracles
  display of, 184n12
  of mahasiddhas, xi–xii
mirrorlike wisdom, 161

mist, as example of way thoughts dissolve, 73–75
monastic universities, Buddhist tradition of, x
Moonbeams of Mahamudra (Tashi Namgyal), 55–56, 95, 153
mother and child, meeting of, 144
mundane things
  abandoning, 124
  examining nature of, 122–23

Nagarjuna, 184n11, 185n24
  brief history of, 124–25
  on emptiness, 79
  Tilopa and, 7–9, 14
Nagatanga, 42
Nagpogowa, 38
Nagpopa, 15
naked awareness, 137–39
Nālandā Translation Committee, xiii
Nalanda University, 117
Naropa
  Ganges Mahamudra and, xiv, 55, 61, 63, 150
  hardships and austerities of, 63, 64, 150
  importance of guru for, 117
  Tilopa's introducing nature of mind to, 24
  as Tilopa's main disciple, xii, 34, 35–36, 185n31
  transmissions to Marpa, 5, 6, 24, 185n30
"nature," meaning of, 185n26, 186n42
nature of mind
  being introduced to, 23–24, 25
  benefits of recognizing, 27–28, 83–84, 126–29
  blissful nature of, 77
  devotion and, 63
  direct experience of, 131
  as distinct from thoughts and feelings, 69–70, 74, 186n41
  familiarization with, 92, 96, 122
  as free from extremes, 107, 108
  as ground of purification, 81
  inexpressibility of, 82–84
  jeweled bridge metaphor for resting in, 31
  looking directly at, 26–27, 28, 70–73, 91
  luminous clarity and, 74, 79–80, 121
  as naked awareness, 137–39

pacification of suffering and, 77–78
relaxation when looking at, 86–87
resting in, 68–69, 95
ultimate reality and, 76–77
as unborn, 24, 26, 185n25
as unity of emptiness and luminous clarity, 78–82
words used for describing, 97–98
negative actions. *See* wrongdoing
nine formless dakinis, 34, 185n30
nirmanakaya, 4, 59, 183n7
nonconceptuality, as veil of awareness, 138
Nuden Lodro (Marti), 37–38
Nyi Öd Dronma, 40
Nyingma tradition, 127, 161

obscurations
  buddha nature and, 24, 25
  pacification of, 109, 110, 128, 135, 141, 152
oral instructions. *See* pith instructions
original mind
  as distinct from thoughts and feelings, 69–70, 74
  as luminous clarity, 74
  See also nature of mind

Padmasambhava, 30, 31
Paldarbum, 75
past, not recalling, 157
path
  of liberation, 33, 185n29
  of Mahamudra, 121, 122
  of ripening, 33, 185n29
Patrul Rinpoche, 138
Pekar Chöjung (Pema Karpo), xii
Pema Karpo, xii, 184n20
phenomena
  emptiness as remedy for fixation on, 78–79, 187n45
  emptiness of, 21, 23, 27, 128
  ground as true nature of, 67
  as indivisible in one essence, 25, 26
  unchanging nature of, 81
  vast and unfathomable emptiness of, 28, 56
physical body, as empty and without meaning, 92–93
physical posture, for meditation, 89–90, 93, 188n50
pith instructions, 126, 183n6

pith instructions (*continued*)
  buddhahood in one lifetime and, 129
  Tilopa and, 4, 12–13, 14–15, 17, 32–34
  of whispered lineage, 30, 32, 185n27
Pointing Out the Dharmakaya
  (Wangchuk Dorje), 93, 146
postmeditation
  applying instructions during, 75
  conduct for, 91, 92
  mindfulness in, 130
  working with thoughts in, 97
Prajnaparamita, 12, 62, 111–12
Prajnaparamita teachings, 21, 23, 78
preliminary practices
  four common, 93, 109, 119–20
  of meditation, 92–93
  ngöndro, 87, 109–10, 120
  relying on a guru, 115–21
present, not thinking about, 157
pride, wisdom nature of, 162
prophecy
  instantaneous, 33–34
  path of ripening and, 33
prostrations, 87, 110
pure realms, sambhogakaya and, 59–60

Rain of Wisdom, The, 75
Raja Udmakemara, 15–16
Rangtong school, 21, 23, 77, 78–79,
  185n24
Ratnasambhava, 13, 162
Rechungpa, 22, 185n30
relative truth. *See* conventional reality
relaxation
  in meditation, 86–87, 95
  in sitting posture, 89–90, 93
renunciation, 116, 119, 123
Rerepa, 34
Roberts, Peter Alan, x
Robinson, James, xiv

Samantabhadra, 127
samaya, key of, 33. *See also* commitments
  (samaya)
sambhogakaya, 4, 59–60, 183n7
Sampopang ("Proper Container")
  sadhana, 71
samsara
  all-basis and, 141
  being continually carried away with, 112

escaping prison of, 108–9, 127
as nature of suffering, 27, 73, 112, 116,
  126
problems with, 93
severing all connections with, 124
stable renunciation of, 116, 119
Tilopa's revulsion with, 12
Sangvadhupa, 14
Sangye Naga, xii
Saraha, xiii, 69, 74, 79, 118, 121
seal, turning emptiness into, 136
secret empowerment, 13–14
self, emptiness as remedy for fixation on,
  79
self-awareness, of mind, 132–33
selflessness
  of persons, 71, 96, 112, 128, 188n56
  of phenomena, 96, 112, 188n56
self-liberation, as final result, 143
sensory consciousnesses (five), 163
sesame oil metaphor, 20, 23–24
seven dharmas of Vairochana, 89, 93,
  188n50
Shamatha (Tranquillity meditation), 93
  compared with Vipashyana, 95
  conceptual fixation and, 104
  luminous clarity and, 153
  stages of, 144
  techniques for increasing, 145–47
  working with thoughts in, 74
Shantideva, 62, 84, 95, 132
shastras (commentaries), importance of, 58
Shentong school, 21, 23, 77, 185n24
siddha tradition, in India, x
siddhis, common and uncommon,
  148–49
Six Dharmas (Yogas) of Naropa, xiv, 4, 5,
  6, 147, 183n5
six perfections (paramitas), 188n53
  view of Mahamudra and, 102, 109
six realms of existence, 42–43, 126, 189n59
solitary retreat, 124
Somapuri, xiv, 12
space
  blue sky as ornamental, 76
  definition of, 76, 186n40
space metaphor
  as absence of solidity, 68–70, 77
  for nature of mind, 98
  as not being obscured, 76–78

as practice of Mahamudra, 70–73
Rangjung Dorje on, 83
speech
  internal conversations, 90
  during meditation, 90–91
spiritual biographies (*namtar*)
  of mahasiddhas, 3–4, 124–25, 189n58
  stories of power of siddhas in, xi–xii
  as stories of realization, xii, 3
  symbolic stories in, 30–31
Spiritual Song of Lodro Thaye, The, 152
spiritual songs. *See* dohas (spiritual songs)
subtle channels and energies, 13–14,
  184n17
  inner heat practice and, 148
  metaphor for mastery of, 31
  physical posture and, 90
suchness
  meaning of, 25–26
  realization of, 16, 20
suffering
  emptiness of, 23, 27
  internal causes of, 83–84
  as nature of samsara, 27, 112, 116, 126
  negative thoughts and, 72
  pacification of, 57, 77–78, 127
  preventing mental and physical, 73–74
suffering of change, 116
Sukhada, 30, 32
sunlight metaphor, for mind's emptiness
  and luminosity, 78–82
Sutra-pitaka, 107–8

Taranatha, xi
temple of fragrance (*gandhalaya*), 32
ten powers, 149, 189n65
thoughts
  as adventitious stains, 81
  allowing to settle, 139, 140
  beginning meditators and, 144
  as distinct from original mind, 69–70,
   74, 186n41
  exhaustion of, 142
  liberation from bondage of, 72
  looking directly at nature of, 26, 71–72,
   74–75, 94–95, 96, 113, 137
  Mahamudra's focus on, 131
  mist as example of dissolution of, 73–75
  self-liberation of, 95, 104
Three Baskets, 107–8

Three Cycles of Doha (Saraha), xiii
three heart spheres, 15, 184n19
thukdam (death practice), xii
Tilopa
  access to pure realms, 60
  biographies of, x–xi, xii–xiii, 125
  childhood of, 7–9
  delight in Mahamudra, 135–36
  depictions of, with fish, 2, 36
  disciples of, 34, 35–42
  as emanation of Chakrasamvara, 4–5,
   30, 32, 34, 185n28
  enlightenment of, xi, xiv, 4, 5, 16–17
  importance of dohas of, 58–61
  important works of, xiv
  marketplace doha of, 17, 19–28
  ordination of, 12
  physical description of, x
  receiving secret teachings, 29–34
  six points for Mahamudra, 157–59
  teachers of, 12–13, 14–16, 29
  as Tilopa Sherab Sangpo, 34
  two aspects of biography of, 29
  Vajradhara and, 2, 4, 29, 32, 58–60
  See also *Ganges Mahamudra*;
   marketplace doha
Tilopa Cave, 37
torpor, in meditation, 146–47, 153
Torricelli, Fabrizio, xii
tranquillity, devotion and, 117
Tranquillity meditation. *See* Shamatha
  (Tranquillity meditation)
Tsangpa Heruka, xii

ultimate reality
  Mahamudra view of, 77, 151
  nature of mind and, 76–77
  Shantideva on, 62
ultimate result, 149
upadeshas (practice instructions),
  importance of, 57–61
Urgyen, secret teachings from, 30–34
Uttaratantra, 107

Vairochana, 13, 161
vajra family, 161
vajra repetition breathing, 146
Vajradhara, 127
  attaining state of, 58, 128–29, 135
  Tilopa and, 2, 4, 29, 32, 58–60

Vajrasattva practice, 87, 110
Vajrayana
  awareness in, 128
  buddhahood in one lifetime and, 22, 28,
    58, 125, 128–29, 135
  direct experience in, 84
  on disturbing emotions, 140
  mother and father tantras of, 14–15
  Tilopa's introduction to, 12–13
  two paths of, 33, 185n29
  view in, 71, 102
Vajrayogini, 5, 6, 30
vanquishing negative behavior stage, 11,
  13, 16, 29
vase breathing, 146
vase empowerment, 13
Vasubandhu, 76
victorious in all actions stage, 11, 29
view
  common vs. uncommon, 67–68
  of Mahamudra as essential for all
    practices, 101–2, 108–10
  monarch of all, 120, 142, 143
  as recognition of the ground, 67, 92
  sutra approach to, 71
view, metaphors for, 67–84
  inexpressibility of mind's nature, 82–84
  mist as way thoughts dissolve, 73–75
  space as absence of solidity, 68–70
  space as not being obscured, 76–78
  space as practice of Mahamudra, 70–73
  summary of six analogies, 83
  sunlight as mind's emptiness and
    luminosity, 78–82
Vinaya, 102

Vinaya-pitaka, 107, 108
Vipashyana (Insight meditation), 93
  as not looking for anything, 96
  resting the mind and, 95
  stages of, 144
  techniques for increasing, 145–47
virtuous actions
  in completely virtuous stage, 11, 12, 29
  happiness and, 42, 77, 108, 116
  limitations of, 108, 111
  Mahamudra samaya and, 103–4
  ten virtuous deeds, 188n54
visualization
  inner heat practice and, 148
  for steadying the mind, 146–47

Waldo, Ives, xii
Wangchuk Gyaltsen, xi, xii
Way of the Bodhisattva, The (Shantideva),
  84, 95, 132
White Annals, The (Gendun Choephel), 3
wisdom
  expanded, of Mahamudra, 149
  inseparability of emptiness and, 57
  that is awareness, 128
  twofold, 80, 149
wisdom of equality, 162
wish-fulfilling jewel, 69, 74, 118, 121,
  186n43
wrongdoing
  karmic seeds and, 77, 128
  pacification of, 109, 110, 128
  ten unvirtuous actions, 109, 188n54

Yonge Mingyur Dorje, 71

Biographical Note
about Khenchen Thrangu

In 1932, the Seventh Thrangu Tulku of Thrangu monastery in Tibet passed away, and a few years later, the monastery began looking for his reincarnation. They visited the Sixteenth Karmapa, who wrote a letter with the following information about his reincarnation: his parents' names, his name, and a description of where he lived. The party then went to the Tai Situpa Rinpoche, who, without seeing the Karmapa's letter, wrote another prediction. Both letters gave almost exactly the same details.

Thrangu Rinpoche was born in 1933, and when he was very young, he was discovered, with the circumstances being just as the letters had predicted, and at the age of five, he went with his parents to Thrangu Monastery and stayed there. He then began to study and was considered the monastery's best pupil. When Rinpoche was ten, he went on a pilgrimage to Lhasa and visited the Sixteenth Karmapa, Rigpe Dorje, in Tsurpu. He asked the Sixteenth Karmapa to become his root guru and was told by the Karmapa to practice White Tara and go on a retreat.

When Thrangu Rinpoche was fifteen years old, Thrangu Monastery, which was under the direction of Thrangu Rinpoche and Traleg Rinpoche, established a monastic college (*shedra*). Thrangu Rinpoche and the students studied under Shechen Gyaltsap, who supported the Shentong view of Jamgön Kongtrul and Mipham Rinpoche. When Thrangu Rinpoche was twenty-one years old, he and Chögyam Trungpa Rinpoche took ordination under the Sixteenth Karmapa, who had just returned from a trip to China.

In 1959, the Chinese started to take over Tibet. Thrangu Rinpoche, along with Khenpo Karthar and several hundred other Tibetans, began fleeing in front of the invading army, undergoing much hardship. Eventually, Thrangu Rinpoche ended up in Baxa, India, an encampment of refugee

Tibetan scholars and practitioners, studying Dharma under teachers from all four sects of Tibetan Buddhism. In a debate in front of 1,500 sangha members, he passed his oral examination on all five divisions of the great treatises. The Dalai Lama conferred upon him the degree of Geshe Lharampa, which is a very high degree in Tibetan education.

At this time, only a few great scholars and rinpoches had escaped from Tibet, many Tibetan religious books had been burned or lost, and the Sixteenth Karmapa was trying to reconstitute in India the second largest Tibetan Buddhist lineage. He asked Thrangu Rinpoche to set up another monastic college in Rumtek, India, which he did with Khenpo Tsültrim, by collecting texts from libraries outside of Tibet. He taught a first class of Kagyu and Nyingma tulkus and continued to teach young tulkus such as Ponlop Rinpoche and Dzigar Kongtrul Rinpoche for several more years.

In 1976, the Gyalwa Karmapa presented Thrangu Rinpoche with a certificate requesting him to teach in Dharma centers outside India. Since then, Rinpoche has tirelessly taught for over forty years in centers and monasteries in over two dozen countries. He has set up over a dozen centers, including ones in North America, Europe, India, Malaysia, Hong Kong, and Taiwan. In addition, he has published forty books in English on many aspects of Buddhism and many more books in Tibetan.

For more information please visit Thrangu Rinpoche's website at www .rinpoche.com, which contains a more detailed illustrated biography of Rinpoche and a list of his centers across the world.